A JOHN RUSKIN COLLECTION

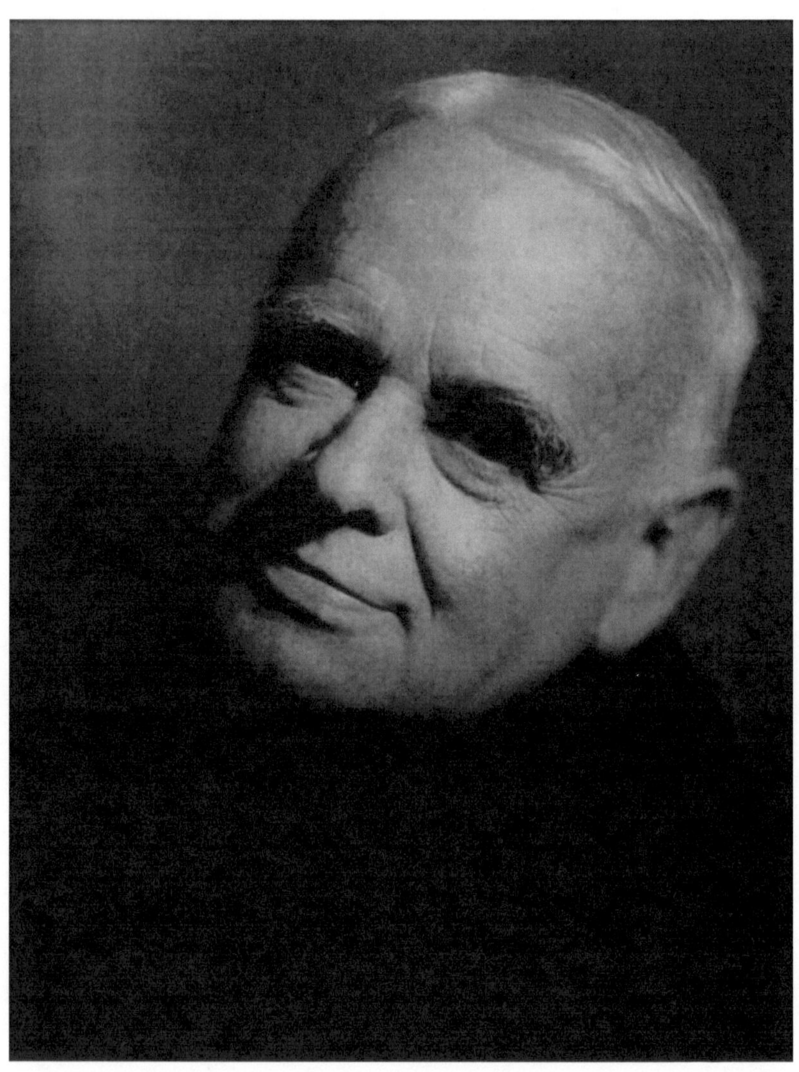

John Howard Whitehouse

A JOHN RUSKIN COLLECTION

JAMES S. DEARDEN

COMPANION OF THE GUILD
OF ST GEORGE

WITH A PREFACE
BY TIM HILTON

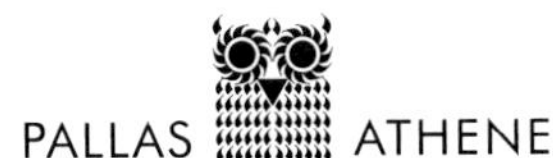

CONTENTS

PREFACE

In thinking about an old, wise and trusted friend I find it hard to distinguish between the qualities of his writing and the virtues of his personality. Do we praise Jim (as we all call him, whether we be Ruskinians, booksellers, printers or Isle of Wight neighbours) for his erudition and long devotion to the causes of specialist publishing; or for his pages-long correspondence and personal generosity, which for decades past has been his gift to all new Ruskin scholarship?

Such qualities are apparent in his articles that are sent to us in this book, as indeed they have been in many other volumes that constitute only a part of a life's work. Looking now at *A John Ruskin Collection*, I suggest that its readers consider not only Jim's vast knowledge but also his memory; for in the present book, as in so many others by James S. Dearden (as he is known in official places and in the acknowledgements of dozens of academic histories), his capacity for recollection makes us pause in respectful wonder. His thoughts of years long gone and the analysis of evidence of the past are not only touching. They have an historical depth that helps us to feel the nature of nineteenth-century life – whether that life is in the clouds of philosophy or, often enough, in the routines of domesticity.

Allow me to distinguish, crudely, between two sorts of memory. The first is that of personal reminiscence. The second is the ability to retain, and then summon, precise information about people and their doings, places, dates, pictures and books. Look now at the moving descriptions of Jim Dearden's visits to Brantwood when he was young and could speak to aged Coniston people who had known the house as it still existed in the years after Ruskin's death. Then consider the account of how Dearden began his bibliography of all the books that Ruskin had ever owned. *The Library of John Ruskin* (2012) is a masterpiece. It has no parallel in the study of nineteenth-century intellectual curiosity. Yet the book itself has no autobiographical introduction. We are not told how the work was begun, nor how its ambition was pursued.

Now, in the essay 'Cataloguing Ruskin's Library', we may discover how years of learning reached a final order. Dearden's research both complemented and extended E. T. Cook's and Alexander Wedderburn's footnotes in the 39 volumes of their classic Library Edition (1903-12). We can follow the expansion of Dearden's first, tentative card index in his own study to the final, printed result. And in this bibliography nearly 3,000 books are impeccably noted.

Jim Dearden's visual memory is one more distinction of his intellectual character. I suggest that his eye is most acute when looking at, or recalling, the smaller artefacts and decorations that belong to libraries, homes, or local museums and family collections. How vividly he can summon, for himself and then for us, book plates, printed illustrations of novels and poetry, typefaces and illuminated manuscripts! And of course he has an especial knowledge of the drawings and watercolours that were in his care when they were hung or stored at Bembridge, as well as of the collection that belongs to the Guild of St George, now housed in the museum in Sheffield.

Dearden is a precise writer who can turn his attention to unhappy emotions. In one disturbing essay we are led beyond the safe confines of Brantwood, Bembridge and Sheffield toward the tragic crisis of Ruskin's emotional life. With firmness and delicacy Dearden lists and illustrates the known portraits of Rose La Touche. Now they call us from their occlusion. Who will not feel some sympathetic terror when looking at the drawing of Rose's insane countenance as she struggled in her deathbed? This intimate portrait, so seldom reproduced, must have troubled Dearden for many years.

So let us now follow our perceptive Ruskin scholar to the hostelry at Bibury in Gloucestershire. There, he tells us, he noticed two small oil paintings of fish, signed by Arthur Severn. This was not the Arthur who was married to Joan Agnew, the director of Ruskin's life in the last three decades of his earthly existence. He was the son of their union. No intellectual, Arthur junior owned a fish farm (perhaps bought with funds from Ruskin's posthumous purse?). And here is Dearden's photograph of that un-Ruskinian modern enterprise, an artificial marriage between nature and commerce.

It is quite proper, and in character, that Dearden has collected and presented this information. His essay on Carshalton and the river Wandle also asks us to value curiosity. Small matters are not necessarily trivial. Historians must be grateful that Dearden knows so much about suburban as well as country places, and introduces us to people who have no grand claims to posthumous fame. We are also in his debt for the careful mentions of unpretentious Ruskin admirers: his schoolgirl friends, for instance, and his secretaries, or the Brantwood servants and their children.

No Ruskin servant was ever cast off, especially since they did not wish to leave his service. So there were often many dependent generations beneath the same roof, or who had retired to neighbouring cottages. Let us think of *A Ruskin Collection* as an elaborate family history: filled with characters, stories, reminiscences, old letters, inheritances, and so on: yet also incomplete, as family histories must always be. And Ruskinians, whether we be writers, dons, local historians, guides to cathedrals or footpaths, Companions of the Guild of St George or book collectors, still form a sort of family. We are not especially numerous, often we know each other and speak of Ruskinians who formed our knowledge, beginning with Cook and Wedderburn about a century ago, and we grieve for those fellow devotees who have now left us. As *A Ruskin Collection* reveals, the guiding archivist of this family – for half a century – has been James S. Dearden. Thank you, Jim!

Tim Hilton

INTRODUCTION

Most of my working life and much of my retirement has been devoted to studying and writing about matter relating to the great Victorian figure, John Ruskin. I have written a number of books and articles on my subject. As it happens, my first three publications – in 1947, 1948 and 1950 – were not Ruskin-related. The first two, on Christmas Carols and Christmas Customs, were published in the *Bembridge School Newspaper*. The third, about my local parish church, was published privately.

However in 1959 I wrote a short article on Brantwood, Ruskin's home at Coniston, which I sent to the Lake District magazine *Cumbria*. To my amazement and delight they not only published it but sent me a cheque too! After that there was no stopping me. I wrote a number of local history articles for the local *North West Evening Mail*, but the greater part of my writing has been Ruskin-related.

A friend once referred to me as 'Ruskin's representative on earth'. I suppose I do now have, in various ways, a slightly more direct connection with Ruskin than most of my contemporaries!

I have written in my *Rambling Reminiscences* of those in the first generation of Ruskinians with whom I either didn't quite overlap, or actually *did* overlap. Among those who I actually met or corresponded with were Sir Sydney Cockerell, Barbara Gnosspelius [Collingwood], Kathleen Olander and the Cork Girls High School's 'Rose Queen' of 1888.

Of course – to me – the principle among these was J. Howard Whitehouse who had visited Brantwood in 1899 to present to Ruskin the National Address of Congratulation on his eightieth birthday. Whitehouse was to build up the world's leading Ruskin collection, of which I write in the first chapter below. I knew Whitehouse from 1945 when I entered Bembridge School, until his death in 1955. As a boy at Bembridge I had the relatively free run of his library. I transcribed Ruskin manuscripts for him when he was writing his *Vindication of Ruskin*, 1950, his reply to Admiral James's book on Ruskin's marriage. I heard him speak of his visit to Brantwood in 1899, and again of his staying at Brantwood with Arthur Severn in 1925 when he was trying to buy the house to establish it as an international memorial to Ruskin. He failed in *that* attempt but finally succeeded in his aim in 1932. I only wish I had asked Whitehouse more about Ruskin the man.

Another important Ruskin collector whom I met on several occasions, was Haddon C. Adams, about whose collection I write in chapter 2. In this chapter I quote from a long letter from Adams to his father about his visit to Coniston and Brantwood in 1928. This letter reveals that Adams knew what he was seeing and what he was looking for. It also reveals how little those in charge of Brantwood at that time knew of its contents – and how ready they were to dispose of them!

Fred Sharp was a carpenter, a teacher and a modest man of modest means. But he too was a Ruskin admirer with an intimate knowledge of Ruskin's books, manuscripts and letters which remained at Brantwood. Buying directly from Brantwood *before* the 1931 dispersal sale (he told me of his regret at not actually being able to attend the same itself) or from T. H. Telford, the Grasmere antiques dealer in the 1930s and '40s, Sharp built up a very important Ruskin collection. I met him on several occasions. Again, missed opportunities. I *should* have taken more notice of what he told me, and showed me on my early visits to him, and I should have asked him more. But originally I was only in my mid-teens, and not *terribly* interested in Ruskin! Following his death in 1957, only weeks after I returned to Bembridge to care for the Whitehouse Collection, the bulk of the Sharp Collection went to America – either to Helen Viljoen (with whom Sharp had been collaborating) or to Yale. However, I *was* able to secure bookcases, books and pictures for the collection at Brantwood, and a number of books from his collection came to me. I have written of Sharp in my *Rambling Reminiscences* and Van Burd contributed a biographical article on him to *The Book Collector* in the Winter 1995 issue.

I have been a book collector from my earliest youth. For many years I collected books relating to Cumbria – with just a smattering of books by or about Ruskin. When I retired and was free to collect Ruskin on my own behalf (as opposed to professionally) that became my speciality. But of course I had already begun to write articles and books about Ruskin. I think my first serious article was on Ruskin's bookplates which appeared in *The Book Collector* in 1964.

In 2009 I 'collected' my Ruskin and book articles into my *Further Facets of Ruskin*. The present volume only includes one bibliographical chapter – on an interesting set of Ruskin's *Stones of Venice* in my collection. All of the other pieces assembled here are not specifically 'bibliographical' although inevitably there are references to Ruskin's books, articles and manuscripts.

The first chapter, on The Whitehouse Collection, as it was then constituted, appeared in *The Bulletin of the John Rylands Library* as it was then titled. Frank Taylor, the Librarian and Editor, used to take his annual holiday on the Isle of Wight, and we met in that way. This article was written at his request. When the Adams Bequest arrived at Bembridge it seemed appropriate that my account of it should appear in the (by now re-named) same publication.

I first wrote about Ruskin portraits in *Apollo* in 1960 and 1961. These articles were finally incorporated into my *John Ruskin in Pictures* in 1999. Meanwhile my interest in portraits – Mary Lutyens had written on the portraits of Effie Ruskin in *Apollo* in 1968 – spurred me into writing on the portraits of Rose La Touche in the *Burlington* in 1978, a piece which is included here.

My article in *Turner Society News* on 'Ruskin and the Splügen' was written soon after the Whitehouse Collection had acquired a number of papers relating to the purchase of this watercolour for presentation to Ruskin. The same journal also printed my piece explaining why Ruskin sold Turner's 'The Slave Ship' wherein I speculated on the price received for it – a speculation which, a number of years later, was to be proved amazingly accurate!

I contributed the essays on 'Margaret's Well' to the 2004 issue of The Guild of St George's *Companion*, soon after a visit to the 'well' at Carshalton.

I have been frequently and generously indulged by the editors of *The Friends of Ruskin's Brantwood Newsletter* and *The Ruskin Review and Bulletin* and I am very grateful to them, and to the editors of the other journals, for allowing me to re-print the articles in this collection. I am also deeply indebted to all of my friends at the Ruskin Library in Lancaster University for their constant and unstinting help.

I am grateful to the various friends and organisations who have made photographs available to me. Particularly I appreciate the help of friends at the Ruskin Library in this connection. Strictly speaking photographs from here should be acknowledged to 'Ruskin Foundation (Ruskin Library, University of Lancaster)'. In the book, for brevity, I acknowledge them to 'Ruskin Foundation'.

I am also deeply indebted to both Patrick Davies and Isi Bogod at Pallas Athene for their enormous help in putting this collection together.

J. S. D.

I

THE RUSKIN GALLERIES AT BEMBRIDGE SCHOOL, ISLE OF WIGHT[1]

BULLETIN OF THE JOHN RYLANDS LIBRARY,
VOL. 51, NO. 2, 1969

I. INTRODUCTION

The Ruskin Collection, and the Ruskin Galleries at Bembridge School which house it, owe their existence to the enthusiasm of the founder of the School, J. Howard Whitehouse.

Whitehouse was born in Birmingham in 1873. In the 1890s he became interested in the life and teaching of John Ruskin and he began to buy and read books by and about Ruskin. In 1896 he founded the Ruskin Society of Birmingham which was just one of several Ruskin Societies which existed in the country at that time. Two years later he established a magazine, *St George*, which was subsequently adopted as the society's official organ. He persuaded many well-known lecturers to visit Birmingham and their lectures are printed in *St George*, or are otherwise preserved.

For example, on 27 October 1898 Dean Farrar, the president, addressed the society on 'Ruskin as a Religious Teacher'. The lecture was originally printed by Whitehouse in 1904. A second edition was published by Arnold Fairbairns in 1907. Farrar's holograph manuscript is now at Bembridge (MS 83), as are the extensively annotated proofs of Professor F. York Powell's 'Appreciation of John Ruskin' from *St George*, 1900 (MS 67).

In 1900 Dr F. J. Furnivall, who had known Ruskin from the 1850s, lectured to the society. The lecture was not printed but Whitehouse kept the shorthand notes of the address together with a transcript of them (MS 73).

The correspondence files and guard books relating to both the

Birmingham Ruskin Society and *St George* are at Bembridge, though as yet they are uncatalogued.

On the occasion of Ruskin's eightieth birthday in 1899, the Ruskin Societies sponsored a national address of congratulation. This is a volume of some 20 pages, beautifully illuminated by Albert Pilley of Sheffield and bound at the Doves Bindery (MS 81). Whitehouse was undoubtedly a prime mover behind the preparation of the address. He and William Wardle, the secretary of the Liverpool Ruskin Society, went to Brantwood to present the manuscript to Ruskin and Whitehouse recorded the details of their visit in his diary.

> Feby 7, 1899 To Coniston to bear to Mr Ruskin the National Address of Congratulation promoted by the Ruskin societies. I left Birmingham at 9 o'clock and reached Coniston at 4. I put up at the Dove Hotel and after tea, I drove to Brantwood to arrange time of presenting address on the morrow. Saw Miss Severn who stated her mother was unwell and in bed and that it was feared that Mr Ruskin could not see us tomorrow, but that Mr and Mrs Severn hoped to receive us on his behalf. I replied that the address I bore was a national one, bearing among others the signature of the Prince of Wales and that I hoped that it would at least be possible for me to hand it to Mr Ruskin personally. Miss Severn thought it might be managed and I arranged to call at 11.30 the next morning.
>
> On my drive to Brantwood I met W. G. Collingwood who seemed rather odd and snappish. Drove back to the hotel through a heavy rain and then to the station to meet Wardle, the secretary of the Liverpool society. The Address also arrived at the station but minus the signatures which should have been sent with it from Sheffield by White. We had therefore to compile another list of signatories, as best we could from memory.
>
> Collingwood came round in the evening and from his manner I gathered that a revulsion of feeling had taken place at Brantwood with regard to the Address and that we should be received by Mr Ruskin. Collingwood said that it had been feared White from the Sheffield Museum was coming with the Address, and Mr Ruskin

did not want to see him. I could not gather what was the precise objection to White, but there was evidently a strong feeling against him at Brantwood. Collingwood further advised us in reading the Address to The Master to omit the reference to the painting of his portrait by Holman Hunt. Ruskin liked his works, but not his portraits and would not care to have his portrait painted by him. Collingwood added that if anyone painted it, it should be G. F. Watts. Under these circumstances we decided to omit the request.

The landlord of the Hotel came in to have a chat about Ruskin. He knows him well, and knew his parents before him. On returning from Italy on one occasion Ruskin gave him some pictures he had brought back, and these now hang in the coffee room.

Feby 8 The morning was fairly bright and clear and at 11 o'clock we started for Brantwood. It is a glorious road, going for some distance by the margin of the lake and commanding exquisite views. At Brantwood we were very politely received by Mr and Mrs Arthur Severn. They explained that The Master felt equal to seeing us and had expressed a wish to do so. Mrs Severn said that he was really wonderfully well and that although we should find him in his bedroom, we were not to conclude from that, that he was ill. They did not want him to come downstairs as the staircase was rather narrow, &c, &c.

We were then conducted to Mr Ruskin's presence. He was dressed and sitting in an arm chair before a little table. As we entered he attempted to rise, but was evidently too feeble to do so. We shook hands and I told him that I was glad to hear he was so well. I then explained that we brought him a National Address, and I read it to him. As I was doing so, I occasionally heard him give a low exclamation half sob it seemed to be. When I had finished he tried to reply but could only utter a few broken words. He was evidently deeply moved and quite overcome with emotion.

After he had looked at the Address we withdrew and when he had become more composed he dictated to Mrs Severn a reply.

What most impressed me when I saw The Master were his wonderful eyes. They are blue and very clear and bright. When, during the reading of the Address, I looked up at him, I found them fixed upon me as though he were searching me through and through. No one who meets his eyes can doubt that his mind is perfectly clear.

Less than a year later Whitehouse was recording another visit to Coniston in his diary:

1900 Jan 20 The Master is dead. Know ye not that there is a Prince and a Great Man fallen this day in Israel.

23 Jan I left tonight for Coniston to attend the Funeral. I travelled all night reaching Coniston soon after 9 on Wednesday morning.

24 Jan Put up at the Waterhead Hotel. The coffin was brought from Brantwood at 11 o'clock and I joined the procession as it passed the hotel, travelling in one of the carriages to the Church, bearing with me the Society's wreath which I placed upon the coffin in the Church. Here the coffin will lay in state until tomorrow morning.

In the evening George Allen, the Master's publisher, arrived, with his son. Allen evidently feels the loss most keenly and has greatly aged within the last few days. In the evening I had a long and most interesting conversation with him. He commenced telling me many of his reminiscences of Ruskin and in talking seemed to lose himself in his subject. I was indeed surprised that he told me many of the things which he did.

He dealt with the divorce between Ruskin and his wife who afterwards became Lady Millais. He stated that the allegations made by the latter were untrue entirely. (The allegations referred to Ruskin's physical inability to consummate the marriage). Had Ruskin liked he could have prevented the divorce being obtained, but he said to Allen, 'Had I done so I should have had the woman on my hands for life'. The truth was, said Allen, that from shortly after the marriage Mrs Ruskin appears to have been maturing plans for getting away from her husband. Millais was a frequent visitor to Ruskin and he took advantage of these visits to get more and more intimate with Mrs Ruskin until the climax came. When the case came before the Ecclesiastical Court Ruskin would have nothing to do with it and went abroad.

Whitehouse resigned the secretaryship of the Birmingham Ruskin Society at the end of 1903 when he went to live in Scotland but his interest in Ruskin was maintained and his collection continued to grow.

He was secretary to, and prime mover behind, the Ruskin Centenary Council, set up in 1919 to organize suitable activities to celebrate the 100th anniversary of Ruskin's birth. The committee arranged a public meeting in London on 8 February and a Ruskin exhibition at the Royal Academy in the autumn. The committee's correspondence files and minute book are in the collection. Among the addresses delivered on 8 February 1919 was one by Professor J. W. Mackail. The holograph manuscript is MS 67. It was printed in *Ruskin Centenary Addresses*. Other addresses were delivered at the exhibition in the autumn. Two, printed in *Ruskin the Prophet*, were by W. R. Inge, Dean of St Paul's, (MS 79) and H. W. Nevinson (MS 67). John Masefield's address is in typescript with holograph corrections (MS 79). This was first printed as a pamphlet at the School's press in 1920 and later in *Ruskin the Prophet*. Bernard Shaw's lecture on Ruskin was delivered in November 1919. The manuscript again is typed with a few holograph corrections (MS 78). This was published in 1921 as a separate booklet, in two editions. The bibliographical ramifications of these will prove confusing to Shavians who do not consult the file on the books (MS 82).

The catalogue of the 1919 exhibition shows that by then Whitehouse owned some two dozen drawings by Ruskin, including the 1874 self-portrait formerly in the collection of Charles Eliot Norton. Among the manuscripts and letters which he lent were 100 letters from Ruskin to George Allen (B 11-IV), proof sheets of *The Pleasures of Deed* and *The Pleasures of Learning* (MS 63-4), and a copy of *Ethics of the*

Dust inscribed by Ruskin, 'A. C. Swinburne, With the old lecturer's earnest regard. Christmas 1865'.

In May 1919 Whitehouse had founded Bembridge School, a public school for boys in the Isle of Wight. By 1929 his collection had outgrown the confines of his study and in that year he built the Ruskin Galleries as an extension to one of the recently erected houses at Bembridge. The galleries are two large rooms, the upper designed as an art gallery, the lower as a library. Both were intended for the use of the School and the upper gallery has always been used for various School functions. But the lower gallery was soon taken over by Whitehouse as his own library. When I returned to Bembridge in 1957, two years after Whitehouse's death, this gallery was crammed to capacity with books and papers of every description. Eventually it was sorted and re-furnished as a library and opened for the use of visitors and members of the sixth forms. This library now houses the printed books of the Ruskin Collection, together with a small art library and a collection of Whitehouse's own publications.

Mrs Severn died in 1924, Arthur Severn seven years later. In 1930-1 a series of five sales at Sotheby's and two at Brantwood and Warwick Square dispersed the Ruskin collection. Whitehouse was an avid buyer and very many important books, manuscripts and pictures were added to the Bembridge Collection as a result of these sales.

The title of the first sale in the series, 'Manuscripts and Remaining Library', reminds one that many of the more important and valuable items from the Ruskin collection, for example most of the Turner watercolours and the illuminated manuscripts, had already been sold privately by the Severns between 1900 and 1930.

Three important lots were bought by Whitehouse at this first sale. They were lot 111, Ruskin's Diaries, lot 115, the bulk of the *Stones of Venice* working notes, and lot 119, which contained parts of the manuscripts or proofs of ten books, among them the 1878 *Turner Catalogue*, *Art of England*, *Mornings in Florence*, part of *Love's Meinie*, *The Eagle's Nest*, and several other fragments. Lot 120, most of the manuscript of *The Bible of Amiens*, was not bought by Whitehouse, but was later acquired by him from Maggs. In addition to these lots, some twenty volumes of printed books from Ruskin's library were acquired.

A further twenty-eight books were bought at the sale of 'The Final Portion of the Manuscripts and Library' at Sotheby's on 18 May 1931. The wealth of the Bembridge Collection lies partly in the Ruskin family correspondence which it contains. The bulk of these letters came in three lots in this sale, a parcel of letters from Ruskin's father, J. J. Ruskin, to his son, 130 letters from Ruskin's mother to his father, and three parcels – some 3,000 letters – from Ruskin to Joan Severn. At this sale, too, Whitehouse bought back the Illuminated Address which he had handed to Ruskin in 1899; by now it lacked several leaves which had been given to the Coniston Museum.

Two days later, again at Sotheby's, Whitehouse bought fifty drawings and 'a parcel' by Ruskin, and forty-four drawings by other artists from the Ruskin collection.

On 15 and 16 July 1931 the remaining contents of the Severns' London house in Warwick Square were sold. Again Whitehouse was lucky in getting a considerable number of pictures by Ruskin and Joseph and Arthur Severn. He also bought fifty-seven volumes and 'a bundle' of books of Ruskin and Severn association and a volume of pressed flowers collected by Ruskin at Chamouni in 1844 (MS 65). He did not succeed on this occasion in buying the 398 letters from Ruskin to his mother (1866-71), catalogued as seven lots but sold together for £90.

In the words of *The Times* report of 4 August 1931, 'The glory that was Brantwood fizzled out last week in circumstances that could not very well have been more depressing or pathetic... It would not be technically correct to state that the sale was, as is usual in such cases, held "on the premises" for the things were sold in the garden, and for the most part in the rain....' Whitehouse was unable to attend the sale personally but he was represented there by Mr Ralph Brown of B. F. Stevens & Brown Ltd., who acted as his agent for thirty-four years. By now all of the important books, manuscripts and pictures had been dispersed, but Whitehouse obtained, amongst other things, forty-six more printed books (a year later he got a further forty-six from a Scottish bookseller who had bought them at the Brantwood sale), twenty-eight drawings by Ruskin and ten by other artists, the Benjamin Creswick bust of Ruskin, and Ruskin's silver christening cup. From

Coniston Brown wrote to Whitehouse on 29 July, 'I must explain that the posts here are awful, the telephone ditto and the weather also'. On the following day he telegraphed, '... Bought all you want but prices much higher to-day'.

In 1932 Whitehouse added the largest piece of Ruskiniana to his collection when he bought Brantwood and some 200 acres of the surrounding estate. The house had been neglected since Joan Severn's death in 1924. Arthur Severn had, thereafter, spent most of his time away from Coniston and the house and its contents had begun to suffer from the damp. Whitehouse had bought a number of pictures and illuminated manuscripts from Severn in the mid-1920s. In 1927 he had tried, on behalf of the Guild of St George, to buy the estate from Severn in order to establish it as a national memorial to Ruskin. But after much correspondence (L 68) the negotiations fell through. In 1932 at the sale of the estate, the house attracted no bidders and Whitehouse subsequently bought it privately with 200 acres of the estate.

Many of the interesting items from his collection were placed in the house which was opened to the public in 1934. With a few short breaks it has remained open ever since. The principal rooms today are furnished with many examples of Ruskin's furniture – his dining table and chairs, his armchair, four of his bookcases (two recently bought from the F. J. Sharp collection), his shell cabinet and collection of shells (bought together with a large collection of other Ruskin relics from Stevens and Brown in October 1933), the desk from Ruskin's rooms at Oxford (from the Rawnsley collection and on loan from the National Trust), a large cabinet made by Snell to house part of the collection of framed Turner drawings, a collection of some 250 drawings by Ruskin and a hundred by associated artists (including the Northcote portrait of Margaret Ruskin and George Watson's John James Ruskin), a number of volumes of Ruskin's letters which are included in the Bembridge catalogue and are referred to elsewhere, and some eighty books formerly in Ruskin's library, and many other association copies. The house and estate are now run as a study centre for adult education courses.

During the years following the Brantwood dispersal sales, many items were offered to Whitehouse which he had missed in 1930-1. In

August 1933 he bought the collection of letters from Ruskin to his mother (B VI) which he had missed at the Warwick Square sale. By now they had been bound by Rivière and Whitehouse had to pay nearly four times the price they had brought on the previous occasion.

A large collection of books by and about Ruskin came to Bembridge from the library of James P. Smart in 1933. Smart had collaborated with Wise in producing the *Ruskin Bibliography* and the part of his library which Whitehouse obtained contained a number of scarce books. Smart, too, had been the secretary of the Ruskin Society of London and included in the purchase were the guard books and minute books of the society and the Ruskin Union, together with several volumes of newspaper cuttings of Ruskin interest.

1934 saw the acquisition of a collection of thirty-three letters from Ruskin to Louise Blandy. In the following year Whitehouse bought another part of the manuscript of the 1878 *Turner Catalogue* and twenty-six letters to Marcus B. Huish, from the collection of Henry Beaumont. Later in the same year he bought eleven letters to the Rev. Edward Clayton and twentyeight to Miss Corlass.

An important purchase at the end of 1936 brought the manuscripts of *Morality in Art*, *The Valley of the Somme*, part of *Love's Meinie*, page proofs of *The Stones of Venice* and part of the *Stones* manuscript to Bembridge.

From the Yates Thompson sale in 1941 Whitehouse obtained sixteen letters to George Smith and in 1943 came thirty-two miscellaneous sheets, parts of the manuscripts of *The Story of Ida*, *Deucalion*, *Love's Meinie*, *Proserpina*, *Comments on Mallock*, *Bible of Amiens* and *Val d'Arno*.

In 1944 Whitehouse bought the two designs by Burne-Jones, exhibited at the Manchester Ruskin exhibition in 1904 (item 188) for the title page of *Sesame and Lilies* and (?) cover of *Munera Pulveris*. These designs were never used, as were the three designs that Burne-Jones made for *Bibliotheca Pastorum*, which are also at Bembridge.

The sale of W. B. Slater's library at Hodgson's in February 1945 was, of course, rich in Wiseiana. Whitehouse bought a Ruskin sketch-book, proof sheets and manuscript relating to *Gold* and *John Ruskin and Frederick Denison Maurice on 'Notes on the Construction of Sheep-*

folds', thirty letters from Ruskin to Furnivall, many of them printed by Wise, and thirty-two other Ruskin letters.

At the end of 1946 the manuscript *Index* to volumes 1 and 2 of *Fors Clavigera* and twenty-five letters to Coventry Patmore and others came to Bembridge.

The Morse collection, bought in 1952, brought much interesting ephemeral matter relating to the Guild of St George to the Bembridge collection, together with a small sketch of Ruskin in 1888 by E. R. Hughes.

It might be assumed from this account that Whitehouse's main Ruskin interest lay in the manuscripts and letters which he bought; this would be a quite wrong impression. He *did* use and publish a small part of his manuscript collection, but it held little interest for him compared with the magnificent collection of Ruskin's drawings which he built up. As an example of this lack of interest I might mention the 3,000 letters from Ruskin to Joan Severn which Whitehouse bought in 1931. Biographically, these are infinitely more interesting than Ruskin's Diaries, yet when I began to care for the collection in 1957 these letters were still as they had been wrapped by Joan Severn and Sara Anderson at Brantwood at the end of the last century and most of the packets had clearly only been opened once – by Wedderburn when he was preparing the *Library Edition of Ruskin's Works.*

Although this account of the Bembridge Collection is chiefly concerned with the books and manuscripts, it would be wrong to omit all mention of the 600-odd drawings by Ruskin or the 200 by associated artists at Bembridge. Brief mention has already been made of the 350 drawings now at Brantwood.

Portraits of Ruskin in the collections include the 1841 cameo cut in Rome (acquired from the Sharp collection in 1959), the 1853 drawing by Millais (bought with Millais's sketch of Sir Henry Acland from the Trevelyan collection in May 1951), the 1864 crayon portrait by Samuel Laurence (from the Lane collection), the *c.* 1866 and the 1874 self-portraits, the 1877 bust by Benjamin Creswick and the 1897 portraits by Severn and Collingwood.

Here, too, is the portrait of Ruskin's father done as a wedding present for John in 1848 by George Richmond.

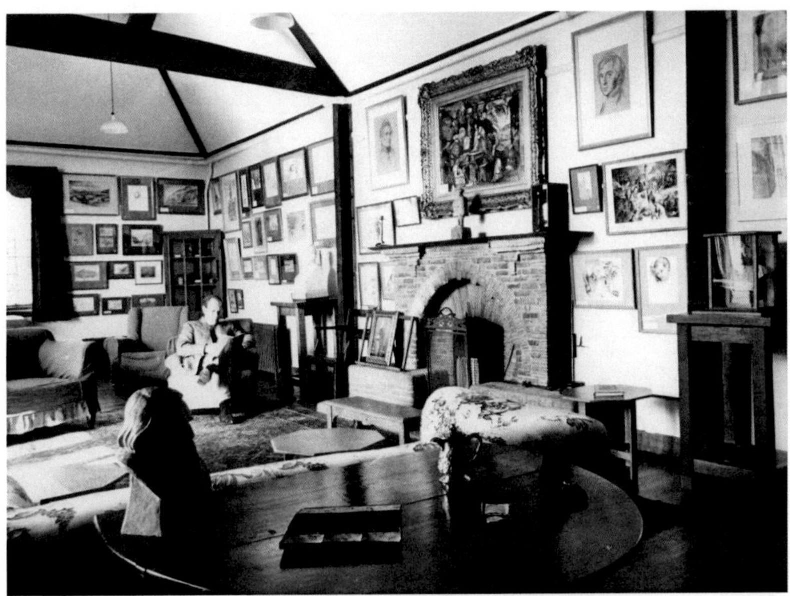

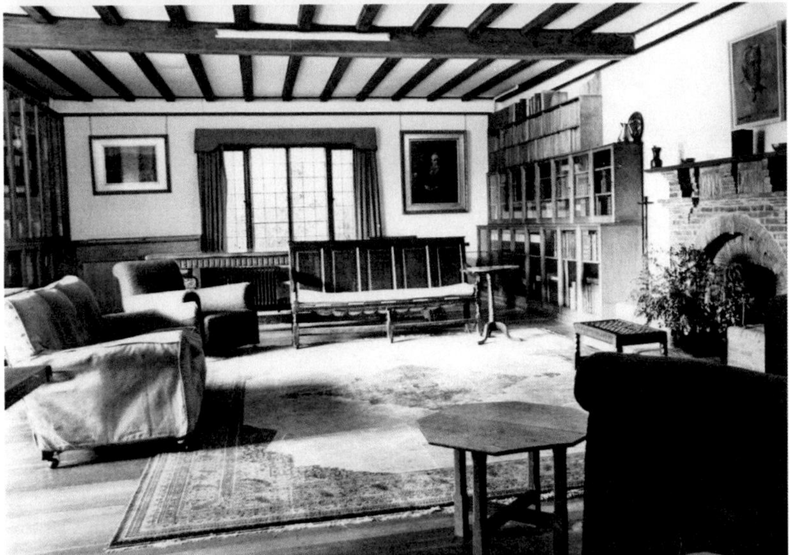

Top, the Ruskin Galleries Upper Gallery, showing part of the collection of Ruskin drawings. Bottom, the Ruskin Galleries Warden's Library; the cases on the right house some of the books from Ruskin's own collection (Ruskin Foundation)

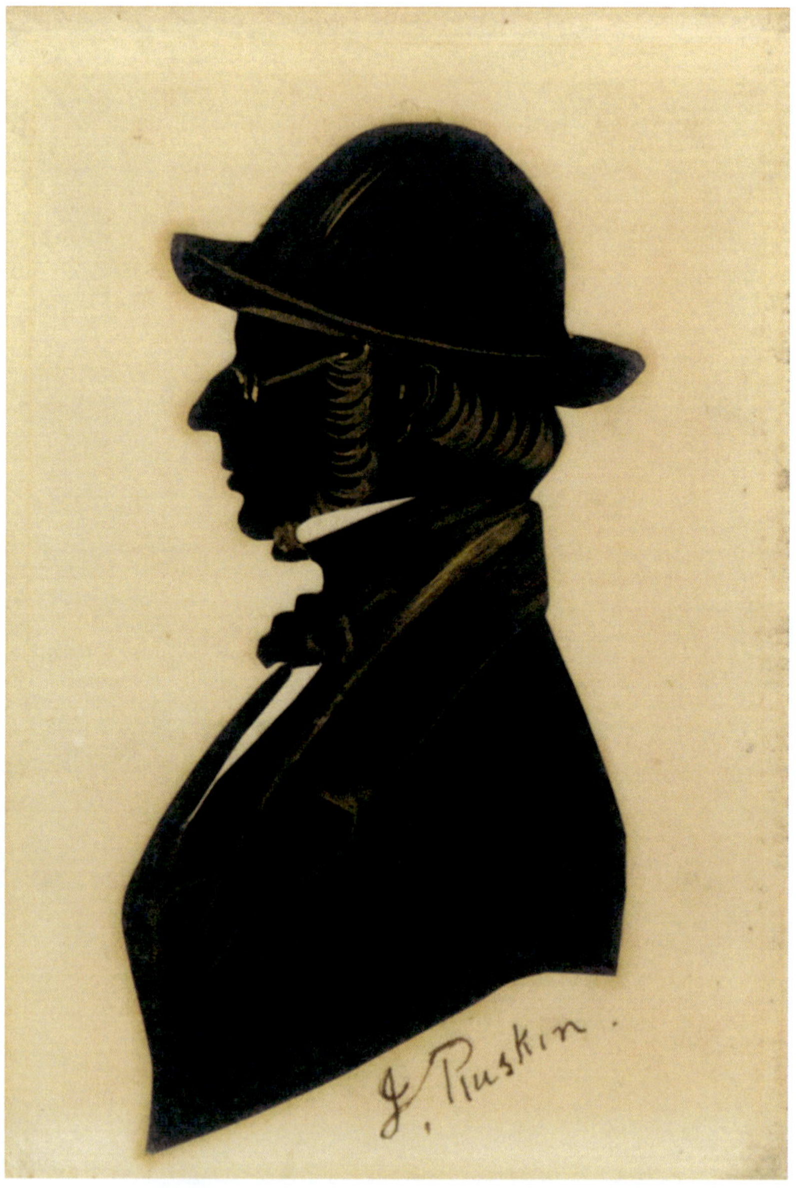

John Ruskin, c. *1870. A previously unpublished anonymous silhouette (Ruskin Foundation)*

I have already referred to Whitehouse's mass purchases of Ruskin drawings at the dispersal sales. The Stevens and Brown files (L. 72-5) show that Whitehouse bought most drawings that were offered to him, right up to the time of his death, sometimes as collections, sometimes singly.

In addition to buying for Whitehouse at Brantwood, Stevens & Brown also bought for Charles Goodspeed, the Boston bookseller. Apart from being a dealer, Goodspeed was a Ruskin collector in his own right and at one time owned many important pieces. In 1935 Whitehouse bought from him his remaining stock of Ruskin drawings. The collection contained 171 items. Some of the drawings were slight or diagrammatic, but there were at least twenty-five important drawings in the collection, as well as three sketch books. One of these was Ruskin's last sketch book containing one of his last recorded sketches, made on 3 June 1889 of the Langdale Pikes. This piece formed a fitting companion to Ruskin's 'first' sketch book of *c.* 1830 which Whitehouse already owned. And by chance the Goodspeed collection also brought back to Bembridge two detached leaves with sketches of Battle Abbey and Rocks at Tunbridge Wells which Ruskin had removed from his first sketch book before giving it to Mrs Talbot in 1885. Whitehouse was later to obtain the two leaves with sketches of Canterbury Cathedral which Ruskin had also removed and given to Miss Gale in 1880.

Another group of drawings, bought as a collection, were ten important ones, including some from the 1830s which Ruskin had given to Sara Anderson. These were bought in March 1951.

Appropriately enough, two of Whitehouses's last purchases for his collection were drawings. In March 1954 he bought a small portrait sketch of Ruskin made by T. Henderson, probably in Manchester, in December 1864. His last purchase, made in November 1954 just ten months before his death, was the important 1837 drawing by Ruskin of 'Cloisters and Pinnacles at the west end of Peterborough Cathedral'. This drawing was one of Ruskin's own favourites and used to hang in his drawing room at Brantwood, among his Prouts.

II. LETTERS

The Ruskin family correspondence is the most important part of the letter collection. Earliest in the series is a twelve-page letter (L 11) dated 'London 5 October 1812' from John James Ruskin to his mother at Bowerswell, which reads 'I cannot conceive what has given you the Idea of my not wishing to come to my Father's house.... Had you seen the Lodgings I have at various times lived in you would have a very different opinion on this head.... Do not you think a person immured for 8 years in a London Counting House would be delighted with a Journey to the Country....' The letter is endorsed by JJR 'I know nothing in this letter that need be kept from Margaret'. J. J. Ruskin and Margaret Cock were first cousins. They had become engaged in 1809 but did not marry until 1818, the year after John Thomas Ruskin, heavily in debt, committed suicide. In the same file is a letter to JJR from one of his father's creditors, with a bill for £30 which had been outstanding for twenty-nine years; to the principal they had added £43 10*s.* interest!

Margaret Cock's mother died on 29 September 1817; nine days earlier she wrote to her daughter (L 30): 'My dear Girl, I think the time Long since you Last rote to me ... and itt Please God to take me there will Be 40 Pounds a year for you the same for Your sister wich Gives Me Some Comfort as I think itt will keep you above want... I cannot walk no where, I ride out in a donkey Chaise....'

The letters from Margaret Ruskin to her husband (L 1) begin with one letter of 1814 prior to their marriage. The second is dated 27 March 1819 and contains the earliest reference at Bembridge to John Ruskin, by then about seven weeks old. 'John grows finely he is just now on my knees sleeping and looking so sweetly I hope I shall not get proud of him but I fear I felt something like pride today....' John's 'first' letter, written by Margaret at his dictation, and signed by him, is contained in Margaret's letter to her husband of 15 March 1823. There are 154 letters in this file, mostly confined to a few for each year from 1814 to 1857, written when JJR was travelling on business, though they are more numerous when Margaret moved to Oxford to be near John. At this period many contain hasty marginal postscripts from John.

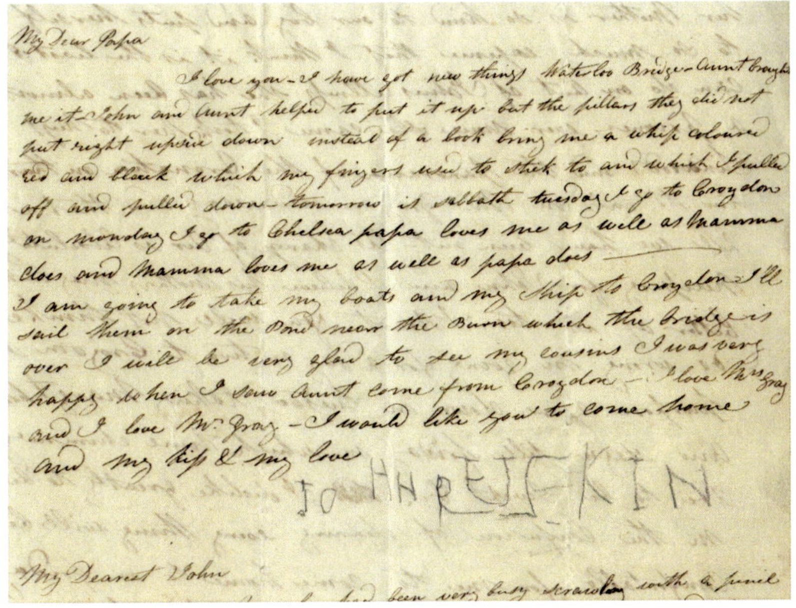

My Dear Papa

I love you - I have got new things Waterloo Bridge - Aunt brought me it - John and Aunt helped to put it up but the pillars they did not put right upside down instead of a book bring me a whip coloured red and black which my fingers used to stick to and which I pulled off and pulled down - tomorrow is sabbath tuesday I go to Croydon on monday I go to Chelsea papa loves me as well as Mamma does and Mamma loves me as well as papa does —

I am going to take my boats and my ship to Croydon I'll sail them on the Pond near the Burn which the bridge is over I will be very glad to see my cousins I was very happy when I saw Aunt come from Croydon - I love Mrs Gray and I love Mr Gray - I would like you to come home and my kiss & my love

JOHN RUSKIN

My Dearest John

… been very busy scrawling with a pencil

John Ruskin's 'First letter', written by his mother at his dictation and signed by himself, 15 March 1823 (Ruskin Foundation)

The series of eighty letters from John James Ruskin to his wife (L 2) runs from 1812 to 1859. Again, they are most numerous during the Oxford period. One interesting letter is dated 20 June 1838 and announces that there is a ticket to the Abbey for the coronation for John. Two days later JJR reported that he had been to the Abbey to examine the scaffolding on which John's seat was located and had found it quite safe. He had then been to Owen's to order John's court dress and he instructed his wife to buy white gloves in Oxford. On 23 June JJR was still worrying about the position of John's seat in the Abbey, though he copied a letter from Blue Mantle Herald, '… Lord Brownlow had two for his sons for the same place today … still I would give my ticket and some cash to have a place in the Body of the Abbey'.

From John James to John there are 264 letters (L 3-4), 1829-62. They discuss a multitude of subjects – criticism of John's writings, the purchase of pictures, Turner's estate, reviews of John's books, financial arrangements, family matters, and many other topics. Most of the other half of the correspondence, John to his father, is at Yale, but there are eight leaves from 1858 at Bembridge (MS 38) in which John writes about the pictures in the gallery at Turin.

Most of the 399 letters from John to his mother, 1853-71 (B VI and L 26) were bought after the Warwick Square sale, as mentioned above. Whitehouse always hoped to publish this series of letters, but time was never on his side. The greater part of the correspondence is dated after 1864 when JJR died; before this John's letters home had usually been addressed to his father. There are also ten letters (L 26), 1842-67, from Margaret to her son.

There are no letters at Bembridge which passed between John and his wife, but there is one from JJR to Effie (L 11) and one from Effie's mother to Margaret (L 11) written on the day following the wedding.

John James's last two letters (L 30), referred to in *Praeterita*, are enclosed in an envelope endorsed by John, 'The two last letters my Father wrote. He sate up till past 12 waiting for me to come in, from London – (Working Men's College I think) – and read these to me. He was struck with his death-illness the following morning – 28th February [1864].'

The largest single series of letters is that from Ruskin to Joan Agnew, later Joan Severn (L 33-54). The letters range from 1864, when Joan first went to live at Denmark Hill as a companion to the widowed Margaret, to 1895, just five years before Ruskin himself died. There are 2,734 dated letters and two files of undated ones. In reply are eight files (L 55-62) of letters from Joan to John, from 1867 to 1899. Clearly there is not space here to go into the details of this correspondence. Suffice it to say that it is of the greatest biographical importance. From 1864 scarcely a day passed when Ruskin and Joan were apart that he did not write to her, on many occasions more than once each day. On a number of occasions when he was abroad, his letters are long and detailed, and written to Joan instead of in his Diary. He specifically tells her to keep them because they are intended as his Diary and will be needed for reference.

George Allen was one of Ruskin's chief assistants, engraving for him, helping him with the Turner sketches in the National Gallery, and finally in the 1870s becoming his publisher. The Bembridge collection contains one hundred letters to Allen, 1857-72 (B II-IV and B IVA). One of the letters is in a special folder and is accompanied by a letter from the *Encyclopædia Britannica* Company presenting it to a purchaser of a set of the *Library Edition* in 1914. The other letters are bound in three volumes by Sangorski and Sutcliffe and include an introduction by William S. Allen.

Charles Augustus Howell was another assistant to Ruskin, with a somewhat roving commission. The collection of sixty-five letters, 1856-67, from Ruskin to him (B I), formerly in M. H. Spielmann's collection and bought for Bembridge in 1949, contain Ruskin's instructions on a multitude of subjects.

Most of Ruskin's twenty-two letters to Frederick Crawley (L 22), his valet and later in charge of his rooms at Oxford, contain demands for the despatch of books, manuscripts, minerals, pictures – from Brantwood to Venice, Oxford to Brantwood, or wherever Ruskin happened to be. The letters of a later valet – Baxter – written from Folkestone to Mrs Severn (L 63) give a quite different picture of Ruskin in their daily reports on his health and activities.

A few of Ruskin's letters in the Bembridge catalogue are kept at Brantwood. Most important among these are the two volumes (B XVI-XVII) containing his 168 letters to Bernard Quaritch, 1867-88. They give a fascinating picture of Ruskin's book-buying habits. The correspondence ends soon after the dispute over the Toggenburg Codex. Another volume at Brantwood (B XIX) contains a number of letters from Ruskin to the Webling sisters.

Letters to friends of long standing, include ninety-two to the Scott family (B V) 1855-80, published by Whitehouse in *The Solitary Warrior*, twenty-eight to Coventry Patmore and his family (L 14), thirty to F. J. Furnivall about Ruskin's marriage, a proposed bust of Ruskin by Munro, Working Men's College business, and other matters (L 17), and twenty-nine to Miss Corlass of Hull, 1843-68 (L 18). These last contain many references to Rose La Touche and in one is an interesting passage on drawing, '... I think you were the first person who showed me how flowers were painted.... The whole difficulty of the art as commonly taught proceeds from the Forbidding the pupil to look at what is to be done....' To Rose La Touche's mother there are ten letters, 1881-9 (B x).

There is only one letter in the collection from Ruskin to his 'old and tried friend' Jean Ingelow (L 13), but there are fifteen from Miss Ingelow to Eliza Fall, the sister of Ruskin's 'first play-fellow and unfailing friend'. Here, too, are two letters from Ruskin to Richard Fall himself (B XIII), and thirty-two to Eliza, as well as six from John James to Eliza (L 13 and B XIII). One of the twenty-three letters from Ruskin to the Rev. F. W. Farrar (B XIII) deals with the subject of a pension for Miss Ingelow.

Of importance to the study of Ruskin's writing, both in prose and verse, are two long series of letters to W. H. Harrison. One group of 180, 1836-80 (B XII), is from John, the other group, 148 (L 5), from John James. Mainly these letters discuss alterations to John's books and poems which Harrison had proposed, or deal with the correction of proofs. One section of the JJR-W.H.H. letters deals with the production of *Poems*, 1850.

Letters to Ruskin's publishers about the printing of his books are represented by sixteen to George Smith, 1869-74 (L 21), and two to Robert Chester (B XV) of Smith Elder & Co. In the 1870s Ruskin's printing was gradually transferred to the firm of Watson & Hazell. The series of 111 letters to Henry Jowett, their printing manager, runs from 1873 to 1889 (L 15). It gives a fascinating insight into the care Ruskin took over the production of his books and the seemingly haphazard way in which some of the serials, such as *Fors Clavigera* and *Praeterita*, were put together. It is interesting to see Ruskin's first draft of the title page for *Praeterita* in one of these letters.

The twenty letters (L 21) in the 1870s to Sir James Knowles, editor of the *Contemporary Review* and founder and editor of the *Nineteenth Century*, deal, among other things, with work that Ruskin was doing – or refusing to do – for his magazines. These letters were bought by Whitehouse in November 1937. For the Arundel Society in 1874 Ruskin visited Assisi to superintend Kaiser's copying of some of the Giotto frescoes. Ruskin's ten letters (B XIV) to F. W. Maynard of the Society report on the progress of the work. Ruskin's friendship with T. C. Horsfall, founder of the Ancoats Art Museum, seems to have begun in 1877. The fifty-four letters to him (L 32) run from 1877 to 1884, and include the eight-page manuscript of Ruskin's introduction to Horsfall's *The Study of Beauty and Art in Large Towns*. Twenty-six letters from Ruskin to Marcus B. Huish, secretary of The Fine Art Society, date from 1875-86 (L 20). They are concerned with Ruskin's Turner exhibition and include part of the manuscript of *A Museum or Picture Gallery*, published in the Art Journal in 1880.

Ruskin's letters to members of the clergy include a correspondence with the vicar of Coniston, the Rev. Charles Chapman (L 23), bought in 1944. Several of the dozen letters deal with parish or school matters; Ruskin was one of the managers of the Coniston School. The Rev. Edward Clayton was Ruskin's tutor. In the eleven long letters of the early 1840s (B XIII) he is addressed as 'Respected Sir', 'Dear Pugnacious Clayton', 'My dear Irascible', 'My dear Good Clayton'. Most of the series deals with religious topics.

We find Ruskin himself in the role of tutor, or rather drawing master, in the thirty letters, 1886-7, to Miss Fortunée de Lisle (L 19). Another pupil – Louise Blandy – pasted thirty-two of Ruskin's letters and many of her sketches and photographs and pressed flowers into a typically Victorian scrap album (B IX). Elsewhere there are fourteen other letters to Louise about drawing (L 23) and several of her sketch-books and drawings bearing Ruskin's comments.

Other series of letters include thirty-one to Henry Willett of Brighton (B XIII), nine to Thomas Carlyle and five from Carlyle to Ruskin (B XIV), and seventy-four to Annie Sumerscales, a school teacher of Hull and Companion of St George's Guild (L 16). There is no room here to mention many other letters in the collection to and from Ruskin and the Severns, or other allied correspondence.

Reference has already been made to Ruskin's 'first letter' which is at Bembridge. It is only right, therefore, to add that we also have what is probably his last letter. Cook and Wedderburn reproduce a letter of October 1893 to Susan Beever (probably now in the Huntington Library) and describe it as the 'last' (they probably meant that it was the last letter from Ruskin to Susan Beever). Later than this are letters of March 1894 to Lady Simon (now in the collection of Dr H. G. Viljoen), June 1894 and May 1895 to Joan Severn (L 53)

BRANTWOOD,
CONISTON LAKE,
R.S.O.

'Last letter' – an attempt to write to Mary Drew on the death of her father, W. E. Gladstone. Probably 21 May 1898 (Ruskin Foundation)

and October 1895 to Sir John Simon (Dr Viljoen). In 1898 Ruskin wrote to Mary Drew on the death of her father, Gladstone. Two drafts for the letter are at Bembridge (L 29). Their faltering words are almost indecipherable. One reads, 'Dear Mary, I am so grieved at your having lost your father'. This is probably Ruskin's last letter. In addition to this the Bembridge collection contains twenty-four autographs, many of them dated, done for Mrs Severn between 1895 and 1898 (L 29).

III. MANUSCRIPTS

(a) Miscellaneous Ruskin Manuscripts

Undoubtedly the most important single Ruskin manuscript at Bembridge is that of his Diary (MS 1-26). It is contained in twenty-nine volumes of assorted shapes and sizes and runs from 1835 to 1889. The chronological part of the 'Diary', which has been published, represents less than half of the contents of the volumes. The miscellaneous unpublished notes include records of his reading, notes on chess games, analyses of his illuminated manuscripts, notes and plans for *Praeterita*, notes on pictures, accounts, and many other subjects. Other miscellaneous manuscripts in this part of the collection are the catalogue of his coin collection (MS 27), the large ledger (MS 45) listed by Cook and Wedderburn containing mythological notes and the first plan of the 1883 Oxford lectures, and Ruskin's holograph 'Statement' to his Proctor regarding his marriage, with its allied documents (MS 66 and L 67).

(b) Ruskin's Literary Manuscripts

Among the earliest literary manuscripts at Bembridge are the early drafts of some of Ruskin's childhood poems, for example, 'The Shipwreck', 1829, which are contained in letters to his father. Probably the earliest independent manuscript is the holograph copy of 'Remembrance' sent to the editor of *Friendship's Offering* for inclusion in the 1838 issue (MS 51/C III). A fair copy of 'The Exile of St Helena', written for the Newdigate Prize of 1838, has been extracted from a longer notebook and bound separately (MS 37).

The bulk of the *Modern Painters* manuscript was in America by the time Cook and Wedderburn edited the *Library Edition*, but they recorded fragments remaining at Coniston which they listed as 'The Brantwood Manuscript'. Several items, most of them unused in *Modern Painters*, from this part of the manuscript, include 'Of size and its effects on the sublime' (MS 50/A), 'Notes on a painter's profession as ending irreligiously' (MS 50/B), a discarded part of the preface to volume 3 (MS 50/C), 'Ideas of Relation' (MS 50/D), notes on tree branches (MS 50/F) and 'Supplementary Notes on Terror arising from weakness of health' (MS 48).

Cook and Wedderburn also noted that part of the *Stones of Venice* manuscript was in America, but they listed a large quantity of working sketches and notes (1636-44), forty-six pages of manuscript and sketches including two drafts of the 1881 Epilogue (MS 76) and the page proofs of volumes 2 and 3 (MS 77) corrected by Ruskin and Harrison. Other proofs corrected by Ruskin and Harrison are those for *The Elements of Drawing* (MS 57/B).

Ruskin's early essays on political economy are represented by the manuscript of 'Government', chapter v of *Munera Pulveris* (MS 51/F). *Munera Pulveris* was first published as a series of essays on political economy in *Fraser's Magazine* in 1863. It was revised for separate publication in 1872. MS 51/F is the revised manuscript of 'Government' though it differs in a number of respects from the version as finally published in 1872. 'Gold', a dialogue connected with *Munera Pulveris*, was published in 1891 by T. J. Wise. The printer's copy (MS 52/B) contains notes by the editor, Buxton Forman. The essays which appeared in *The Art Journal* in 1865 under the title, 'Cestus of Aglaia' were reprinted in *Queen of the Air* and *On The Old Road*. Chapter III was read by Ruskin as part of his 1884 series of Oxford lectures and the corrected proofs (MS 56/C) show that it was set with the intention of re-printing it, probably as chapter 5 of *The Pleasures of England* – but the idea seems to have been abandoned. No doubt a study of the Ruskin/Jowett letters would throw additional light on the subject.

Ruskin's poem 'Ah sweet lady' (MS 51/C II) was addressed to Rose La Touche on her eighteenth birthday in 1866.

The first exhibition of Ruskin's drawings was that which he

prepared himself, one hundred years ago, to illustrate his lecture of 29 January 1869 on *The Flamboyant Architecture of the Valley of the Somme*. The exhibition catalogue was printed in 1869 but the manuscript of the lecture (MS 42) was printed for the first time in the *Library Edition*. In the following year another exhibition was arranged to illustrate 'Verona and its rivers'. The lecture was included in the volume *Verona and other lectures*, edited in 1894 by W. G. Collingwood, whose page proofs are MS 71.

What little remains of the *Fors Clavigera* manuscript is widely scattered. At Bembridge we have the manuscript and partial page proof of Letter 91, 'Dust of Gold' (MS 49), corrected proofs of part of the Second Series, Letter 5 (MS 58/A) and the manuscript of the *Index* to volumes 1 and 2 (MS 50/G).

Probably all that remains of the manuscript of *The Eagle's Nest*, 1872, are the revised proofs of Lecture 1 and part of Lecture 2 and the manuscript of Lecture 4 and part of Lecture 5 (MS 56/A).

The three parts of *Love's Meinie* were issued between 1873 and 1881. The manuscript of the first lecture, 'The Robin' (MS 43) was formerly in Wedderburn's collection. MS 50/H contain a large part of the manuscript of lecture 3, 'The Dabchicks' and three leaves of the 'Appendix'. There is also a copy in Crawley's hand of part of 'The Chough'. Another Oxford lecture series was *Val d'Arno*, of which one leaf of manuscript, the end of chapter 10, is MS 51/L. MS 57/A contains proof copies of Lectures II, V, VI and VIII, all with extensive manuscript revisions.

Ruskin's *Academy Notes* were first published in 1855. In the manuscript preface (MS 56/B) to the 1875 issue he wrote, 'It is now just twenty years since I wrote the first number of these notes and fifteen since they were discontinued'. The 1875 issue was the sixth and last in the series. MS 56/B are galley proofs of the whole pamphlet, heavily annotated, together with a number of manuscript additions. Parts 1-4 of *Mornings in Florence* were also published in 1875, parts 5 and 6 following in 1876 and 1877. The thirty-nine leaves of manuscript (MS 46) comprise most of part 1 and sections of parts 4 and 5.

'Bibliotheca Pastorum' was to be a series of 'classic books which I hope to make the chief domestic treasures of British peasants'. So

Manuscript of the first draft of the Editor's Preface to The Economist of Xenophon
(Ruskin Foundation)

wrote Ruskin in the preface to *The Economist of Xenophon*, the first volume in the series. The manuscript of the preface (MS 41) is an interesting example of the chaos which Ruskin's secretaries, editors and printers had to cope with. The volume contains the first draft of the preface which Ruskin sent to Wedderburn to copy for the printer, Ruskin's fair copy of the first four leaves of the preface (no more of this was done), and the first and second proofs corrected by Ruskin. His corrections bill today would be enormous!

'The Three Colours of Pre-Raphaelitism' first appeared in the November and December 1878 issues of the *Nineteenth Century*. It was subsequently re-printed in *On the Old Road*. Of the existing manuscript of the second paper (MS 51/K) one leaf was facsimiled in the Library Edition, vol. XXXIV, page 166. The manuscript and revised proofs of *Notes by Mr Ruskin on his drawings by the late J. M. W. Turner Esq.*, 1878, have been re-united at Bembridge. The bulk of the manuscript is contained in one volume (MS 39), given by Marcus Huish to Henry Beaumont. The remainder of the manuscript, thirty-nine leaves in all (MS 50/I), containing the Introduction and the Epilogue, came to Bembridge as a result of the Brantwood sales.

Arrows of the Chase is a collection of Ruskin's letters to the Press. Naturally much of the original manuscript is lost. The book seems to have been printed from manuscript copies of the printed letters, and a bundle of these, in various hands, is now MS 55.

Cook and Wedderburn record 'no manuscript' for *The Elements of English Prosody* but MS 51/O contains five leaves of manuscript for the work and MS 62 comprises page- and galley-proofs of pages 1-51.

The bibliography of *Letters to the Clergy on the Lord's Prayer*, both printed and in manuscript, is one of the most complicated in the whole Ruskin field. In 1880 Ruskin wrote a final letter as Epilogue for the first edition of the complete book. Wedderburn was evidently unable to find the whole manuscript of this Epilogue at Brantwood in 1908 when editing volume XXIV of the *Library Edition*. Subsequently the missing leaves must have come to light, for all eighteen are now MS 51/M. The detailed history of *Our Fathers have told us* is almost equally complicated. Suffice it to say that the bulk of the manuscript – 124 leaves – almost all of part 1, *The Bible of Amiens*, together with notes for *Valle Crucis* and *Candida Casa*, are in MS 46. The publication of *Proserpina* began in 1875; volume 2 began to appear in 1882. Twelve leaves from the first chapter of the second volume are at Bembridge (MS 51/J).

1883 saw the publication of *The Art of England* of which we have the manuscript of parts of Lectures 3, 5 and 6 and Appendix, together with the corrected proofs of lecture 5 (MS 51/E). In the same year Ruskin wrote the preface (MS 51/G) for Francesca Alexander's *Story of Ida*. *The Pleasures of England* contain four lectures given at Oxford in the Michaelmas Term, 1884. They were published in 1884-5. MS 64 and 63 are corrected page proofs of lectures 1 and 3 while MS 57/C is the corrected galley proof of lecture 2, marked by Ruskin, 'For Reporter'.

Praeterita, Ruskin's last major work, was published in parts between 1885 and 1889. Not a lot of the manuscript remains. A study of the Ruskin/Jowett correspondence reveals Ruskin's method of writing the book. The type for some sections was standing for a long time before it was used and the whole was put together rather like a jigsaw puzzle. There are two fragments of the manuscript at Bembridge (MS 51/DI, 51/DII) and corrected proof copies of three parts (MS 59, 60, 61). Additionally one or two of the later volumes of the Diaries contain notes and plans for the work.

Other late fragments of manuscripts are parts of the *Catalogue of Drawings for St George's Guild* (MS 51/A) and proof copies of *Christ's Folk* (MS 68, 69).

(c) Manuscripts of Ruskin Association

Mention has already been made of several manuscripts of Ruskin association. Others in the collection include one of the few remaining Rose La Touche documents (MS 36). This is a small black notebook in which Rose wrote notes on several of Ruskin's Oxford lectures of 1872 which she had evidently attended.

Another interesting little manuscript is W. J. Linton's Inventory of the contents of Brantwood (MS 53/A) made in 1867 when he left Coniston to emigrate to America. Many of these contents were in the house when Ruskin bought it in 1871. The Inventory is not only of interest for its own sake, but also because it enables us to know, in the absence of early plans, just exactly what was the lay-out of the house which Ruskin bought.

In 1854 Ruskin was prevailed upon to help with the Working Men's College and to teach art there. He says in *Praeterita*, 'I took two special pupils out of its ranks, to carry them forward all I could. One I chose ... a carpenter of equal skill and great fineness of faculty; but his pride, wilfulness, and certain angular narrowness of nature, kept him down...'. This favourite pupil was George Butterworth. His Diary of 1855-6 (MS 35) contains some interesting accounts of Ruskin at the college as well as accounts of many of Butterworth's conversations with Ruskin.

(d) J. J. Ruskin's Manuscripts

Invaluable to the study of Ruskin's early life and to the lives of his parents is a group of eight notebooks kept by John James Ruskin.

Three of these are Diaries. The earliest, a small half-calf volume (MS 33/A), recently presented to the collection by H. C. Adams, Esq., is a travelling diary used between 1833 and 1846. It contains a seventy-four page account of the 1833 continental tour, a short diary from 14-31 May 1844, and a diary of the 1846 tour starting on 2 April, 'by railroad to Dover, Bad weather', and finishing on 21 September at Dijon.

The next diary is a thin volume in marbled paper covers (MS 32) inscribed by Ruskin, 'My Father's account of the journey of 1835 – beginning at Poligny'. Five leaves have been removed from the beginning, leaving twenty-six pages and the back cover. The diary begins on 30 June 1835 with the entry, 'Left Poligny at 8 o'clock & never passed a more delightful day...' and ends on 24 September. The final leaf has been torn out, but written on the inside back cover is the diary for 4-6 October. This forms a useful supplement to Ruskin's own diary of the same tour which finishes on 25 September.

The most interesting volume in this group (MS 33) runs from 1845 to 1864. Many of the entries are merely a record of the senior Ruskins' dinner guests, with occasional references to John's activities. Typical random entries are, '27 April 1853 Dinner Mr & Mrs Pritchard, Sir W. & Ly Trevelyan & Millais. Jn & E at Rogers & Wigram', '9 June

1861 John unwell but at Church with me – Runciman Harrison & Furnivall not admitted'. But the diary also contains many longer entries, as well as JJR's account of his last illness, finishing on 26 February 1864, five days before his death, '... Legs swelled. Nervous – little sleep till 3 o'clock great pain – up at 3 & at 6'.

There are many non-diary entries in the notebook. For example, the first two and the last four leaves contain presentation lists for a number of John's books – *Poems* 1850, *King of the Golden River* (Effie Ruskin, for whom the story was originally written, getting six copies), *Academy Notes* 1858, *Stones of Venice*, volumes 1, 2 and 3, *Harbours of England*, *Modern Painters*, volume 5. Then there are many pages of précis of letters to John and others, two pages of accounts with Smith Elder for John's books, and a list prepared in 1852 of the pictures in his possession. This lists sixty-nine pictures valued at £4595 17s. and records where they were hanging and when they were bought.

Two further picture lists are to be found in JJR's account books, 1827-63 (MS 28, 29). These two volumes contain a very detailed account of JJR's income and expenditure, the latter divided into annual groups under general headings, Sundries, Charities & Gifts, House Keeping, Country & Doctors, Garden, Wines & Spirits, Wages to Servants, Coal, Clothes – Mrs R., my own, John's Education – &c. These accounts make very interesting reading and often enable us to date events in John's life with precision. And they pose many interesting little problems. What, for example, caused the entry of 13 August 1852, 'Recd R.E. Insurance for Hopkinson's carriage lost at Sea, less £20 pd Corben packg. £130', or why did JJR need to buy twenty-one umbrellas between 1830 and 1839? JJR was a very generous man as is illustrated by his Charities account. In the last year of his life his gifts to charities amounted to £4,109. These accounts seem to have been written up annually from small pocket notebooks like the one for 1862 (MS 31). MS 30 is another account book which records, among other things, JJR's account with his own business of Ruskin, Telford & Domecq from 1826 to 1863 ('1 Jan 1863 To balance due to me this date £32,263-0-2d.'). 'Amount of all my property at this date 31 December 1827 £21,938-2-10', 'Clear value of my entire property & that of my son given to him by me,

1 Sept 1863, £161,416-18'. A summary of his charities begins in 1825 with 'Pd for my Father till now, £3,203-18-2'. The total charities between 1825 and 1853 are £20,579-1-6.

The final volume in the group of manuscripts belonging to JJR contains copies of his letters to his business partner, J. P. Domecq, from 1839 to 1842. It is complementary to the two files of Domecq letters (L. 9-10), which contain forty-five letters from to various members of the Domecq family, a large number of letters from the Domecq family to JJR, 1836-43, and a complete set of the printed circulars which the firm of Ruskin, Telford and Domecq distributed to its customers between 1816 and 1864. Also in the collection are photocopies of memoranda of agreements (T. 40) which relate to the later history of the firm.

IV. TRANSCRIPTS

There are some sixty volumes or files in this section of the Bembridge catalogue. It seems that when Cook and Wedderburn were preparing the *Library Edition* they first typed all the letters and manuscripts which they found at Brantwood and elsewhere. Their editing was then done from these transcripts. Twenty-eight volumes of their transcripts are at Bembridge. In the case of the fifteen volumes of Diary transcripts, the original manuscripts are also at Bembridge, but the Cook and Wedderburn transcripts at Bembridge include, in addition, *Early Prose Writings*, *Harry and Lucy*, *The Puppet Show*, *Notes on Frederick William*, *Iteriad*, two volumes of *Poems*, 1826-38, and three volumes of *Modern Painters*. The original manuscripts of these works are in other collections and so it is of particular value to have the transcripts at Bembridge, available for reference to students who may be unable to reach the originals.

The originals of much of the other material present in this section of the collection are in other private or public collections. The transcripts or photocopies have been lodged at Bembridge for reference. In one or two cases the whereabouts of the originals is no longer known to Ruskin students, the manuscripts or letters now being available only from these copies.

This section forms a valuable supplement to the original Ruskin material at Bembridge.

V. PRINTED BOOKS

Whitehouse must have started collecting books by and about Ruskin from the time that his interest was first aroused. One of his first seems to have been a copy of W. G. Collingwood's *Life and Work of John Ruskin* (2 vols, 1st edition, 1893). This copy has twice been re-bound and contains Whitehouse's early signatures on the fly-leaves of both volumes. From this early acquisition his collection of Ruskin books grew as the result of many purchases, sometimes of individual volumes, sometimes of complete collections – the latter resulting in many duplications. An attempt is now being made to complete the collection. Very few titles are lacking, but a number of the later editions of Ruskin's books remain to be found.

A few statistics may help to describe the extent of the collection. There are some 900 volumes by Ruskin, including two different sets of the *Library Edition*, occupying some eighty-eight feet of shelving. The 200-odd books about Ruskin take up another twelve feet. These hundred feet of shelves contain no duplicates. The duplicates – two more sets of the *Library Edition* and four cases of miscellaneous books – are housed elsewhere.

A considerable number of volumes were formerly in the libraries of other Ruskin admirers – William Ward, Selwyn Image, J. P. Smart (secretary of the Ruskin Society of London and joint editor with T. J. Wise of the *Ruskin Bibliography*), John Morgan (Ruskinian and well-known book collector of Aberdeen), S. W. Bush (another ardent Ruskin collector) and Michael Tomkinson. To these I have been able to add a number from the library of W. G. Collingwood.

(a) Books by Ruskin

Ruskin's earliest published pieces, the poem 'On Skiddaw and Derwent Water' from the *Spiritual Times* of 1830,* and articles from

* A situation rectified several years later!

the *Magazine of Natural History* of the early 1830s, are not in the collection. But his early poems and other pieces are present in an 1829-44 run of *Friendship's Offering* and various volumes of the *Keepsake*, Heath's *Book of Beauty* and other annuals.

The earliest independent piece to bear Ruskin's name is *Salsette and Elephanta*, 1839, reprinted with its own title page and pagination by J. Vincent from his *Oxford Prize Poems*, 1839. The blue paper covers of the Galleries' copy bears the inscription 'R. Fall Esqr' in Ruskin's hand. The poem was reprinted in 1879.

The first collected edition of Ruskin's youthful poems was prepared in 1850 by John James Ruskin and W. H. Harrison and has been the subject of a separate study.[2] The Bembridge copy is in the green 'female' binding. Two unauthorized editions by Ruskin's principal American pirate, Wiley, were published in 1882 and 1884. Both volumes, *The Old Waterwheel and other Poems*, and *Poems*, were edited by J. O. Wright. The next authorized English edition was that edited in two volumes by W. G. Collingwood in 1891. The 'special' edition on handmade paper, and the 'ordinary' edition both contain a fine series of reproductions of Ruskin's drawings. The 'small' edition only contains the facsimiles of manuscripts.

Collingwood's page-proofs (MS 70) of the 1891 edition, in their home-made binding of rather violently-patterned curtain material, are carefully dated. The proofs of the earliest signatures arrived in September 1890 (A, 19th; BC, 22nd; D, 23rd; E-L, 1st Oct; MN, 3rd), until finally the last signature (vol. II, Z) was with the editor at Coniston on 19 November. The Prospectus shows that the 'Special' and the 'Small' editions were published on 21 October 1891. The 'ordinary' edition was issued two weeks later.

Other editions of Ruskin's poetry include *A Walk in Chamouni and other Poems* by John Ruskin, published by J. R. Tutin of Hull, and the Waverley Book Company's edition of *Poems*, with an introductory essay by G. K. Chesterton; and, of course, there are copies of the *Pigwiggian Chaunts*, *The Pheasant* and *Ah Sweet Lady*, the last with its initial and decoration by Margaret Adams.

The first edition of *Dame Wiggins of Lee*, 1885, contains additional verses by Ruskin and is present in the collection in grey, red and green bindings, with a large-paper copy in brown and a third edition in green.

In the case containing the poetry is also to be found *The King of the Golden River*. Ruskin wrote this fairy story in 1841 for his future wife. It is still read by the lower forms of the John Ruskin Grammar School at Croydon. *The King of the Golden River* was first published in 1851 with illustrations by Richard Doyle. The first two editions are in pictorial boards. The third and subsequent editions are in paper or cloth boards printed with a different design. We have twelve copies ranging from the first edition to the 34th thousand, with the Doyle illustrations. In addition there are the editions published by Collins' Penny Library (T. H. Robinson illustrations), Oxford Story Readers (unillustrated), The Studio, 1930 (F. H. Horvath illustrations), Harrap, 1932 (illustrated, signed and numbered by Arthur Rackham) and Edward Ward, 1958 (Charles Stewart illustrations).

It was the first volume of *Modern Painters*, first published in 1843, which brought Ruskin to prominence. The first two editions of volume 1 were published in a large crown 8vo. In 1846, when volume 2 was ready for publication, Ruskin decided that he was going to include illustrations in volume 3. In order to accommodate the illustrations it was decided to increase the size of the book to imperial 8vo, and so, to be in series, volume 2 was issued in this size. In the same year the third edition of volume 1 was being prepared and this was also increased to imperial 8vo. The final part, volume 5, was not published until 1860. By this time the previous volumes had been through several editions – volume 1 (editions 1-7), volume 2 (editions 1-5), volume 3 (not in fact published until ten years after it was decided that it would include illustrations, editions 1-2), volume 4 (editions 1-2), volume 5 (one edition only). Not until 1873, when the 'Autograph' edition appeared, were the five volumes published as a complete set. In 1888 the 'complete' edition was published, in a general and a large-paper edition. In the meantime, 'Re-arranged' editions in a smaller format had appeared in 1883 and 1885, and again in 1891. During this time Wileys of New York had been producing innumerable pirated editions. George Allen continued to issue the various authorized editions in various formats in this country, and subsequently other publishers issued their own versions of the book or selections from it.

In 1875, with the author's blessing, 'The Younger Lady of The Thwaite', Ruskin's friend Susan Beever, compiled her own volume of selections from *Modern Painters*, under the title of *Frondes Agrestes*. By 1890, 18,000 copies of this title had been printed in ten editions. By 1902, the date of the latest edition in the collection, the book was in its 38th thousand. Ruskin, too, produced his own selections from *Modern Painters*. *In Montibus Sanctis*, studies of mountain form, was published in two parts in 1884 and 1885; *Coeli Enarrant*, studies of cloud form, in 1885.

The complex publishing history of *Modern Painters* and its allied books is a typical example of the way in which most of Ruskin's books were issued. In the 1870s when he took over his own publishing and began issuing his books in parts, the situation became even more confusing. Here there is neither space nor necessity to go into it all in detail. Suffice it to say that almost all the early editions and many of the later editions of Ruskin's books are at Bembridge. But perhaps I may be allowed to mention a few of the scarcer items.

Of interest, though of no great scarcity, is the first edition of the pamphlet printed in an edition of about 600 copies by F. J. Furnivall and given, as a manifesto, to those attending the Working Men's College. This was part of the sixth chapter of the second volume of *The Stones of Venice* and was entitled *On the Nature of Gothic Architecture: and herein of the True Functions of the Workman in Art*. It is interesting to compare this small, shabby, typically mid-Victorian production on cheap paper with small margins, with the 1892 Kelmscott Press edition of the same work, with its Golden type, its woodcut initials and borders, on handmade paper and bound in vellum with green ties.

Another beautifully produced Ruskin book is the Doves Press edition of *Unto this Last*, 1907. *Unto this Last* was considered by Ruskin to be his most important work. It originally appeared in parts in the *Cornhill* in 1860, until Thackeray told Ruskin that he had to end the series with the fourth part. As editor, Thackeray could not endanger the future of his journal by continuing to publish such heresies of political economy. Ruskin issued it in book form in 1862; between then and 1905, 43,000 copies were issued in authorized editions. In addition there were many unauthorized editions. In 1902 it was translated into French, German and Italian. In 1904 it was read by Gandhi who translated it into an Indian tongue and said that he immediately determined to change his way of life in the light of its teaching. We have nineteen different editions at Bembridge ranging through the Cornhill parts, the first edition, the Doves (1907), Collins' Penny Library, Ballantyne (1902 – one of eleven copies on vellum), to a new 1967 edition published by the University of Nebraska Press, and a 1968 Everyman's re-issue.

Ruskin's Oxford *Lectures on Art*, delivered in 1870, were published in the same year as a demy 8vo of 189 pages. It is quite a common book. Much scarcer, at least in collections on this side of the Atlantic, is the export edition printed from the same setting of type. For export purposes the leads were removed from between the lines, the half titles were dropped, and the result was a crown 8vo volume of 155 pages.

The Crown of Wild Olive is another confused book. When it was first published in 1866 it contained three lectures, 'Work', 'Traffic' and 'War'. An additional lecture, 'The Future of England' was included in the fourth edition of 1873. The book itself is of little bibliographical interest, though the second pair of lectures is. Both were delivered at Woolwich, 'War' at the Royal Military Academy in 1865 and 'The Future of England' at the Royal Artillery Institution in 1869. When *The Crown of Wild Olive* was printed in 1866 Ruskin had a number of extra copies of *War* run off with its own pagination, title page and imprint, 'Printed for Private Circulation'. The Bembridge copy contains a slip tipped to the title page stating that Ruskin had presented the committee of the R.A. Institution with 100 copies of the booklet for distribution. This slip is not referred to by either Wise or Cook and Wedderburn. The half title bears the signature of the original owner, Lt.-Col. A. I. T. Green, R.A., of Plymouth, with the note, 'Recd. 19.6.66'. Wise says, 'This little book is exceedingly scarce', and Cook and Wedderburn, who were not prone to exaggeration, described it as 'one of the scarcest Ruskiniana'. *The Future of England* was originally printed as a pamphlet in 1870 by the Royal Artillery Press at Woolwich and is scarce. A type-facsimile of it is one of the group of seven Ruskin pamphlets forged by T. J. Wise. Copies of all the Wise/Ruskin forgeries are at Bembridge, except

The Queen's Gardens and the variant 'Reprint' *Future of England.*

The Wise forgeries add a little spice to Ruskin bibliography; his editions of Ruskin's letters are a valuable contribution to the study of Ruskin biography for without these printed volumes a number of the letters would be unknown. All were printed in limited editions of about thirty-three copies on paper and seven on vellum. There are copies of all the letter books at Bembridge, both on paper and on vellum. A number of them are finely bound by Zaensdorf, de Sauty, and other leading binders.

Copies of most of Ruskin's published correspondence are in the collection, to C. E. Norton (*Atlantic Monthly*, May-September 1904, and in book form, 2 volumes, Boston, 1904) to William Ward (Boston, 1922), to Francesca Alexander (Boston, 1931), to Bernard Quaritch (London, 1938), to Kathleen Olander (London, 1953), Letters from Venice 1851-2 (Yale 1955), to Lord and Lady Mount Temple (Ohio, 1964), to Dearest Mama Talbot (London, 1966), and several others. Based on the correspondence of Ruskin and his wife are *An Ill-Assorted Marriage, The Order of Release, The Vindication of Ruskin, Effie in Venice,* and *Millais and the Ruskins.* Here too, of course, are the volumes of letters published in Ruskin's lifetime by his official publisher – *Hortus Inclusus* (both the general and the large-paper editions of 1887), the various editions of *Letters to the Clergy, Three Letters and an Essay* (general edition and large-paper limited edition of 1893), and *Letters to a College Friend* (1894 in both the green and brown bindings).

An attractive example of modern American private press work is the Adagio Press edition of *The Contemptible Horse*, 1962, which is Ruskin's letter to 'Tinie' Horn of 31 August 1857.

Out of the ordinary are the two letter volumes of the *Library Edition* (volumes XXXVI and XXXVII) printed on thin paper. From their binding I would judge them to have been formerly in the Wedderburn collection. They have printed paper wrappers bound in. Unusual also is *Additional Letters* (1827-1889) set up for, but crowded out of, volumes XXXVI-XXXVII. These are just three examples of by-products of the *Library Edition.*

Either Cook and Wedderburn or George Allen produced a pamphlet which must be scarce in other collections because over half of the edition is at Bembridge! Ruskin's 1838 *Essay on the Comparative Advantage of the Studies of Music and Painting* exists in two very similar manuscript versions. In the first volume of the *Library Edition* they printed the 'fair copy'. They then altered a word or two of the type and ran off an edition of twelve copies of the 'original draft' – 'Privately Printed 1903'.

(b) Books about Ruskin

The collection of biographies and criticisms of Ruskin contains some 200 volumes but there is little that is particularly scarce. The complete sets of Ruskin exhibition catalogues, 1869-1966, and the Ruskin dispersal sales, 1869-1932, are of particular value in cataloguing and tracing books, pictures, letters and manuscripts. Many of the sale catalogues are priced. One copy of the 1904 Manchester exhibition catalogue was Collingwood's and contains many interesting annotations by him. In this category, too, are several printed catalogues of collections containing Ruskiniana. Catalogues of current sales containing Ruskiniana are retained in the collection.

Bibliographies of Ruskin are those by Shepherd (various editions between 1878 and 1881), William Axon (*A Bibliographical Biography*, 1879, second edition 1881), and T. J. Wise (1889-93). William Ward's and W. G. Collingwood's sets are both here.

There is a large quantity of pamphlets, leaflets and cuttings relating to Ruskin and the Guild of St George and the various Ruskin Societies which still awaits cataloguing. There is also an invaluable collection of thirteen volumes of newspaper cuttings about Ruskin from 1884 to date.

One section of the collection of printed books contains biographies of Ruskin's friends and associates – Henry Acland, Gutzon Borglum, Edward Burne-Jones, Sydney Cockerell, E. T. Cook, Walter Crane, Lady Eastlake, Kate Greenaway, Octavia Hill, Mrs La Touche, E. Lynn Linton, George MacDonald, J. E. Millais, Mary Russell Mitford, C. H. Moore, William Morris, Coventry Patmore, Richmond, Rossetti, Severn, Simon, Webling, Whistler and others. These are kept apart from the Galleries' small art library which is strong in works on English artists and the artists admired by Ruskin.

Two miscellaneous books with a Ruskin association, which may be mentioned, are W. J. Linton's *Ferns of the English Lake Country*, dated from Brantwood, 1865, and Susanna Beever's *Remarkable Passages in Shakespeare*, London, 1870.

VI. BOOKS FROM RUSKIN'S LIBRARY AND OTHER ASSOCIATION COPIES

The Bembridge collection contains some 400 volumes of close Ruskin association, of which 320 were in Ruskin's own library. The bulk of these were bought by Whitehouse at the 1930-1 dispersal sales; others came when the S. W. Bush collection of Ruskin books was bought in 1937. Occasional volumes are still being added to this part of the collection, either by gift or purchase.

Among the books which Ruskin inherited from his father is the latter's *Book of Common Prayer* (London, Samuel Bagster, 1829), a two volume *Bible* (Edinburgh, 1806) with JJR's map of Jerusalem drawn on a fly leaf, and a *Bible* (Oxford, 1846) inscribed by Margaret Ruskin to her husband in 1850. Here, too, is the 1749 Baskett *Bible* mentioned by Collingwood with the paste-down leaf from the *Apocrypha* on which Ruskin's great grandfather has written the names and birth dates of his seven children.

A book evidently used by the family when on continental tours is M. Reichard's *Itinerary of Italy*. This contains many notes by JJR and, careful business man that he was, he has underlined an early passage reading, 'When the traveller arrives at an inn, he should make an agreement with the landlord about the price of his meals and apartments, or he will be liable to imposition or unpleasant altercation'.

Associated with Ruskin's youth is a copy of Pharsalia, *De Bello Civili* (London, 1719) inscribed, 'To Mr J. Ruskin Jnr with J. Rowbotham's best respects and best wishes for his welfare and happiness'. Rowbotham, who kept a 'young gentlemen's Academy', was appointed in 1831 to teach young John mathematics. Between 1833 and 1835 Ruskin attended a day school in Camberwell kept by the Rev. Thomas Dale. He later attended Dale's lectures at King's College and also read privately to him. A copy of Dale's *Sermons ... delivered in St Matthew's Chapel, Denmark Hill* (London, 1836) is in the collection. Another book from Ruskin's early period is a Xenophon, inscribed 'John Ruskin, Herne Hill, Aug 1834'.

From Ruskin's university days is the Rev. S. W. Waud's *Treatise on Algebraic Geometry* (London, 1835) signed 'J. Ruskin, Ch Ch'. There are three pages of mathematical notes on the fly leaves – and drawings of three ships' mainmasts in full sail on the title page!

In 1847 Ruskin contributed a long review of Lord Lindsay's *Sketches of the History of Christian Art* (London, 1847, 3 vols) to the *Quarterly*. His review copy of the book, stamped 'With Mr Murray's compts' is at Bembridge. Works on history from Ruskin's library include a twelve volume Gibbon's *Decline and Fall* (1838), Green's *The Making of England* (1881), Keller's *Histoire de France* (1876, 2 vols), Napier's *History of the War in the Peninsula* (1832, 6 vols), de Sismondi's *Histoire des Républiques Italiennes* (1838, 3 vols only) and Turner's *History of the Anglo-Saxons* (1836, 3 vols). All, in common with most of Ruskin's books, contain annotations and marginal scoring. Someone has noted in the first volume of Bussey and Gaspey's *History of France* (1850, 2 vols), '130pp. scored or noted by JR'.

The same hand has noted in Cary's *Dante* (London, 1870), '93 pp with notes or scoring in J. R.'s hand'. The Greek and Latin classics from Ruskin's library are well represented at Bembridge. One set which may be mentioned is Bekker's *Plato* (London, 1826) in eleven volumes. Plato's *Laws* which occupy part of volume 7 and all of volume 8 are copiously annotated and Ruskin has numbered the lines on each page for easy cross-reference to his notes and translations which occur in two of his Diary volumes.

Several volumes of travel, well-known to Ruskin scholars, are at Bembridge. These include Forbes's *Travels through the Alps of Savoy* (1845), copiously annotated, Gaullieur's *La Suisse, Historique et Pittoresque* (1855), Tyndall's *Glaciers of the Alps* (1860) and David Roberts's *The Holy Land* (1855, 3 volumes).

Ruskin's predeliction for the works of Scott is well-known. Unhappily none of the Scott manuscripts which Ruskin owned is at Bembridge, but we do have innumerable printed copies. In most cases Ruskin owned several copies of Scott's books, a bedroom set, a drawing room set – and so on. Present in the collection as first editions are *Anne of Geierstein*, *Fortunes of Nigel*, *Marmion*, *The Monastery*, *Peveril of the Peak*, *Redgauntlet* and *Woodstock*. Most of these are well annotated, the notes in *Nigel* and *Woodstock* comparing the printed text with the manuscripts. In his notes in *Marmion* Ruskin draws parallels between the characters and himself and Rose La Touche. The 48-volume set of *Waverley Novels* (1865-8) appears well used but contains no scoring or notes. I would assume that this was the bedroom set.

Next to the *Waverley* set at Bembridge is the 10-volume *Life of Sir Walter Scott* by Lockhart (1869). I think this, too, may have been from Ruskin's bedroom for he has noted inside the front of the first volume, 'Contents of Bedroom Bookcase drawers, 1 (lowest) Packet of spare Turner pen and ink, Spare Do. Liber Stud. Photos Abbeville Rheims'. This first volume has almost escaped Ruskin's annotating pencil, but the other nine are full of his notes and scoring and he has added his own index to the back of the volumes. On the spine of each he has pasted a large paper label with the volume number painted an inch high.

Another biography with an interesting provenance is Thomson's *Life and Works of Thomas Bewick* (1882). This is dedicated to Ruskin and on the dedication page is the inscription 'From the Author, Sept 14th 1882'. To the same page Ruskin has added 'Mary Beever, with John Ruskin's love, Brantwood, January 8th 1883'. Other than this Ruskin seems to have left no mark on the book!

The same is not the case with one of Ruskin's favourite books, De Queux de Saint-Hilaire's *Le Livre des Cent Ballades* (Paris, 1868). Ruskin at one time contemplated publishing an English edition of this collection of early French romantic poetry and his copy, which he subsequently gave to Norman Hay Forbes, is covered with notes and translations.

Cook and Wedderburn have pointed out how few books on art were to be found in Ruskin's library. Of the seven important titles which they list, three are at Bembridge: Lord Lindsay's *Christian Art*, Westwood's *Miniatures and Ornaments of Anglo-Saxon and Irish Manuscripts* and Lenormant and De Wittes' *Élite des Monuments Céramographiques* (1844) in 4 volumes.

These last two titles illustrate Ruskin as a user (or mis-user) of books, rather than as a collector. The Lenormant and De Witte is extensively annotated, many of the plates are loose and some two inches have been trimmed from the fore-edges of almost all the text pages so that Ruskin could easily find the plates. The mutilation of Westwood is worse. Not only are almost all of the plates loose, several are missing, presumably given to Ruskin's friends, and the head and tail of the book have been cut off by Ruskin so that it would fit its shelf. Other books that have suffered the same ill-treatment are his Chaucer, Turner's *Anglo-Saxons*, and the two volumes of Bussey and Gaspey's *History of France*. In this case the saw-marks can still be seen on the lower edges.

It is well known that Ruskin's adeptness with the saw and scissors was not confined solely to the ordinary working copies in his library. His medieval manuscripts were no safer than a nineteenth-century Chaucer. A collage in the collection, prepared by Ruskin, consists of twenty miniatures cut from the pages of a French fifteenth-century *Book of Hours*, and a larger miniature attributed to the School of Bourdichon, all pasted on to strips of marginal decoration cut from a later Italian manuscript. This item was subsequently in the collection of Hugh Walpole and was bought for Bembridge in January 1947.

Other ex-Ruskin manuscripts in the collection are *Regula della scola del sanctissimo corpo de d. Iesu* (Italian, sixteenth century) and a Dīwān of Mushtāk (Persian, A.D. 1814). This latter has an interesting history. It was given by Ruskin, in a disbound state, to W. G. Collingwood, who in turn gave it to his daughter. After her death I obtained it for the Bembridge collection. Purely by chance I found that the back cover of an oriental binding already at Bembridge fitted exactly to the remnants of the spine of the *Diwan*. This cover must have been bought with other miscellaneous material from Brantwood in 1931. The manuscript and its binding have now been re-united by Bayntun of Bath.

Incunabula from Brantwood are Gregorius Magnus, *Liber dyalogorum* [*c.* 1478], Hain 7958, and Hyginus, *Poetica astronomica* 1485, Hain 9063.

Interesting among association copies of Ruskin's works is his father's copy of the *Architectural Magazine* (1837-8) in which the 'Poetry of Architecture' first appeared. On the fly leaf JJR has indexed

'Kataphusin on Architecture'. Ruskin's Oxford copy of Aristophanes (1835), contains, in addition to a few translation notes, several sketches made when he was writing *The Poetry of Architecture*.

The collection contains an interesting copy of the 1880 edition of *The Seven Lamps of Architecture*. It was the publisher's own copy and is one of the seventy-five large paper copies printed on Whatman's hand-made paper. On the half title is the inscription to George Allen 'With John Ruskin's grateful love'. Bound in it is the three-page manuscript of the new preface which Ruskin wrote for this edition, with his note at the top, 'Here we are – I've knocked it off before breakfast'. The manuscript and corrected proof of the 'Advice' is also bound in, as is a letter of 1879 from Ruskin to Allen, 'I've made myself quite sick and ill in trying to revise 7L. – the utterly useless twaddle of it – the shallow piety and sonorous talk are very loathsome to me ... the actual teaching of it is all right and some bits are good – but it is all Fools Paradise...'. Bound in at the end is one of the two copies of the 1891 *Index* by Alexander Wedderburn printed on large Whatman's hand-made paper.

An interesting copy of *Sesame and Lilies* has recently been acquired. This is the fifth (1882) edition and it contains the bookplate of Sara Anderson. On the end papers are two wash drawings by Ruskin of the Maritime Alps. This is probably the advance copy of the book which was sent to Ruskin when he was abroad. He disliked the blue-grey cloth which the binder had used. He also decided that the words 'Small Abridged edition' on the title page were a mistake, and he noticed a few minor errors in the preface. The edition in its original form was not issued. A cancelling title page and preface were printed and the binder's cloth was changed to red. This Bembridge copy has the uncancelled preliminaries, with Ruskin's manuscript corrections to the preface, and is bound in a faded grey cloth. Copies of the fifth edition in this state must be rare.

Three copies of the first edition of *Ethics of the Dust* (1866) contain Ruskin's inscriptions to A. C. Swinburne, Joanna Agnew and Jessie Rowe ('Lucilla' of *Ethics*). This book was, in fact, issued in December 1865 and the inscriptions in two of the copies are dated 'Christmas 1865'.

Two Christmases later Ruskin inscribed a copy of *Time and Tide* (1867) to Joan Agnew. Two other copies of *Time and Tide* contain long inscriptions from Thomas Dixon, the 'working man of Sunderland' to whom the letters in the book were addressed. One is inscribed to J. Stokeld. After Stokeld's death, Dixon re-inscribed the copy to T. C. Horsfall, for whose *Study of Beauty in Large Towns* (1883) Ruskin wrote the preface. (A copy of this pamphlet inscribed by Horsfall to James Russell Lowell is at Bembridge). The other copy of *Time and Tide* has Dixon's inscription to William Bell Scott. This later belonged to John Morgan.

Alice Tollemache's (later Lady Mount Temple and one of Ruskin's closest friends) copy of *Queen of the Air* (1869), Arthur Burgess's *Sesame*, *Aratra Pentelici* and *Fors Clavigera* VI are all inscribed to their owners by the author, while Ruskin's Oxford colleague, C. L. Dodgson, had to write his own name in each of his volumes of *Praeterita*. These volumes were later in the Harmsworth library. Five parts of *Praeterita* bear Mrs La Touche's signature, as do one of *Proserpina* and thirteen of *Fors*. Her daughter, Rose, signed her own copy of *Queen of the Air* but her *Val d'Arno* (1874) is inscribed by Ruskin 'To Briar-Rose, Fleur de Lys, 31 October 1874'. Also in the collection are her copy of Shelley's *Minor Poems* (1868), her ivory bound *Prayer Book* with its inscription from Lady Mount Temple, and a copy from Brantwood of the book she wrote herself, *Clouds and Light* (London, 1870).

Two incomplete sets of *Fors Clavigera* belonged to Ruskin and Alexander Wedderburn. The former's is a much annotated indexing copy, with the reference at the head of Letter LXXIX, p. 201, 'Whistler, Mr – impudence of'. Wedderburn's set, also much marked, was evidently used when he was working on the *Library Edition*.

Hortus Inclusus (1887), a selection of Ruskin's letters to the Misses Beever, is inscribed from Susan Beever to W. G. Collingwood. Near to it in the collection is one of Susan Beever's sketch books full of delightful bird and flower drawings, which she gave to Ruskin.

Among other association copies I will only mention Shelley's *Essays, Letters from Abroad, Translations and Fragments* (London, 1845), inscribed to Ruskin from Joseph Severn, father of Arthur and friend of Keats, and a small volume containing Italian and Russian translations of Ruskin's *King of the Golden River*, given to Ruskin by the translator, Barbara Charlton, 'with kind regards & Xmas Greetings 1891'.

VII. RUSKIN RELICS

I have already mentioned many of the Ruskin relics now at Brantwood. Among the relics at Bembridge are his mother's watch, his grandfather's walking stick, his wife's silver and agate seal, his own silver christening cup, a selection of his cutlery and drinking glasses, and his travelling writing desk (according to Arthur Severn, the only piece of luggage that Ruskin ever packed himself!). Of Ruskin association are some examples of 'Ruskin Pottery', 'Ruskin Linen', an Arcadian ware coffee cup printed with an inscription by Ruskin and sold at the end of the last century as 'a present from Coniston', one of the fragments of slate from the Ruskin Cross, and the gold cross designed by Arthur Severn and presented to the Cork High School's Rose Queen of 1888. There are also in the collection many photographs of continental scenes collected and used by Ruskin, and photographs of Ruskin and the Severns and their homes.

REFERENCES

1. This chapter is a general survey of the Whitehouse Collection as it was in 1969. The addition of the Adams Bequest in the early 1970s greatly extended the collection. Two major purchases, at Philip's in 1971 and Bonham's in the following year, of the Mack Collection added very many more letters and watercolours to the collection. The Whitehouse Collection moved from the Ruskin Galleries at Bembridge to the newly custom-built Ruskin Library at Lancaster University which was opened in May 1998. The old Bembridge catalogue number were preceded by the abbreviation 'Bem'. At Lancaster the cataloguing system is retained, but the numbers are now preceded by the letters 'RF' (Ruskin Foundation). The prefix has been omitted in this chapter for the sake of convenience. All of the illustrations of this chapter are reproduced by courtesy of the Ruskin Foundation (Ruskin Library, Lancaster University).
2. J. S. Dearden, '*Poems* 1850', *The Book Collector*, summer 1968, subsequently reprinted in J. S. Dearden, 'Further Facets of Ruskin', 2009, Ch. 3.

II

THE HADDON C. ADAMS RUSKIN COLLECTION AT BEMBRIDGE

BULLETIN OF THE JOHN RYLANDS UNIVERSITY LIBRARY OF MANCHESTER, VOL. 55, NO. 2, 1973

1. THE FORMATION OF THE COLLECTION

Haddon C. Adams was an admirer of John Ruskin for many years and built up an important collection of Ruskiniana. His interest may have been aroused in the first instance by attending Quiller-Couch's 'Milton' lecture printed in the second series of *The Studies in Literature*. In an undated letter to Quiller-Couch written in autumn 1931[1] Adams told him, 'collecting Ruskin is my one luxury'. Adams became a member of the Ruskin Society and this brought him into contact with J. Howard Whitehouse, the president of the Society and founder of Bembridge School and its Ruskin collection. Mr Adams made no secret of the fact that he intended bequeathing his collection to Whitehouse's Education Trust Ltd., to be added to the Trust's collections at Bembridge or Brantwood. In fact, by the time of his death, Mr Adams had already passed several interesting items to Bembridge.* Finally, in September 1971, the remainder of the Adams Collection came to Bembridge.

Haddon Clifford Adams was born at Salisbury in 1898 and was at school in Ipswich. In the first World War he served in France with the Royal Flying Corps and was awarded the M.C. At the end of the war he went up to Jesus College, Cambridge, in the Easter Term 1919. He took his degree through the Mechanical Sciences Tripos. Mr

* He had also given, in 1946, to Ruskin's college – Christ Church, Oxford – Ruskin's certificate of his appearance before the Vice Chancellor, his subscription to the Articles, and taking the oath of obedience to the University, his Matriculation, his Sponsoring certificate and his Public Examination in Greats (see Whitehouse, *Ruskin Renascence*, 1946, pp. 24-25.)

Adams married Miss Kathleen Snare and after leaving Cambridge went to America, in 1922, where he became an assistant highway engineer in a bridge department at Illinois. In 1926 Mr and Mrs Adams returned to England. He obtained his M.I.C.E. and was later awarded his Fellowship.

In 1931 he joined the Ministry of Transport as an assistant and was ultimately appointed their chief bridge engineer, an appointment which he held until his retirement in 1963. Bridges were his abiding interest. He was the co-author, with C. S. Chettoe, of *Reinforced Concrete Bridge Design* (London 1933), and other books on concrete.

Mr Adams's chief hobby was golf, a game which he played regularly until illness forced him to give it up. Three and a half years later he died, on 14 June 1971, at his home, Allington Lodge, 1 Sheridan Road, Merton Park, S.W.19. His home itself had distant Ruskin associations in that it was built by Thomas Carlyle as a wedding present for his nephew Alexander.

Because of his great interest in Ruskin, Haddon C. Adams had long wished to visit Coniston. There Ruskin had spent the last years of his life at his house, Brantwood, which he had first occupied in September 1872. On Ruskin's death in 1900 Brantwood and its contents were inherited by Mr and Mrs Arthur Severn, Ruskin's distant cousin and her watercolourist husband. After his wife's death at Brantwood in 1925 Arthur Severn spent most of his time in London. His daughter Violet continued to live at Brantwood, the house and estate being cared for by members of the Wilkinson family.

Two years after Mr and Mrs Adams returned from America the opportunity to visit Coniston presented itself, and the focal point of a motor-cycle holiday in the summer of 1928 was a few days spent in the village. In a long letter to his father,[2] Adams described his visit to Coniston, his impressions of Brantwood, and his meetings with the Wilkinsons:

> We passed through Kendal, Windermere and came round the north end of the lake, just below Ambleside and on to Coniston which is a pretty little village at the foot of the hills and close to the lake.
>
> We reached Coniston about 11 a.m. Friday [22 June 1928] and

took room and board at a little hotel* just opposite the church where Ruskin's grave is.

In the afternoon we went round the lake to see Brantwood. Visitors are not allowed in without previous permission from Mr Arthur Severn (86 years old and husband of Joan of 'Joanna's Care'. She died here three years ago and is buried near Ruskin.) However we persuaded the man in charge of the house, a 'Miles Wilkinson' to take us in as he had just taken in a man and his crippled wife (he was a Ruskin lover through 'Unto this Last' and has read all the books. He is a mechanic.) We saw the study, dining room, drawing room and bedroom. I will give more particulars later.

We then walked on in the lane and looked at the garden through a five bar gate in the stone wall, and I got into conversation with the old gardener† who had been there with five others in Ruskin's time. He was the only one retained now and being old and without help, absolutely unequal to the task. He seems so sad at the place going down. The Severns seem in financial straits and the house, with priceless Turners etc. on the walls is in disrepair – paper peeling from ceilings – it is heartbreaking to see. The gardens are hardly kept, but the old gardener does his best.

We walked on a little way to where Ruskin had a little wooden seat by the lake – a favourite spot. Walking back, the gardener's wife and daughter came out, and fetched us into the lodge – a small house designed by Ruskin for his valet Baxter‡ who died some years

* Probably the Crown Hotel.

† Joseph Wilkinson (1859-1952), uncle of Miles Wilkinson. Joseph Wilkinson began working for Ruskin as his post boy. After a short break, he returned to Brantwood in his early twenties as an under-gardener, eventually becoming head gardener. He and his family had moved into the Brantwood Lodge soon after the death there in 1918 of Peter Baxter, Ruskin's valet. After Brantwood was bought by J. Howard Whitehouse in 1932, Wilkinson continued to live in the lodge, eventually dying there on 28 October 1952.

‡ The lodge was, in fact, built by Ruskin for an earlier valet, Frederick Crawley, in 1873. Crawley was replaced as valet by Peter Baxter in 1876. He remained in Ruskin's service until the death of the latter in 1900. Thereafter he remained in the Severns' service for several years.

ago. They kindly showed us the garden, but in one of the greenhouses we came upon Miss Severn and thought it best to retire. She came up just as we were leaving the lodge. The gardener's wife, Mrs Joseph Wilkinson, lent me an umbrella as it was raining heavily, and I left my card. (I heard later that Miss Severn saw the card, and expressed the hope that we had seen through Brantwood.) By the way, Mrs Wilkinson had *given* us a good tea before we saw the garden.

Next day we took a ride round the lake and I left the umbrella at the lodge and brought Miss Wilkinson in in the sidecar, to tend the graves. I was able to get a few roses and place on the grave. We then went back to Brantwood and were shown again through Brantwood much more fully.

We went into the dining room by the French windows. There hang some famous pictures. The fine pair of oils of his mother and father by Northcote, and the first one of himself, with 'the blue hills'. The fine full length Richmond watercolour of 'The Author of Modern Painters'. A copy of Titian's Doge of Venice, a Raphael and several more. The old furniture which was Ruskin's father's and mother's is still in use throughout the house.*

In the drawing room we saw many interesting pictures and books and furniture, including the little chair from which the little boy gave his 'first sermon'.† There were several of the original Kate Greenaway pictures where the little children have such beautiful faces. We also went into an inner room off the drawing room.

* James Northcote, *Margaret Ruskin* (still in the Brantwood dining room), *John Ruskin at 3½*; George Richmond: *John Ruskin*, 1842 (called 'The Author of *Modern Painters*'). *Doge Andrea Gritti*, though produced as a Titian at the Whistler v. Ruskin Libel action, is now attributed to Catena. It is now in the National Gallery. Before the Severns sold it, about 1917, W. G. Collingwood made the copy referred to here; it is still at Brantwood. The Raphael was probably a copy of Raphael's self-portrait. The dining table and two of the sideboards are still in use in the house.

† 'People, be dood. If you are dood, Dod will love you. If you are not dood, Dod will not love you. People be dood'; delivered, according to W. G. Collingwood (*Life of Ruskin* (1893), I. 21) when Ruskin was not quite 3 years old.

Then into the study! His desk and the little circular table where he did so much writing. I saw the original notebook of a diary and poems, some of the famous books referred to in his works – i.e. Dante (Cary),* George Herbert, etc., a Dürer drawing etc.

Upstairs in a bedroom from the ceiling of which the paper was hanging because of the damp, were wonderful drawings, etc., the miniatures referred to in *Praeterita*, a little picture of Keats by Severn (father of the present one).†

In Ruskin's own bedroom everything was as left when he died in it – bed, etc. Some priceless Turners were there, but I am afraid they will spoil with damp. In a drawer was Ruskin's waistcoat, trousers, blue cravat. On a little table was his bedroom bible‡ with notes on the fly-leaves – one entry, the last, was: –

'ten minutes past two by my mother's watch 1867'

(I quote from memory and am not quite certain. I believe it to be the entry of his mother's death.).

We saw one or two more things of interest and then went into the garden where the old gardener took me round and up into the wood at the back.

* Adams was to add two copies of Cary's *Dante* from Ruskin's library to his own collection *The Vision* (London, 1819, 3 vols) and *The Vision* (London, 1844, 1 vol.). Another copy, of 1870, came to J. H. Whitehouse from the Brantwood sale.

† This was probably the 'Turret Room', the first bedroom on the left at the top of the stairs, so named from the small turret which Ruskin had built onto the angle of the room in 1871. Ruskin used this room as his bedroom, later moving into the room next door, where he died. Arthur Severn took over the Turret Room when Ruskin vacated it, although Ruskin seems to have used it as a sitting room towards the end of his life.

‡ Probably the 1846 O.U.P. *Bible* inscribed on the fly-leaf by Ruskin's father, 'Margaret Ruskin to her Husband John James Ruskin 1850'. This *Bible* was subsequently in the Adams Collection and was passed to Bembridge on 8 May 1964. Among many annotations by Ruskin is (on the reverse of the title page) 'Ten minutes past two by my mother's watch April 28th? 1887 John Ruskin'. And again on the end fly-leaf, 'Two minutes past 3 a.m. by my mother's watch 27th April 1887 John Ruskin'. There does not appear to be any particular significance in either note.

Everything was wild and overgrown. I saw a stone-flag seat which Ruskin used to sit in to watch a waterfall. A little stone arch bridge I saw had a history. A bridge had to be built over a small stream during Ruskin's absence. When he returned he was furious to find a huge slab of stone had been thrown across and a squared up hand rail of pitch-pine had been made by the joiners. He sent for a sledge hammer and had it all smashed up, and another bridge built by packing together small pieces of rock.

Sunday morning we climbed the Coniston Old Man and in the evening walked over again to the lodge at Brantwood where Mrs Wilkinson told us several anecdotes and showed us several things of interest. She also gave me an old Art magazine of 1891* with a long article in about the different pictures of Ruskin (i.e. drawings and paintings and photographs of him.)

We were to leave Coniston Monday morning but rain prevented us and I spent the morning in the little Ruskin Museum which is very interesting. In the little antique shop I picked up, on the Saturday, a few early sketches of Ruskin's† (unsigned – but I believe them genuine.) Miles Wilkinson, who looks after the Severns and has charge of the house declares them genuine too (he is a nephew of the gardener). I saw him in the village on Saturday night, where he made his weekly visit to the pub, and asked him to come up to my room to look at them. He told me of the eccentricity of the older Severn and told me that he had had a lot of Ruskin's sketches and Turner's engravings destroyed. In one pile of things to be burnt, Miles Wilkinson had picked out a tiny box and on opening it he took out a short chain with Ruskin's seal on one end and Ruskin's father's seal on the other. Severn, for his honesty in taking it to him gave it to him and he pulled it out of his breeches pocket in evidence! saying he always carried it on his person. An American

* *Magazine of Art*, January 1891, pp. 73-79. M. H. Spielmann, 'The Portraits of John Ruskin – I.'

† Drawings and sketches by Ruskin were readily available at this time. From time to time the Severns had given Ruskin drawings to local charity sales. Several exhibitions in Coniston, notably the 1900 Ruskin exhibition, had also included works for sale.

had offered him a great deal of money for it but he would not part.

The old lady* who kept the antique shop had been a maid at the Beevers and knew Ruskin well. She spoke of gossip in the village about the art treasures being secretly dispersed from Brantwood. A beautiful old illuminated psalter had been sold, it seems, to an American for a few hundreds and shortly after in the United States re-sold for about £15,000. It is terrible to think of. We were told (with what truth I don't yet know) that Ruskin left £1,000 a year for the upkeep of Brantwood,† and you know his first action on buying the place was to put it in thorough-going repair. Now the rain goes through and is rotting the place. The Severns have made it a good bit larger since Ruskin died.‡ The sons are away, spending the proceeds presumably, and have no interest in the place.

I saw the famous coach in the stables in which Ruskin as a little boy used to tour England and France.§ It is still in fine condition,

* Mary Ellen Wilkinson (*née* Robinson). Her antique shop was in Yewdale Road, opposite the Institute, on a site now occupied by the Fire Station. In the 1880s, as a young girl, she had been in service at The Thwaite, the home of the Misses Susanna and Mary Beever, 'The Ladies of The Thwaite' to whom Ruskin had addressed the *Hortus Inclusus* letters. Ruskin was a frequent visitor at The Thwaite and had met Mary Robinson there. He had liked her and had occasionally given her small drawings and other things. Her son, Mr H. Wilkinson of Coniston, still [in 1973] owns a small ammonite, a Greek coin which his mother had had made into a brooch, and two key rings inscribed 'John Ruskin' and 'John James Ruskin', which Ruskin had given to Mary Robinson. This Wilkinson family is not related to the Wilkinsons of Brantwood.

† Under the terms of his Will Ruskin had directed that the first £1,000 annually from his royalties was to be devoted to the upkeep of Brantwood.

‡ After Ruskin's death the Severns extended the drawing room and built on to its corner the heptangular room entered from it, together with the room above it entered from Joan Severn's bedroom.

§ In fact, at this time the Ruskins used to borrow a coach from J. J. Ruskin's business partner, Henry Telford, or hire one from Hopkinson, the coach-builder in Long Acre. The carriage which Adams probably saw is the one which is still at Brantwood. It was built in 1875 by Tucker of Camberwell for the posting tour which Ruskin made in the following year with the Severns from London to Coniston. At the time of the Brantwood sales it was given to J. H. Whitehouse by Miss Violet Severn.

> but mould is standing on the outside of it for want of care, and it will go like the rest.
>
> Professor Collingwood* lives about a mile away in the same lane, by the lake, but he is not wealthy. It must be heartbreaking to him to see the place so let down.

While he was at Coniston, Adams had arranged for Wilkinson's daughter, Edith Isabel Wilkinson, to make two samplers for him. Both are embroidered on linen, 18 ins. x 10 ins., and signed 'E. I. Wilkinson, Brantwood Lodge, Lake Coniston'. One comprises 'Unto this Last' within a wreath of wild roses;† the other, 'To-day' repeated three times and separated by two panels of Ruskin lace.

The series of sales which dispersed the contents of Brantwood began at Sotheby's in July 1930 and continued there in May of the following year. At the sale of pictures, Adams probably bought one or two of the early 'parcels'. He also bought lot 103, 'J. J. Ruskin: Lake scene with a castellated building on an island, and Conway Castle'. The Conway Castle is an interesting picture. Ruskin exhibited it at The Fine Art Society with his Turner collection in 1878 and wrote of it in the catalogue:[3]

> 1 R Conway Castle
>
> Drawing by my father, made in Edinburgh drawing class under Nasmyth the elder, and showing the way in which young people were in those days taught: the first tints being laid in grey; then the warm colour laid on the lights, and no 'effects' of light, or of *local* colours ever thought of. The great Hakewill drawings by Turner are nothing more than the perfect development of this method.

* William Gershom Collingwood (1854-1932), Ruskin's secretary, editor and first biographer, who lived at Lanehead, a short distance from Brantwood. For some years he was Professor of Fine Art at University College, Reading.

† A similar motif had been used in the embroidery on Ruskin's pall, made by members of the Keswick School of Industrial Arts and Ruskin Linen Industry.

Ruskin also wrote about the picture in *Fors Clavigera* in 1875:[4]

> I was particularly fond of watching him [JJR] shave; and was always allowed to come into his room in the mornings (under the one in which I am now writing), to be the motionless witness of that operation. Over his dressing-table hung one of his own watercolour drawings, made under the teaching of the elder Nasmyth. (I believe, at the High School of Edinburgh.) It was done in the early manner of tinting, which, just about the time when my father was at the High School, Dr Munro was teaching Turner; namely, in grey under-tints of Prussian blue and British ink, washed with warm colour afterwards on the lights. It represented Conway Castle, with its Frith, and, in the foreground, a cottage, a fisherman, and a boat at the water's edge.
>
> When my father had finished shaving, he always told me a story about this picture. The custom began without any initial purpose of his, in consequence of my troublesome curiosity whether the fisherman lived in the cottage, and where he was going to in the boat. It being settled, for peace's sake, that he *did* live in the cottage, and was going in the boat to fish near the castle, the plot of the drama afterwards gradually thickened; and became, I believe, involved with that of the tragedy of 'Douglas', and of the 'Castle Spectre', in both of which pieces my father had performed in private theatricals....
>
> I remember nothing of the story he used to tell me, now; but I have the picture still, and hope to leave it finally in the Oxford schools,* where, if I can complete my series of illustrative work for general reference, it will be of some little use as an example of an old-fashioned method of water-colour drawing not without its advantages; and, at the same time, of the dangers incidental in it to young students, of making their castles too yellow, and their fishermen too blue.

* In the event, the picture remained at Brantwood, hanging over the fireplace in Ruskin's bedroom.

Mr Adams must have written to tell the Wilkinsons of his success at the sale for he had the following reply from Mrs Wilkinson:[5]

> I hasten to answer yours of yesterday to tell you that the picture *Conway Castle* is not only attributed to Turner but is a Turner and if you take the back off you will find Turner's name there, Miles thinks, and it was him (Miles) who wrote Hut Castle but he found out that it was Conway Castle it being over the fireplace in Ruskin's bedroom and Mr Ruskin gave over £100 for it – I think it was £120. As there is receipts for all he bought and the prices he paid, he was so honest and straight-forward, Mr Ruskin I mean, in all his dealings, Miles is going to look for the receipt it is amongst a lot more and then you shall have it which adds to the value. The other two pictures only one is by his Father the more highly coloured one …

Adams must have written again when he realized that the Wilkinsons thought the picture was by Turner and he had the following reply:[6]

> I cannot tell you how sorry and disappointed we were to hear from your letter the picture was not a Turner and I told Miles as soon as I was able to see him but he will scarcely believe that it isn't a Turner. He says that Mr Agnew Severn had a secret code of knowing when they were Turners and if you come which I hope you will do *soon* if only for a *weekend* (bring the picture with you, Miles says) he has found the Companion picture to the one you bought done by Ruskin's Father but he said it isn't in a frame but there is plenty of frames at Brantwood and he will send it to you if you don't come soon. I said you had paid plenty for the others so you are having this for nothing as Miles knows you thought the 2 you bought were by Ruskin's Father…

And on the same day Miles wrote to say that he would 'send the companion picture done by J. J. Ruskin to match the one you bought at Sotheby's', and three days later he wrote again:[7]

> I am sending these two pictures of Ruskin the other one by his father the same style as the one you got from Sothebys …

Thus the Adams collection now contains four water-colours by J. J. Ruskin. Another picture from the bedroom is Arthur Severn's copy of J. M. W. Turner's 'Flint Castle' – '… the loveliest piece of pure water-colour painting in my whole collection…'.[8] When the original Turner was sold from Brantwood its place on the bedroom wall was taken by Arthur Severn's copy; it was this copy which was reproduced in 1906 as plate 11 in *Works*, XXII.

A large part of the library remained at Brantwood after the sales at Sotheby's. Mr Adams must have mentioned his interest in buying some of the books to Mrs Wilkinson because in her letter to him of 23 May 1931 she offered him 'a first edition of Scots life, 7 volumes by Lockhart, bound in leather' for £1. She also offered 'Cambells poems with *Turners* signature in *first page*' for £3.

> I asked Miles particularly about the price, anyone who makes a likely offer can have books, I told Miles to keep these books untill I hear from you as I think they will be worth while but you know best. Any one who speaks for things before the sale will have the first chances but if you are coming over next month as you thought of doing you could select anything you would like as I guess there will be a lot of drawings etc.

Adams must have rejected the Turner item but asked for several other books, which Miles must have sent him on 1 June.

> I am sending off to-day the books you mentioned to my aunt also one or two more that you will see. I used these to fill up so the parcel would travel better. If there are any more that you should think of, I will only be too pleased to send. There are a few more small items enclosed also.[9]

A receipt for £2 signed by Wilkinson on Violet Severn's behalf is enclosed with his letter of 12 June. Adams seems to have visited

Brantwood towards the end of June and this visit must have resulted in the purchase of more books and possibly some letters.

The final dispersal sale was held at Brantwood on 28, 30 and 31 July 1931 and the Adams copy of the catalogue[10] is marked with the prices he was prepared to pay for several items. He commissioned Miles to bid for him, but he was only lucky with one bid, for 'lot 56. Walnut writing table 4 feet 10 inches with 2 drawers', a table which had stood in the dining room below the Watson portrait of J. J. Ruskin. Mrs Wilkinson reported on the sale on 5 August:

> The sales were quite a success. The books were in *great demand* & fetched good prices we were glad you were able to come & choose for people seemed ready to cry about the books they wanted & couldn't get. I feel sure you will never regret coming for there will never be another chance.... I wonder if Miles has got written to you to tell you he got Ruskin's *beautiful* writing table for you £3 10s.*... These sales here made roughly £1000, not bad was it.

Mr Adams does not seem to have added very much more to his collection of Ruskiniana after the sales other than keeping up to date with new publications, though one gift from a friend added some Ruskin/Leighton letters to his collection.

Such then is the story of the formation of the Adams Collection. It remained in his home for the next forty years. During the war much of it was packed away for safety and when I visited him at Merton Park in 1964 I only saw a small part of it. Not until it arrived at Bembridge for cataloguing was it possible to see how carefully he had made his selection from Brantwood.

II. THE COLLECTION

(a) General

In addition to the writing table, which Mr Adams was to use in his

* Adams had marked this table in his catalogue at £2, so that he had to pay more than he had expected. Another priced catalogue of the sale in the Whitehouse Collection shows that in fact the table brought £3.

study for the rest of his life, he also had a marble paper weight engraved with Ruskin's initials, and Ruskin's travelling writing desk – a large, leather-covered writing case.* Of the various certificates which Mr Adams owned I have already referred to those which he presented to Oxford in 1946.

Ruskin was appointed to honorary membership of many organizations. The Collection already has his certificates of appointment to the American Institute of Architects and the Académie Royale des Beaux-Arts d'Anvers. These are now joined from the Adams Collection by his certificate of honorary membership of the Pennsylvania Academy of Fine Arts (22 July 1862) and Accademia Fiorentina delle belle Arti (9 September 1861).

The collection's illuminated addresses to Ruskin from the members of the Cork High School for Girls of May Day 1887 and 1895 are now joined by an address for 1885. There is also an undated letter of thanks decorated with a water-colour of apple blossom from a group of girls of the Nottingham High School. Mr Adams also had an interesting group of photographs of Brantwood and Ruskin, including an unpublished photograph of Ruskin standing on the ice of the frozen Coniston Lake.

(b) Manuscripts

There are one or two very interesting manuscripts in the Adams Collection. The holograph preface for *Hortus Inclusus*[11] is contained in an envelope endorsed by Joan Severn, 'original MSS of "Hortus" in which it is 'her master of the rural industries at Loughrigg' meaning Susie Beever's – for which A[lbert] F[leming] substituted '*his*' giving quite a different impression to the public! – implying that he was Ruskin's 'master' &c –'.†

Ruskin's mother died, aged 90, on 5 December 1871. For some time before this her health had been causing concern and on 'Monday

* According to Arthur Severn, this was the only item of luggage Ruskin ever packed for himself. (J. S. Dearden, *The Professor* (1967), p. 53)

† This mistake was continued in *Works*, XXXVII. 80, where the extract is printed 'she has permitted my Master of the Rural Industries…', as opposed to 'her Master' in the MS.

afternoon 30th Oct [1871]' Ruskin wrote down what he must have thought was to be his last conversation with his mother.[12]

> (Mama dear, I must tell you true – I think if you have anything to say to me, it should be said.)
>
> I've nothing to say, but to do good and be good.
>
> (I wanted to tell you they say I am to be Lord Rector at Glasgow,[*] – and to-day Mr Liddell announces my gift of the Oxford Mastership[†]... Do you not like me to be the Lord Rector)
>
> I like it for your Father's sake....

Another manuscript connected with Margaret Ruskin is a small scrap of paper endorsed by her '10 May My Husbands third Birthday after his death 1866'. On the reverse is a list of names and amounts, showing that Mrs Ruskin maintained the custom of giving gifts to her servants on the anniversary of her husband's birthday. It is also useful in showing the number of servants in the household at this time.

6 Incloset Females[‡]	1 : 10 :
Mrs Crawley for herself & Husband[§]	: 10
Mrs Dowries[⁋]	: 10 :
Hersey, Edward & Charles[△] each 5/	: 15 :
David and Mrs David[●] each 5/ Children 5/	: 15 :
Caroline & children	: 10 :
	4 : 10 :

[*] Ruskin was also a candidate in 1868 and 1880, but was never elected.

† Ruskin's endowment of the Drawing Mastership.

‡ From John James Ruskin's accounts for 1863 (MS 29), one can infer that these six were 'Cook, Lucy, Ann, Jones, Elizabeth, Mary'. § Frederick Crawley, Ruskin's valet.

⁋ Presumably the wife of David Downes, the head gardener.

△ Under-gardeners. ● David Fudge, the coachman. Unidentified.

A small volume[13] containing John James Ruskin's travelling diary for 1833, 1844 and 1846 was sent to the Whitehouse Collection by Mr Adams in March 1968. A volume[14] of similar size which came with the bulk of the bequest is a commonplace book kept jointly by John James and John. The first twelve pages are in John James's hand and include 'Elegy in a Country Churchyard' and 'The Passions'. After this the extracts are in the hands of father and son and to judge by the latter, the volume must date from about 1830. A partly-dismembered sketch book[15] of Ruskin's contains ten leaves of notes on the frescoes in the Spanish Chapel at Florence and probably dates from about 1874. There is also a proof copy of *Christ's Folk*, part IV, containing several of Ruskin's corrections.

Alexander Wedderburn was a frequent visitor to Brantwood after 1876. During his visit in August 1879 Ruskin was engaged in making a translation of Plato's *Laws* from vol. VIII of his Bekker edition of 1826. At the same time Wedderburn compiled an index to the *Laws*, the manuscript of which remained at Brantwood until acquired by Mr Adams.

Two sheets of George Allen's note-paper[16] contain a statement of costs and circulation for the first year of *Fors Clavigera* (1871). They show a steadily declining sale, from 821 copies of the January part, to 446 copies in December. In all, 7,098 parts were sold in the twelve months. Packing and carriage expenses for the second half of the year amounted to £7 6s.

(c) Letters

Miscellaneous letters in the collection include three to J. J. Ruskin.[17] One, of July 1855, is from Jane Welsh Carlyle, accepting an invitation to Denmark Hill. On 13 October 1830 James Northcote acknowledged J. J. Ruskin's

> praise [which] you are so good as to bestow upon me and the volume of Conversations … the book was published against my consent and in its first appearance in the magazines totally without my knowledge. I have done all in my power to prevent its coming before the public because there are several hard and cruel

> opinions of persons that I would not have them see in a printed book....

In a letter of 2 July 1843 Samuel Prout wrote about the first volume of *Modern Painters*.

> Permit me to say that I have been indulged with a hasty perusal of a work on art and artists by 'a Graduate of Oxford'. I read the vol. with intense interest, the sentiments and language rivetting my attention to every page. But I mourn that such splendid means of doing eminent service to art should be lost. Had the work been written with the courteousness of Sir Joshua Reynolds' lectures, it would have been a standard work.... Pardon, Dear Sir, this presuming to tire your patience with my humble opinions and should it be true, what I have just heard, that you know the author, I will rely on your goodness to forgive my objection to opinions in which you are so much interested....

After the death of John James Ruskin in 1864 his two clerks, Watson and Ritchie, became partners in a new agency for the importing of Domecq sherry. Writing in 1871[18] to Mrs Severn at Matlock where Ruskin lay seriously ill, Henry Ritchie asked for news of 'your eminent invalid' and mentioned that 'six bottles of purest old sherry is being packed for travelling – it is of all wine perhaps the most wholesome...'. And in a letter[19] of August 1875 to Ruskin, Ritchie told him that 'not one brick is left standing upon another that composed the walls of No. 7 Billiter Street, in case your steps were directed to that locality and the fact be a startle to you.'

This second letter from Ritchie is one of a series of letters in the bequest addressed to Ruskin by fifty-eight different correspondents including Henry Acland, Helen Duchess of Albany,◇ Peter Bayne,◇ Rawdon Brown, Elizabeth and Robert Browning, the Burne-Joneses, Madame Blayne de Bury,◇ Thomas Carlyle, Olive Cockerell, J. D. Forbes, J. A. Froude, Mary Gladstone,◇ Kate Greenaway, Hubert Herkomer,◇ E. L. Hicks,◇ Holman Hunt, Jean Ingelow,◇ Caroline Kerrison,◇ Edward Lear, George MacDonald,◇ Charles Newton,◇ C. E.

Norton, Bernard Quaritch,◇ W. R. Richardson,◇ George Richmond, Edward Sharpe,◇ C. H. Swinburne◇ and Lilias Trotter. Most of the letters are ones which particularly interested or pleased Ruskin and which he had put into separate envelopes endorsed with the name of the writer and, in some cases, the subject. Fourteen of the envelopes, containing letters from those correspondents marked above with diamonds, are marked by Ruskin with a 'D', almost certainly indicating that he intended to use them in *Dilecta*.

The three Burne-Jones letters[20] are written from Winnington Hall in Cheshire. Two of them, one from Edward and one from Georgiana, are letters of condolence, written in March 1864 on the death of J. J. Ruskin.

> What can I possibly write to you – I want to do everything you wish, and stay or go where you wish, but now I want to be in London even if I could only see you once or twice this spring – it is so hard not to do anything for one I love as I do you – I am so grieved for we loved your father and admired him, and shall never forget him....

And from Georgiana,

> The surprise of your letter this morning makes it no worse to bear for us, but what must it have been to you. We love you so, and we don't know what to do or say – how can we be any comfort to you? We cry too for our little selves – not to see him again, for we loved him dearly, and now we thank you more than ever that you let us know him....

On 4 January 1866 Henry Carlyle acknowledged the receipt of a copy of *Ethics of the Dust* while on 4 March 1861 his brother Thomas acknowledged J. J. Ruskin's gift of 'yr exquisite cognac'. One bottle had been set aside 'that the house, in case of real emergency, may never be without *Brandy that can be depended on*'. Associated with the Carlyle letters are five from J. A. Froude including one written on the death of Carlyle.

> He rallied and lived for a week longer, the heart … being kept in action by the power of the brain…. His [face in death] was grand but gentle and loving – Boehm wished to take a cast from it and I would have well liked that the expression should have been preserved – but Mary shrank from allowing him to be touched, and I did not urge it.

In a letter of 4 February 1896 Kate Greenaway wrote of Lord Leighton's funeral, of St Paul's, of Swinburne ('such a pity he had not a nice mind, for he has such a clever one'), of Handsel and Gretel and fairies and witches, and accompanies her last page with a drawing of a little girl.

The JJR/JR/Miss Fall/Miss Ingelow[21] correspondence already at Bembridge is now joined by four letters from Jean Ingelow to Ruskin. One is accompanied by the holograph sonnet *Though all great deeds*, 'which arose mainly out of a conversation, nearly the first I ever had with you'.

In Ruskin's correspondence in the *Pall Mall Gazette* about Sir John Lubbock's 'Best Hundred Books', he wrote in February 1886[22] 'I really don't know any author to whom I am half so grateful, for my idle self, as Edward Lear. I shall put him first in *my* hundred authors.' Now from the Adams Collection comes Lear's letter to Ruskin of 1 March 1886.

> I believe you will begin to repent having written so kindly about my 'Nonsense', if your having done so entails more interruption of your time. I sent off, because you asked me for some notice of the A[lfredl T[ennyson] work, a packet with a set of Lists of all 200 illustrations,[23] also a Dedication I had written to Lady Tennyson…. And now it had occurred to me – as you have taken an interest in my 'Nonsense' – that you may only hitherto have seen the first original part … the 3 succeeding absurd whims … are now very rare books … because the horrid man Bush who published them (as he did my 'Corsica') became bankrupt – & the whole machinery collapsed. Therefore if you wish for these three later books of Bosh – namely 1 *Nonsense songs & stories*, 2

More Nonsense, 3 *Laughable Lyrics*, you have only to say so....

Four of the five letters from Charles Eliot Norton deal with the Ruskin exhibition which Norton arranged at Boston, Mass., in October 1879. Norton sought Ruskin's permission to arrange the exhibition on 9 November 1878; permission must have been sent by return of post because on 28 December Norton was thanking Ruskin and calling him 'the best of fairy godmothers'. On 20 May 1879 Norton wrote, 'I mean to make the catalogue as permanently valuable as it can be made, as a record of your work'. An examination of the catalogue shows that Norton did not fail in his intention.

There are letters from Ruskin[24] to four named and two unnamed correspondents. In both of the letters to Dawson Herdson, the head gardener at Brantwood (15 May, 13 December 1882), Ruskin encloses cheques for his accounts and in the second says that he is 'vexed at having no word from you about the one thing I care most about – the *moor*. Mr Collingwood tells me everything has failed – Will you please tell me to what extent and as far as you know, why.' Ruskin had been trying to reclaim part of the fells behind Brantwood and bring them into cultivation. But the corn which he sowed would not grow and he had to content himself with planting fruit trees in his clearing.

Two letters to Arthur Severn show how carefully Ruskin looked after Joan's well-being. Arthur Severn was on trial as a suitor for Joan's hand for some time before they became officially engaged. In a letter of 21 March 1868 Ruskin wrote, 'After this, I shall allow Joanna for all arrangements of meeting – or other matters needing intervention of post – to be your correspondent....' And even after they were married and their first child was born, Ruskin expected to still take an active part in the running of their lives. On 2 April 1873 he wrote to Severn,

> I am not well today myself – (stomach wrong) – and am much tired – I write with rude brevity that I am sure Joanna ought to give up nursing. even were she well, her constitution is not one which she ought to wish her child to inherit more than it will by birth – an entirely strong wet nurse would be far better for her child – You can hint this to her perhaps – at all events, act on it.

(d) Books

The Adams Bequest contains two boxes of books by and about Ruskin which will help to fill gaps in the Bembridge and Brantwood collections. Then among the twenty-five volumes of Severn and Ruskin association are books about Ruskin by Mrs Meynell, Collingwood, Spielmann, Marwick and Kitchin, inscribed by their authors to Joan or Arthur Severn. Joan Severn's copies of *German Popular Stories* and *Notes on Prout and Hunt* are inscribed to her by Ruskin. There is Arthur Severn's Latin *Dictionary* with its end papers covered by drawings of boats, and Susan Beever's copy of *Harbours of England* inscribed to her by Joan.

However, the bulk of the books in the collection – 185 volumes – came from Ruskin's own library. Most of them have a particular significance and their presence here shows how carefully Mr Adams made his selection from the books at Brantwood.

Mr Adams had already passed to the Collection two Bibles in which I had expressed interest in 1964. Both of these are mentioned by Collingwood,[25] one is the Baskett Bible of 1749 with the leaf from the Apocrypha pasted down, on which are recorded the dates of birth of Ruskin's grandfather and his brothers and sisters. The other is the Bible given by Margaret Ruskin to her husband and referred to in the third footnote on p. 52.

There are two *Books of Common Prayer*. One, of 1844, contains J. J. Ruskin's signature and has his notes on all the endpapers and fly leaves, and over these notes on the front pastedown Joan Severn has written 'Brantwood. Used by him when last he came to this (Coniston) church – It was his Father's.' The slightly larger 1860 edition has only three notes by Ruskin on the final fly-leaf. A *Psalter* from the Brantwood library is the 1823 Chiswick Press edition of Sir Philip Sidney's translation, used by Ruskin to prepare *Rock Honeycomb*, vol. II of *Bibliotheca Pastorum*.

Other books which may be mentioned at this point are the 14th edition of Cruden's *Concordance* (1865) – only sparingly annotated by Ruskin, but characteristically cut down to fit its correct shelf in his study. Finden's *Landscape Illustrations* of the Bible (Murray, 1836, 2 vols) contains the label of a Leamington bookseller. Perhaps Ruskin bought them there in 1841 when he was staying in the town under Dr Jephson's care. He owned the original Turners of several of the plates. *Old Bibles* by J. R. Dore (Eyre & Spottiswoode, 1888, 2nd ed.) is inscribed 'May it please Mr Ruskin to accept this book from the author'. J. Ker's *The Psalms in History and Biography* (Edinburgh, Elliot, 1886) contains quite a lot of notes by Ruskin, while *The Legends of St Patrick* (London, King, 1872) was written and presented to Ruskin by his Coniston neighbour Aubrey de Vere.

Juvenilia is represented by *Little Jack* (London, Bysh, 1820) containing some *very* early 'drawings' and showing that Ruskin was a mutilator of books from an early age! A favourite author of Ruskin's youth was Maria Edgeworth; here is a late (1856) copy of *Harry and Lucy* with a sketch by Ruskin on the pastedown of what appears to be a comet over Wetherlam at 3.30 a.m. on 2 October 1881.

Another favourite author was Sir Walter Scott. Here is his *Memoirs of Jonathan Swift D.D.* (Paris, 1826, 2 vols). Lockhart's *Memoirs of the Life of Sir Walter Scott, Bart* (Edinburgh, 1837, 7 vols) must be the set from the Brantwood study because the bedroom set is already in the Collection. It is evident from some of the annotations that this was originally John James's set. Other biographies include Knight's *Life of Dante Gabriel Rossetti*, 1887, inscribed 'with the writer's compliments', H. S. Marks's *Pen and Pencil Sketches*, 2 vols, 1894, and C. H. Spurgeon's *Autobiography*, 2 vols, 1897. *The Life of Lord Byron* by an English Gentleman in the Greek Military Service (3 vols, 1825), may have been his father's. William Smart's *John Ruskin: His life and work* is inscribed 'with the writer's compliments, 6th Dec 1880'.

Art and architecture are represented by five volumes of the *Magazine of Art*, MacGibbon & Ross's *Castellated and Domestic Architecture of Scotland*, 2 vols, 1887, the *Catalogue* of the London Art Gallery's Turner exhibition, 1899, specially bound and inscribed 'with much humility', and Richardson's *Essay on the Theory of Painting*, 1715. Julia Boyd's *Bewick Gleanings*, 1886, is heavily bound in morocco and has an author's inscription which fills the fly-leaf. An interesting manuscript is *The Proportions of Ancient and Modern Architecture drawn by W. Wilkins*. On the fly-leaf is the inscription 'Henry Wilkins the gift of his brother W. Wilkins 1801'. William Wilkins was the architect of the National Gallery and Ruskin wrote somewhat disparagingly of his work in the *Poetry of Architecture*. Ongania's monumental work on St Mark's, Venice, is present in its six parts. There are several books of engravings: Turner's *Liber Studiorum*, 3 vols, 1875, Prout's *Hints on Light and Shadow*, 1848, and *Sketches at Home and Abroad*, 1844, and Harding's *Elementary Art*, 1838.

Under the heading of general literature comes one of the scarcest books of Ruskin association, Rose La Touche's *Clouds and Light* (London, 1870), but unhappily, although it was Ruskin's copy, it contains no markings by either him or the author. Also in this category we have two sets of *The Thousand and One Nights* (London 3 vols, 1859, and Paris, 7 vols, 1824), three of George Elliot's first editions and Sale's *The Koran*, 1836, but the strongest section is poetry. There is Cowper in two volumes (1811), Dante's *Vision* translated by Cary in three volumes (1819) and one volume (1844), Victor Hugo's *Odes et Ballades*, 2 vols, 1838, Pope in four volumes (1835), Thomson's *Seasons* (1793), Falconer's *Shipwreck* (1796), and Young's *Night Thoughts* (1824). William Morris's *Earthly Paradise* is inscribed on the fly-leaf of volume 3 'John Ruskin from his friend the Author'. Inserted in Tennyson's *The Foresters*, 1892, is a printed slip, 'From the Author'. Wordsworth's *Yarrow Revisited*, 1835, is inscribed on the half-title 'To Anna Braithwaite from Dora Wordsworth with grateful and affecte. remembrances, Dec 16th 1835'; inserted is a letter from C. W. S. Goodyer to Joan Severn, giving the book to Ruskin on 7 February 1898. Coventry Patmore's *The Unknown Eros*, 1877, is bound in full blue velvet and has an extra title page of vellum beautifully illuminated by Patmore's daughter Bertha. Her 'exquisite work' was nevertheless criticized by Ruskin* 'Never reduce Angelico angels to blow trumpets in a letter B.†… Are there no leaves on the earth but ivy-leaves….'

Geology and allied sciences are represented by fourteen volumes including Reynold's *Geological Atlas of Great Britain*, liberally anno-

* In a letter of 10 June 1881 to Patmore, thanking him for the volume (*Works*, XXXVII. 365).

† Mistranscribed by Cook and Wedderburn. In fact the angel is in the initial 'U'.

tated, and by works by Conybeare, Phillips, Trimmer, Allan, Brance and Miller.

There are a few copies of Ruskin's own works – *Poems* (the large paper edition of 1891), *Usury*, 2nd ed., 1885, in a heavy vellum binding, *Mornings in Florence*, 2nd ed., with some of Ruskin's notes in part v, and *Two Letters concerning 'Notes on the Construction of Sheep-folds'*, 1890, inscribed 'To John Ruskin in memory of old times. F. J. Furnivall 17 Jan. 1891.'

(e) Drawings by Ruskin

There are forty-nine drawings in the Adams collection which are definitely the work of Ruskin and several more that could be attributed to him. Generally speaking they are a mixed lot and do not include any examples of Ruskin at his best. However, the collection does include a number of particularly interesting drawings which we are delighted to have as additions to the Collection.

The earliest drawing in the Collection is dated '1 September 1831 JR.' This is one of the earliest of Ruskin's contemporaneously signed and dated drawings. It shows a road curving past a ruined tower and wall, with hills suggested in the distance. An old lady walks along the tree-lined road. Very much in this same style are five drawings in a sketch-book and a further three loose ones clearly by the same hand. Unfortunately, none is signed or dated but a certain amount of circumstantial evidence can almost persuade one that they are early Ruskins done in imitation, or at least in the style, of Runciman. This group of drawings merits further research. Meanwhile, one is on firmer ground in identifying the 1832 *Tunbridge Castle*, described by Collingwood as being in Ruskin's 'drawing master style'.

The most important group of drawings are the eleven which date from the 1835 continental tour. These are a particularly welcome addition to the Whitehouse Collection because we already have twenty-nine drawings from the same tour. At this time it was Ruskin's habit to make on-the-spot sketches during the day and then work them up into finished drawings in the evenings or during the winter after the family returned to London. Two of the drawings from the Adams collection fall into the latter class – *Mont Velan from the windows of*

Hospice of the Great St Bernard,[26] and *Hospital, Pass of St Gothard.*[27] The other drawings are sketches showing varying degrees of finish. Most combine landscape using his 'line and dot' style, with architectural studies in the style imitative of Prout. One sketch shows a fireplace and massive French bed in *Interior of a bed chamber, Hotel du Palais, Chalons S. Marne*. Others show *Lauterbroonn and Staubbach* [*sic*], *Grindelwald & Wetterhorn*, *Lucerne from a suburb*, and *Wellhorn, Wetterhorn, Glacier de Rosenlau & Reichenbach from Meyringen*. The drawing of the *Lake of Como* has another of the *Tower and Vale of Meyringen* on the reverse. A view *On the Rhine* has two slight mountain studies on the reverse, marked by J. J. Ruskin as 'Done'. Two copies of churches, one at Cologne, by Ruskin after Samuel Prout, must also date from about this period.

From the 1850s comes a sheet of diagrams and notes on the balustrade of the Ca d'Oro. There is a later watercolour of the *Sea Walls* of Venice, and, also probably from Venice, is a drawing of arches with a shield and carved figure. A pencil and wash study of *Gneiss Rock* may have been made at Glenfinlas in 1853, while a drawing of the *Aiguille Charmoz*, Chamouni, is dated 1854.

Malham: Source of Aire rejoins the four other studies of 1875 of the same subject already in the Collection. There are two drawings made at Schaffhausen – *The Rhinefall*, apparently in the frame behind the *Roslin Chapel Prentice Pillar* when it was exhibited at Coniston in 1919 (no. 33), and *Houses at the left hand of Falls of Schaffhausen in Turner's drawing*.

A drawing which came to the Collection from the Adams Collection in 1964 is one of Ruskin's many studies of the effigy of Ilaria di Caretto at Lucca; now we have a small sketch of a road, dated *Lucca 3rd Oct., '82*. Also from this tour come two studies of the *Walls of Fiesole*.[28] There are eight drawings of carvings or mouldings including one of St Symmaelius.

In addition to the Ruskin drawings in the Adams collection is a part ream of Ruskin's unused drawing paper. It is a cream laid handmade paper, 17 ¼ ins. x 13 ½ ins., 17lb., with a Britannia watermark. The wrapping paper is inscribed by Joan Severn, 'Hand made drawing-paper of John Ruskin's, for Arthur Severn'.

(f) Drawings by other artists

As far as I am aware, all of Mr Adams's drawings came from the Ruskin or Severn collections. Thus, in this section are detailed a cross-section of the miscellaneous drawings from Brantwood. Inevitably there are several uninscribed drawings to which it may never be possible to ascribe artists since they are probably the work of amateurs.

From the drawings actually 'collected' by Ruskin may be mentioned *Wenlock Priory*, by P. S. Munn, 1802, and Prout's *Wakefield Church.* Of Moritz Retsch's *Poetry and the Swan* Ruskin wrote in the *Art of England*,[29] 'The drawing which I possess by his hand, of the Genius of Poetry riding upon a swan, could not be placed in my school [the Ruskin Drawing School at Oxford] with any hope of deepening your impression either of the beauty of swans, or the dignity of genii'. In the same lecture Ruskin referred to Retsch's illustrations to Goethe's *Faust*; Ruskin's copy of the 1843 edition is in the collection. Another interesting drawing is a study in pencil, ink and wash of two figures, inscribed on the reverse by Joan Severn, 'Original sketch by Sir Joshua [Reynolds]'.

I have already referred to the four watercolours by John James Ruskin, and to Arthur Severn's copy of Turner's *Flint.* The drawings by Severn form the largest single group in the collection after the drawings by Ruskin himself. There are twenty-one of them, in addition to the *Flint.* Undoubtedly the most interesting of the group is a small water colour of the interior of the drawing room at Brantwood, possibly dating from 1877. It is evening and on the table in the window stand five tall silver candlesticks. Seated around the table are Ruskin and three other people who could be Alexander Wedderburn, Sara Anderson and Joan Severn. At the time that M. H. Spielmann was preparing his *Magazine of Art* articles on Ruskin's portraits, Arthur Severn wrote to him about this portrait on 16 July 1889, 'I have two [portraits of Ruskin] by myself, but not very good – one is interesting – of Ruskin reading in the evening Sir Walter Scott, with six* tall candles! But it is only a small watercolour done more to show the contrast of black cold mountains outside windows (blinds are up) with

* Severn is in error; there are five. The letter and *Memoir* are printed in *The Professor.*

warm light inside – this one, I hope to use some day – if ever I write something about Ruskin!' I searched in vain for this drawing when I was editing the Rylands manuscript[30] of Severn's *Memoir of Ruskin*, but at last it has emerged.

Other drawings of Brantwood or Coniston include a small wash drawing of Brantwood from the front drive made in the early 1870s when the only Ruskin addition to the house was the turret room, and an attractive view of *Coniston Old Man and the Copper Mines Valley from Brantwood.* Severn must have had a mental blockage where fives and sixes were concerned! His later *Coniston Lake and Old Man from Brantwood* only shows five instead of the six cypress trees planted by Ruskin, in the foreground. There is a nice water-colour of the garden behind No. 28 Herne Hill, the house which was the Ruskins', and which was given to the Severns as a wedding present; and on two sheets of notepaper are four small sketches, the front and back of Herne Hill, the interior of Ruskin's bedroom there, and the view of Forest Hill from the room.

An interesting association item is Severn's sketch of Loughrigg, Ambleside, the home of Albert Fleming, who edited the *Hortus Inclusus* letters. Other pictures connected with Severn are a study of stained-glass windows by his wife, a drawing of Sydney Harbour by his brother Henry, and a mountain study by his brother-in-law, Sir Charles Newton.

Drawings by Ruskin's friends include two watercolours by Mary Beever, a landscape and a view near The Thwaite, Coniston, where she lived with her sister Susanna. From the large collection of Kate Greenaway's at one time in the Ruskin collection come an uncharacteristic leaf study signed with initials, and pencil drawings of a lady with a girl picking flowers (1883) and a girl with a skipping rope ('Found in a book I draw flowers in. K. G.'). To this group Mrs Adams has very kindly added a sketch of a lady with a muff from her own collection. She tells me that she can remember seeing this picture hanging in Ruskin's bedroom when she and her husband visited Brantwood in 1928. Also by lady artists are a study of daisies by Emily Warren (1884), who was later to illustrate Cook's *Homes and Haunts of John Ruskin*, *Savoy* after Turner by Isabel Jay and three pictures by Lilias

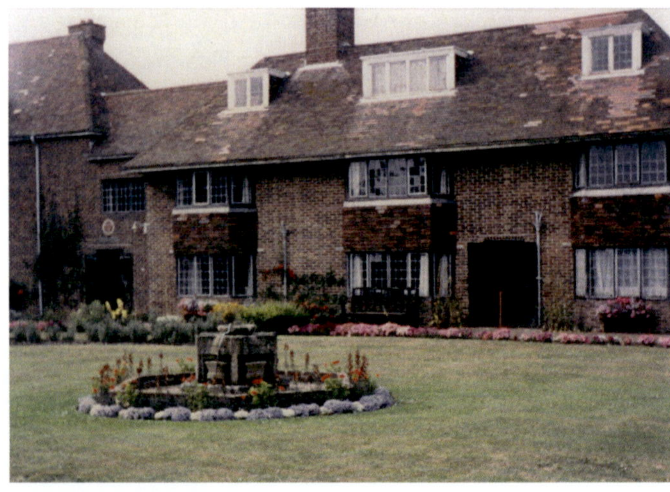

New House and Ruskin Galleries, Bembridge

Trotter, the 'quite provokingly good lass' whom Ruskin once thought of setting up, with Kate Greenaway, in a London girls' drawing school.

There is a small landscape with trees by Laurence Hilliard, one of Ruskin's secretaries, who died just as he was beginning to make a name for himself as an artist; a study of a capital (1874) by Thomas Wade who also drew in 1876 for Ruskin 'a cottage at Coniston, likely to be soon destroyed by "improvements"',[31] and two leaf studies (1884) by George Butterworth, 'a carpenter of great skill and fineness of faculty, but his pride, wilfulness, and certain angular narrowness of nature, kept him down...'.[32] Butterworth was one of Ruskin's students at the Working Men's College; another was J. W. Bunney, who was later to do work for Ruskin and the Guild of St George in Venice. He is represented in the collection by a chiaroscuro study of books dated 1869.

Other artists who worked for the Guild were Angelo Alessandri, represented now at Bembridge by *Mosaic of St George, St Mark's Venice*, and two other watercolours; H. R. Newman, study of two fish and two small and microscopically-detailed landscapes; Frank Randall, studies of spheres; and William Ward, with a study after Turner and three architectural studies, including one of the *Ponte Pietra, Verona*.

The Adams Bequest has added more interesting and valuable material to the Whitehouse Collection than any other single accession since the bulk purchases made by J. H. Whitehouse in the 1930s. Many of the books, letters, manuscripts and drawings fill gaps in that collection, while others are re-united with their companions after a break of over forty years.

REFERENCES

1. Now part of the Adams Bequest in the Whitehouse Collection in the Ruskin Library at Lancaster University, RF L 81. Lancaster catalogue numbers are prefixed by the abbreviation 'RF', which hereafter has been omitted for the sake of convenience.
2. L 81, begun Monday, 25 June 1928, continued 'two weeks later 8/7/28'.
3. *Library Edition of the Works of John Ruskin* (hereafter referred to as *Works*), XIII. 489.
4. *Works*, XXVIII. 346 ff. This extract, with the omission of the final paragraph, was repeated in *Praeterita*, *Works*, XXXV. 37 ff.
5. Mary J. Wilkinson-H. C. Adams, 23 May 1931, L 81.
6. Mary J. Wilkinson H. C. Adams, 1 June 1931, L 81.
7. Miles Wilkinson H. C. Adams, 3 June 1931, L 81.
8. *Works*, XIII. 442.
9. Miles Wilkinson-H. C. Adams, 1 June 1931, L 81.
10. MS 91.
11. MS 91.
12. MS 91.
13. MS 33A.
14. MS 88.
15. ADD.S/48.
16. MS 91.
17. L 81.
18. L 81.
19. L85.
20. L 83, which contains correspondents Acland to L'Estrange, L 84 Forbes to Martin, L 85 Newton to de Vere.
21. L 13.
22. *Works*, XXXIV, 585.
23. This holograph dedication and list are filed as MS 91.
24. L 82.
25. W. G. Collingwood, *Ruskin Relics* (London, 1903), pp. 197-8.
26. Reproduced in *Works*, I. 520.
27. Reproduced in *Works*, II. 436.
28. Exhibited Coniston 1919, no. 207.
29. *Works*, XXXIII. 334.
30. Rylands English MS 1264/13.
31. *Works*, XXVIII. 583.
32. *Works*, XXXV. 488.

III

CATALOGUING RUSKIN'S LIBRARY*

THE FRIENDS OF RUSKIN'S BRANTWOOD NEWSLETTER, AUTUMN 2013

It must have been in 1960 or '61 when I catalogued the three hundred and eighty volumes from Ruskin's library then in the Whitehouse Collection at Bembridge. In 1962 I printed the catalogue as *Ruskin Association Books*. All of the books from Ruskin's library then at Brantwood came from the collection of F. J. Sharp of Barrow, the noted Ruskin collector who died in 1957. These I also catalogued, printing *their* catalogue in 1967 as *Books from John Ruskin's Library.*

Soon after I had catalogued the books at Bembridge I decided that it might be a useful and interesting exercise to try and list all of the books once owned by Ruskin. I cut up copies of my 1962 and 1967 pamphlets and pasted each entry onto a 4" x 6" library card. This became the foundation of my catalogue of Ruskin's Library.

Originally housed in one card-box, the Catalogue rapidly grew. Whenever I saw an ex-Ruskin book offered for sale in a bookseller's or auction house catalogue the information was added to my cards.

My project gradually became known to scholars internationally and from time to time they told me of other ex-Ruskin books. For example one very important find was made by Paul Tucker when he was engaged in research in the Working Men's College in London. He was shown their early Library Accessions Register wherein was recorded a large number of books which Ruskin had given the College from his own library when he taught the College's art class. Fortunately Paul transcribed all of the entries in the Register and sent me a copy. When I visited the College a short while afterwards they disclaimed all knowledge of an Accessions Register. I was allowed to go into two small

* This piece was written at the request of the Editor to accompany his review of my book.

and extremely filthy book stores in the basement adjacent to the boiler room. I found quite a few of the books on Paul's list – and since there was no order in the room, I foolishly assembled most of the ex-Ruskin books in one place. I returned a few weeks later to find most of these books gone. A few have subsequently appeared on the market.

I wrote to all of the librarians in the world at libraries or museums with Ruskin holdings and obtained details of their ex-Ruskin books. I obtained photocopies of the pages of Ruskin's own 1868/1873 catalogues from the Beinecke Library at Yale. I also had copies of occasional lists which he made in his diaries. Thomas Telford, the Grasmere antiques dealer who bought at the Brantwood sale in 1931, knowing of my work gave me the two volumes of the 1894 catalogue prepared by Ruskin's secretary, Sara Anderson. But none of these catalogues was complete. Some only catalogued books in the study in glazed bookcases but not on open shelves. One only listed books in the drawing room - and so on. Ruskin never had a complete catalogue of his own library, and his library was never static. He was adding to it as quickly as he was dispersing it.

Ruskin gave a number of books from his own shelves to The Guild of St George's collection at Sheffield. I spent a couple of days going through this collection. For various reasons Ruskin was interested in several educational establishments. He gave books for the use of students at Cheltenham Ladies' College and a friend there supplied me with details. More were given to Whitelands College where Ruskin was instrumental in establishing a May Day Ceremony. Judith Peacock and others kindly supplied me with lists of those.

The only occasions on which some attempt was made to list *all* of the books was in the various 1930 and '31 dispersal sales of the contents of Brantwood and the Severns' house in Warwick Square, London. The catalogues of the Brantwood sales at Sotheby's were fairly accurate. The Warwick Square books were a mixture of Ruskin's and the Severns' books, and were difficult to separate. The listing of the books in the catalogue of the sale at Brantwood was totally incompetent and many of the lots included '... and 30 other'. Many of the listed titles themselves were quite incomprehensible.

Many of the entries on the various lists which I had were very brief – often just a surname, a one word title and a date. It rapidly became obvious that I needed access to the British Library catalogue to flesh out these brief entries. No library within striking distance held a copy of the catalogue. I had resisted ownership of a computer for some years, but the time had clearly come when I must invest in one. I quickly found the programme COPAC, which is a union catalogue of not only the British Library catalogue but also of the catalogues of most of the academic libraries of the country. This was enormously helpful in identifying titles on my lists.

When the lease of 28 Herne Hill expired the Severns moved to their larger house in Victoria. There were still quite a lot of Ruskin's books in the house and Joan Severn gave a number of them to the local public library in memory of Ruskin's association with the area. Through enemy action and council reorganisations, most of these books have ended up in the Southwark Local Studies Library where I catalogued them. Others, which must have found their way into another library and which I hadn't been identified, appeared on the market when my catalogue was almost being printed! Of course I had already listed the volumes from Ruskin's library which had found their way into the Coniston Museum.

As a quite separate venture, I had catalogued the medieval manuscripts once owned by Ruskin and this had been published in *The Library* in 1966. This was updated and incorporated into my cards.

The Ruskin *Library Edition* was searched for book titles appearing in both Ruskin's and Cook and Wedderburn's footnotes. This in itself was interesting in showing that Cook and Wedderburn did not always cite the same *editions* which Ruskin had used.

From these and other sources my single box of cards had grown to ten boxes. I knew of no further sources to explore. Further additions would only be made by chance. The time had come, some forty years later, to try to do something about publishing my catalogue. I couldn't face the prospect of typing all of the details from my – now 2969 – cards and I found someone willing to undertake the task for me. She also typed the eight chapters of my lengthy introduction. I approached several possible publishers – but they all fell about laughing at the prospect of publishing such a book!

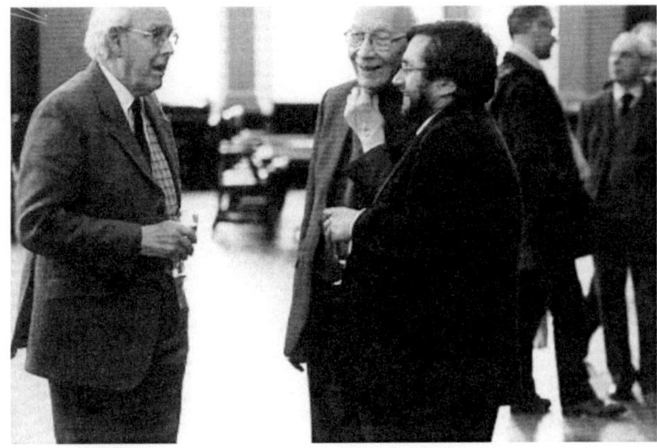

At the publication party, the author (left) talking to his editor (right)

One of the final collections to be checked was the Cook and Wedderburn Collection at the Ashmolean Museum at Oxford. Both Cook and Wedderburn knew Ruskin and both had formed their own extensive collections of books by him. When they began the task of editing the Ruskin *Library Edition* they formed as third joint collection for that express purpose. I knew that the Cook and Wedderburn Collection included a volume of newspaper cuttings relating to Ruskin that had been assembled by his father. This must have come from Brantwood. I wondered if there were any of Ruskin's own copies of his books, also from Brantwood, now at Oxford.

I went to examine the collection and found several volumes to include in my catalogue. By a happy chance the Cook and Wedderburn Collection is housed in Dr Colin Harrison's office – because he had happened to have some empty shelf space! During the course of conversation I told him of my inability to find a publisher. He explained that the publishing of library catalogues was just the thing that the Oxford Bibliographical Society specialised in. He suggested that I wrote to their editor, Dr Scott Mandelbrote – and the rest, as they say, is history. A little over fifty years since I began my project, I attended its publication party in the Upper Library at Christ Church, Oxford, situated in Peckwater Quad, where the undergraduate John Ruskin had his rooms.

IV

HOW DID JOHN JAMES RUSKIN GET TO THE OFFICE?

RUSKIN REVIEW AND BULLETIN, VOL. 9, NO. 2, 2013

We all know that John James Ruskin went daily to his office at 7 Billiter Street in the city of London and returned home 'always punctually'. 'He dined at half past four, in the front parlour, my mother sitting beside him to hear the events of the day'.[1] What Ruskin does not tell us is just *how* his father travelled to and from his office.

When the Ruskins lived at 54 Hunter Street, Brunswick Square, John James may well have walked the bare mile and three quarters to Billiter Street. However, with the move in 1823 to 28 Herne Hill, 'four miles south of the "Standard in Cornhill"'[2] a new mode of transport must have been adopted. At that time Herne Hill was on the edge of open country, and was not served by public transport. Although their new house incorporated a coach house and there was a stable at the end of the garden, it is improbable that the Ruskins had a carriage at this date because John James was still working – until 1828 – to pay off his father's debts. It was in this stable where in 1829 Ruskin's pony Shagram lived and where Ruskin was bitten on the mouth by their Newfoundland dog Lion.

From 1796 there were stagecoaches running regularly, if infrequently, between Camberwell and Westminster and the City. After 1835 there were three omnibus operators running services between Camberwell and the City.[3] It seems probable that John James Ruskin walked from Herne Hill to Camberwell, from where he took a stage to the City. He *may* have hired a carriage to take the family to Beresford Street Chapel on Sundays as that was a substantial distance from Herne Hill. But whether they walked or drove, the distance may have accounted for their occasional arrival at the chapel 'when those short prayers were half over'.[4] They certainly would

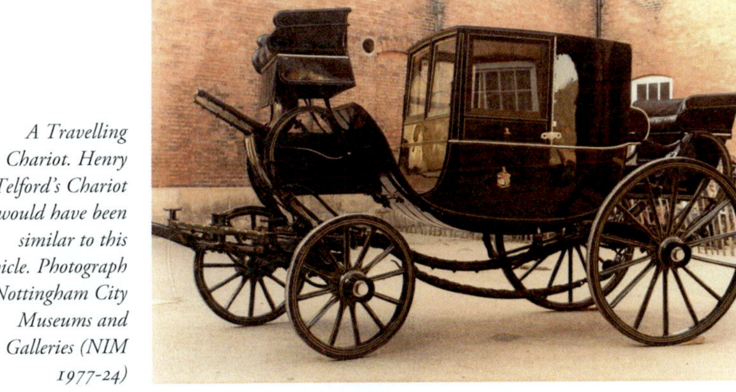

A Travelling Chariot. Henry Telford's Chariot would have been similar to this vehicle. Photograph © Nottingham City Museums and Galleries (NIM 1977-24)

have needed to drive to the Camden Chapel in Peckham Road.

When John James travelled in England in the course of his business we know that he used the extensive network of stagecoaches and, after the development of the railways, a combination of both. Writing to his son from Penrith on 8th March 1831, he described the Liverpool and Manchester Railway which had been opened six months earlier. 'I do think you would be delighted to be one of the passengers. I do believe we should scarcely be able to keep Mamma from taking a journey', he wrote.[5] However he soon came to dislike railway travel.

For example in February 1840 he travelled by coach to Worcester, but from Worcester to Birmingham he took the train. 'I came here … very fast by train … it is the dullest of all travelling – not a soul or object of interest near you & at night more dreary.'[6] Writing from Stone a month later he told his wife:' I begin to detest Railroad travelling too for its mere stupidity.'[7] Writing to his son from Liverpool a couple of years later, he confided: 'I find Railways very tiresome as far as waiting is concerned. We waited for an hour beyond time at Warr[in]g[to]n.'[8]

In the years before the canny John James Ruskin 'thought it right to hire a carriage'[9] for the family's summer tours of England and Scotland, they used Henry Telford's travelling Chariot (see image above). Telford's Chariot was possibly an elderly vehicle, but well-designed for travelling. There was no driving seat, the pair of horses being driven by a postillion who would have ridden the near-side horse. Thus there was a fairly uninterrupted view from the coach's front window for the three Ruskins inside. Anne Strachan, Mrs Ruskin's maid, travelled outside on the wide dicky seat at the back, which had ample space beneath it for all the luggage. On fine days John James, to obtain better views, would join Anne on the dicky seat. Presumably young John was kept inside for safety with his mother.

When the family began to undertake longer continental tours they needed a larger and more sturdy carriage. This they hired for the occasion from 'the hireable reserves at Mr Hopkinson's of Long Acre'. They possibly first hired a coach from Hopkinson for the 1825 journey to Paris and Brussels. They would certainly have hired one from him for the long continental tours of the '30s when Mary Richardson lived with the Ruskins. There was space inside the carriage for all four of them.

The carriage chosen for the 1833 tour[10] was fitted with an outside front seat, occupied on nice days by John James and Mary; Mrs Ruskin and John rode inside, and again Anne Strachan occupied the dicky seat now accompanied by their courier. The carriage was driven by a postillion. Setting out from Herne Hill, in full view of the neighbours, they took a pair of horses, probably quite adequate for travelling through the lanes and villages of south London. Ruskin said[11] that an extra pair of horses would be waiting for them at the foot of Greenwich Hill. In fact here they would probably have joined the main London-Dover road and changed from one pair to two pairs of horses at what would have been one of the first posting houses out of central London. The original pair, with the coachman, would have returned whence they came. On later family tours, probably for John's greater convenience, they also took a second carriage for him. This *may* also have been hired from Hopkinson but more possibly was hired on arrival in France.

Luke Hopkinson's premises were at 77 High Holborn; since Ruskin described him as being 'of Long Acre', he may also have had premises there. Hopkinson elevated coach making to a profession. He was consulted as an advisor on his customers' special needs and he gained a footing of personal friendship with many of them. It was he who obtained John Ruskin's Westminster Abbey ticket for Queen

Victoria's coronation. Hopkinson introduced the landau into England from Germany in 1838. In his Britzka-Landau the two hoods could be folded flat while the seats rose six inches to give the occupants a better view. Luke Hopkinson was Master of the Worshipful Company of Coachmakers and Coach Harness Makers in 1822. He seems to have ceased trading in the early 1850s.

The second-hand 'Fly' which John James bought from Hopkinson for £27 10s[12] was probably the first carriage which the family actually owned. John James Ruskin left home for one of his business trips on 9 February 1835 (the day after John's birthday) so he must have arranged for the purchase of the carriage before he left home. The carriage is first mentioned in a letter of 21 February from Mrs Ruskin to John James, sent for his collection at the Post Office at Whitehaven in Cumberland.

> I have been twice out in the Fly. I believe it is a very nice looking one but you know I am no judge of carriages[.] Its colour is a very pretty brown, wheels and all, a little red on the wheels lined with a full blue [,] the steps and bottom newly carpeted. It has also had a little new paint & varnish[,] a comfortable seat in front for Coachman which will hold two very well. Mary [Richardson] thinks it is a very neat decent looking vehicle but not striking. John says it is one which every body would consider genteel but that no person would sit down to draw the form of.[13]

A 'Fly' is not a *design* of carriage. The word is a generic term such as 'taxi' or 'cab'. A Fly was usually a light carriage designed for rapid motion and such a vehicle could have been described as a Fly, even though it was not for hire. In the case of the Ruskins' 1835 Fly, it was probably a 'Four Wheeler' or 'Growler', a coach pulled by one horse in shafts and driven by a coachman on the box, and with room inside for four adults.

From the letter quoted above it is evident that the carriage was being used for pleasure during John James's absence from home. We do not know if its use continued thus, with John James going to the office in his usual way, or whether he used it daily for travelling into the City.

The use of a carriage presupposed the presence of a horse and coachman/groom. At this date I think the vehicle was only used for occasional pleasure.

An invaluable source of Ruskin family biographical information is the group of account books[14] kept by John James Ruskin. One of the sections in his annual accounts is headed 'Country and Doctors', and includes details of John James's out-of-London travelling. A new section, 'Carriages and Horses', was introduced into the account books in 1848. I assume from this that expenditure of this nature had reached the level at which it need recording in more detail. The new section in 1848 itemised expenses such as food, shoes, the hire of a Brougham (below), and wages for the coachman, Powell, 26/- per week (£67 12s for the year). The annual total for the 1848 was £234 10s. If they still had the 1835 Fly, then they had become a two-coach family. Perhaps by now John James was travelling to Billiter Street in his own carriage.

Coachmen had to be dressed as befitted their employers and John James Ruskin recorded the appropriate expenses in his accounts. The coachman Powell features in the 1849 and 1850 accounts; on 12 July 1850 his 'Dress' cost £6 15s. However by November 1850 'Frank' appears in the accounts when his 'livery' cost £5 12s. He continues to feature in the accounts until 1856; in January 1857 Powell

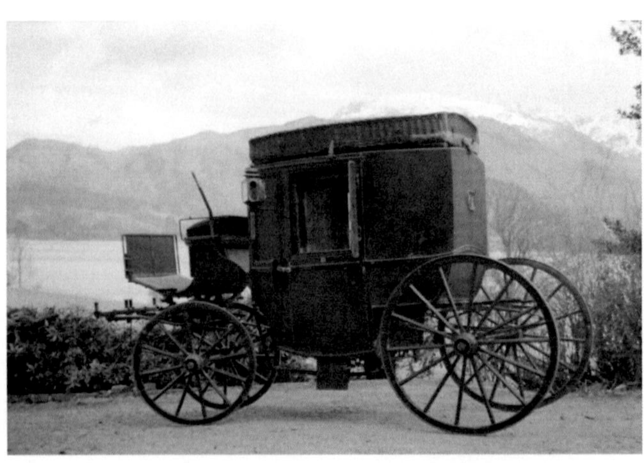

Brougham, built for John Ruskin in 1875 (Brantwood Trust)

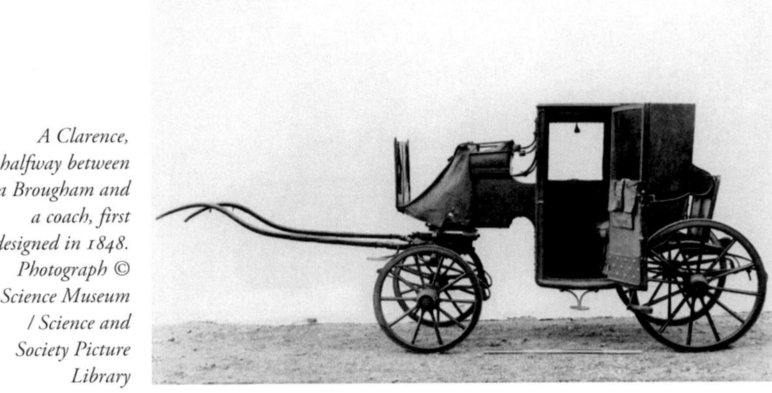

A Clarence, halfway between a Brougham and a coach, first designed in 1848. Photograph © Science Museum / Science and Society Picture Library

reappears for a short while, to be replaced in 1858. The accounts record 'January-September coachman Vincent £1 15s per week, £38 15s'. In September 1860 David Fudge appears for the first time when his 'clothes' cost £13 1s 6d.

The annual accounts reveal that John James had realised that it was more economical to *hire* rather than *buy* carriages and horses. An entry for October 1849 confirms that the Brougham was hired annually at £42. In August of the following year he hired a 'new Clarence'* (above) for £45 and this hire charge was repeated a year later, while in October 1851 he paid £42 for the hire of a Brougham. July 1852 saw the hire of a 'Large Clarence' at £45 for the year and in October a 'Small Clarence' was hired for the following twelve months. The accounts show that the pattern of hiring carriages by the year continued, although there *was* a change in 1854 because in that and in succeeding years, carriages were hired from 'Corben'. It must have been at this time that Luke Hopkinson went out of business.

It is evident that John James not only dealt with Hopkinson on his own behalf, but also on behalf of his Spanish business partner,

* He also had an old Clarence. Perhaps this was an error. The Clarence and the Brougham are very similar in outward appearance. Usually a Brougham just has seating for two people whereas a Clarence seats four. The carriage now at Brantwood, which Ruskin had built to his own specifications in 1875, is a Double Brougham – a cross between a Clarence and a Brougham.

Pedro Domecq. It seems that Domecq bought a carriage from Hopkinson in 1836 for on 26 May he wrote from Paris to John James Ruskin:

> I cannot yet send Hopkinson the Arms* for carriage for which I am not in a great hurry but shall bear it in mind.[15]

Perhaps it was also while riding in this same carriage that Pedro Domecq met with a fatal accident. He suffered from a rheumatic or arthritic complaint, the pain from which was alleviated by heat or steam. In his carriage he travelled in a hammock suspended over a bath of boiling water which was heated from below. Travelling in Spain 30 January 1839 the hammock broke and he fell into the bath of water, surviving after the accident for twelve days.

Pedro Domecq's brother, Juan Pedro, took over his business interests in the firm of Ruskin Telford and Domecq. Perhaps John James also looked after Juan Pedro's carriage requirements. This may explain the Income page entry in JJR's accounts[16] on 13 August 1852:

> To Recd. Of R[oyal] Ea[gle?][17] for Hopkinsons's carriage lost at sea less £20 pd Corben pack[ing] £130

John Ruskin was in Venice at this time and his father told him of the accident in a letter which I have not seen. Ruskin responded:[18]

> I am sorry bye the bye to hear of the fate of the old carriage – the more because it alarms me for my Tintoret† – which I am forced to send by sea … . If it gets home it will be a great delight to me – if it goes to the bottom I can do without it.

Charles Corben (1794-1879) was a coachmaker of 30 Great Queen Street, St Giles; in 1851 he was employing twenty-three men. By 1871

* Presumably the Domecq coat of arms, to be painted on the carriage doors.

† Ruskin bought two Tintoretto paintings while in Venice. This particular one was probably Dominico Tintoretto's 'An Allegory of Faith', now in the Fogg.

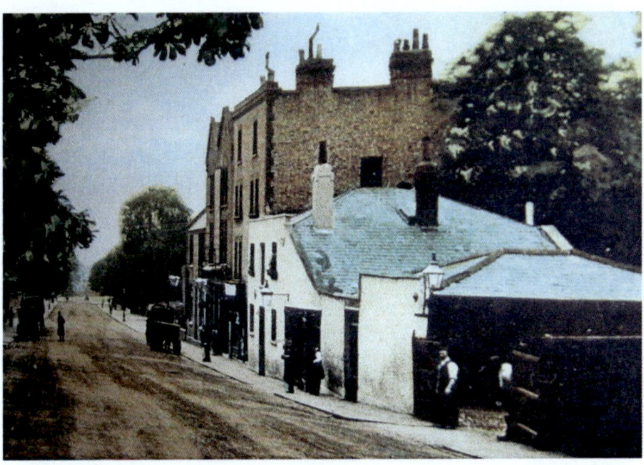

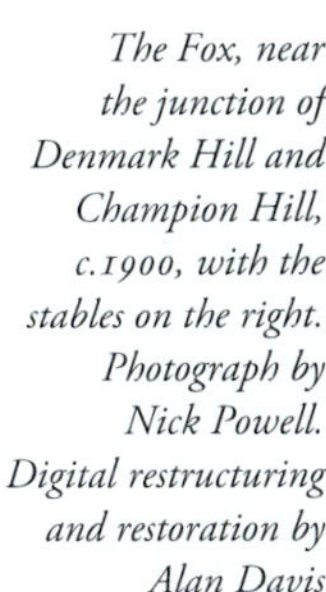

The Fox, near the junction of Denmark Hill and Champion Hill, c.1900, with the stables on the right. Photograph by Nick Powell. Digital restructuring and restoration by Alan Davis

he had retired and two years later he was the Master of the Coachmakers Company.

Perhaps Corben was a better salesman than Hopkinson! In 1855 John James hired a 'new carriage' (of unspecified type) for the increased sum of £55 while also re-hiring the small Clarence for £42. A similar pattern of carriage hire continues until the final set of accounts in 1863.

Carriages need horses, and again John James Ruskin hired rather than bought his horses. I assume if you hired a horse for a year and something went wrong with it, the livery stables replaced it! By chance there was a livery stable kept by John Bullock adjacent to the old hostelry, The Fox-under-the-Hill,* near the junction of Denmark Hill and Champion Hill, some five hundred yards from the gates of 163 Denmark Hill (above). In 1849 he was paid 'for horses to 18 March £15' and in 1850 the breakdown of this figure was clarified

* The old Fox was demolished in 1865 during the construction of the South London Railway's line. H.J. Dyos, *op.cit.*, 64. I am indebted to Dr Cecilia Powell for telling me that it was rebuilt on the same site in 1874, and demolished again by bombing in 1941. It is evident, from one of the photographs kindly taken for me by Nick Powell, that the old stables adjoining the Fox survived the 1865 demolition of the original inn. The original stables can be seen, adjoining the 1874 Fox, in the turn of the century photograph which I reproduce. Probably after the war the present inn was built on higher ground a little further south, in the fork of Denmark Hill and Champion Hill, and logically was re-named 'The Fox on the Hill'.

by the entry '18 June Bullock to 18 Sept for two horses at £60 per year, £15'. The pattern of hiring horses continued. By 1860 George Creed had taken over the stables.

In an era when the price of commodities changed little from year to year, we can judge the increasing use that John James made of his carriages and horses by comparing the annual totals of the 'Carriages and Horses' section of the accounts. When the new section was introduced into the accounts in 1848 the total was £234 10s. By 1863 this figure had risen to £446 7s 6d.

We can assume that from at least the mid to late 1840s John James was travelling between his home and his office in his own carriage. It would have been uneconomical to have travelled by any other means. But what happened when he arrived in Billiter Street? You can't just park your horse and carriage outside for the day! The answer appears to lie in the small 1862 account book.[19]

This small 1862 account book shows that John James spent a considerable amount of money – some £99 – on flies. The hiring of a Fly was not as simple as hiring a taxi today. The taxi comes complete with driver. John James had to hire the Fly for a fixed sum and additionally had to hire the coachman. What the account book *doesn't* show are any regular payments for stabling in London (except in the large account book for March 1859 when there is an entry 'City Stable £7').

Based on all of the evidence I think that John James was driven from home to Billiter Street in his own carriage with his own coachman, which, having deposited him, then went back to Denmark Hill. At the end of his working day it returned to collect him for the homeward journey. I think the small account book's record of flies and coachmen must be for excursions daily from the office to elsewhere in London. For example the note made on Saturday 1 February 1862 shows that he hired '3 Flies 7/- coachman 9/-'; on '18 February Flies £4 1s. coach[man] 10/-' and on 15 March 'Flies £7, coachman 7s'. The cost of the Fly doesn't seem to be in any regular proportion to the charge for the coachman.

It is often difficult to interpret the account book entries. For example the entry in the big account book in March 1859 for 'City stable £7' *could* be for stabling a horse daily at a livery stable near Billiter

Street, but it *does* seem out of proportion to the £15 per quarter for hiring two horses. There is a further alarming entry in the 1863 accounts when in June JJR spent £120 on 'Flies [for] Mr Domecq and John'. The entry is all the more amazing when one realises that at the time John was in fact in Italy!

John James's last coachman, David Fudge, remained in John's employment. He often drove Ruskin through the Surrey lanes, dropping him at a picturesque spot. Before setting off on a cross-country walk Ruskin would give Fudge a sketch map showing where he was to be met.[20] Even after the sale of the Denmark Hill house, when Ruskin was living at Oxford or Brantwood, David Fudge continued to be his 'coachman in London', receiving £60 per annum.

With Ruskin away from London much of the time, Fudge's duties after 1872 could not have been too onerous. No doubt he served the needs of the Severns when they cared to hire a carriage, but he was there when Ruskin needed him. In an undated letter from Oxford Ruskin wrote to him:

> Please be at Paddington Station to meet the train leaving here at 4 – getting to London at ½ past 5 I suppose … Tell Sarah I shall not be home till about eleven, – I'm going to the Grosvenor Hotel dinner.[21]

Ruskin always looked after his servants. In *Fors Clavigera*, he writes:[22]

> I have got two Davids, and a Kate[23] that I wouldn't change for anybody else's servants in the world; and I believe the only quarrel they have with me is that I don't give them enough to do for me.

Hearing of Fudge's illness Ruskin wrote to him from Brantwood on 19 October 1883:

> I am so very sorry for your illness. I wish I could come to see you – but every hour is fixed in town just now. If I could do you

good I would come – but it would only queer both of us. I send you five pounds in case you can get any comforts with it to relieve present pain. Ever your affectionate Master, J. Ruskin.[24]

Like all of Ruskin's old servants, David Fudge, his father's coachman, was provided for in his old age, receiving a regular cheque from Brantwood. As Joan Severn complained to George Allen in March 1889, 'you know this is always a heavy month with Pensioners wages &c.'[25]

In connection with Ruskin carriages, an outstanding question remains. The carriage now at Brantwood did not return to London after the 1876 posting tour to Coniston. Ruskin told Joan Severn that it was for country, not London, use. But where did it live? The original Brantwood coach house and stables were pulled down when the lodge was built in 1872 and the present stable block was not built until 1881-2. I think the carriage *may* have been housed in the stables at the Waterhead Hotel, from where Ruskin hired carriages when he needed them.

These are all fascinating, if trivial, byways in Ruskin biography.

REFERENCES

1. *Works*, XXXV, 39. John James Ruskin must have been taking a late lunch. Elsewhere (*Works*, XXXV, 61) Ruskin refers to joining his parents for tea at 6 p.m. If John James had to stay late at the office 'old Maisie' would cook a chop for his lunch (*Works*, XXXV, 133).
2. *Works*, XXXV, 34.
3. H. J. Dyos, *Victorian Suburb. A study of the growth of Camberwell* (Leicester: Leicester U.P., 1977), p. 66ff. One of the principal omnibus operators was Thomas Tilling. He began with one horse in 1845; by 1880 he had 1500 horses.
4. *Works*, XXXV, 72.
5. *Ruskin Family Letters*, ed. by Van A. Burd (Ithaca and London: Cornell U.P., 1973) [Hereafter referred to as *RFL*], pp. 236-7. Extract first printed in *Bembridge School Newspaper*, vol. 42, no. 124, Christmas Term 1960.
6. *RFL*, 639.
7. *RFL*, 670.
8. *RFL*, 713.
9. *Works*, XXXV, 29.
10. *Works*, XXXV, 107.
11. *Works*, XXXV, 108n. This information is in a passage excluded from the original edition of *Præterita*.

12. John James Ruskin's account book, RF MS 28, paid May 1835.
13. *RFL*, 302.
14. Particularly RF MSS 28, 29 and 31. RF MSS 28 and 29 contain itemised and classified annual accounts. They are so detailed that one can fall into the trap of believing that they detail *every* item of JJR's expenditure. It is not until one looks for specific items that one realises that this is not *exactly* the case! These two volumes were written up annually, clearly from the notes kept at the time. RF MS 31 is such a notebook. This records JJR's expenditure in 1862. It becomes clear from internal evidence that this notebook was written up weekly, usually on a Saturday but occasionally on a Monday.
15. RF L 10.
16. RF MS 29.
17. JJR's abbreviations are unclear.
18. *Ruskin's Letters from Venice*, 1851-1852, ed. by J.L.Bradley (New Haven: Yale University Press, 1855), p. 286.
19. RF MS 31.
20. Interview for the *Daily Chronicle*, 22 January 1900 (*Works*, XXXIV, 717).
21. RF L 91.
22. *Works*, XXVIII, 520; *Fors Clavigera* Letter 62, February 1876.
23. David Downs, David Fudge and Kate Smith.
24. RF L 91.
25. Mitchell Library, Sydney, N.S.W. The letter will be quoted in my forthcoming *George Allen and John Ruskin*.

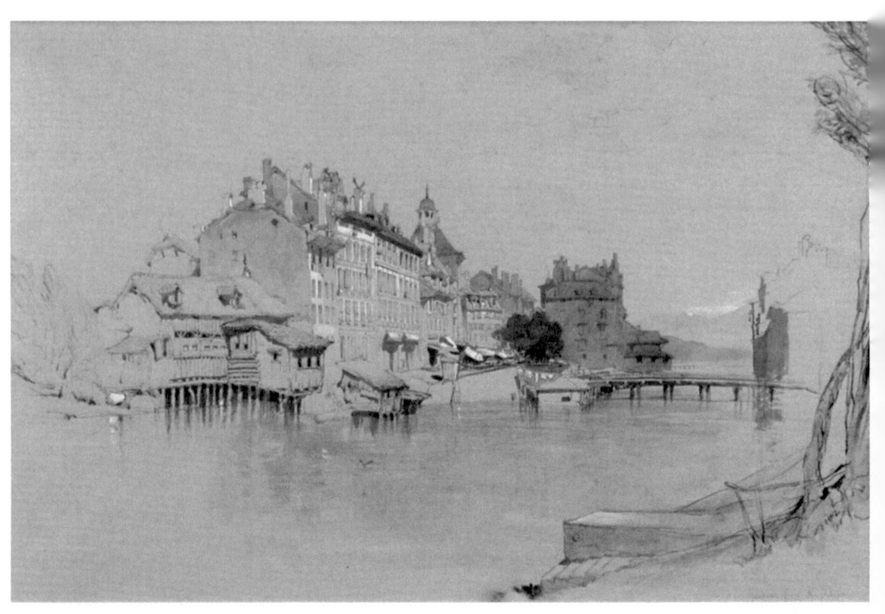

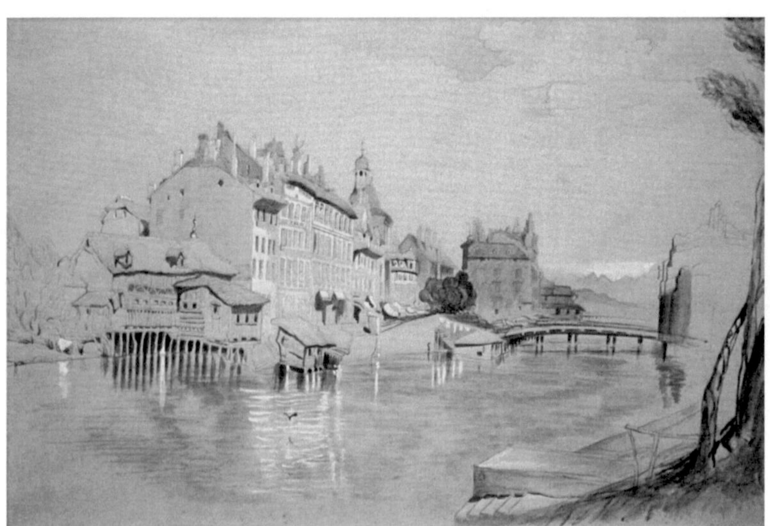

John Ruskin: Geneva from the Rhône, 1842 or 1846; pencil and wash, 330 x 482mm (Huntington Art Collection, 59.55.1137); bottom, Agnes Harrison: Geneva from the Rhône, after John Ruskin; pencil and wash, 310 x 436mm (Ruskin Library, RF 1290)

V

THE TWO MISSES HARRISON

RUSKIN REVIEW AND BULLETIN, VOL. 8, NO. 2, 2012

❧

It is well known that Cook and Wedderburn were not always as open as they should have been when editing the Library Edition of Ruskin's works. By chance I have stumbled upon another point on which they can be taken to task. This is not a question of concealment, but a shortcoming in indexing and laxity in using second-hand information.

I obviously had seen the name, but was not really *aware* of 'Miss Harrison' until John Hayman's *John Ruskin and Switzerland* was published in 1990. In this valuable study he reproduced a wash drawing by Ruskin of Geneva from the Rhône, which he described as being in the Huntington Library.[1] I had provided him with a number of photographs for the book of drawings in (what was then) the Whitehouse Collection at Bembridge. When I saw this drawing of Geneva, my immediate reaction was that he had ascribed it to the Huntingdon in error. This drawing was hanging in the upper Ruskin Gallery at Bembridge. But when I read his caption, and then referred to Cook and Wedderburn's 'Catalogue of Drawings',[2] I realised that we had a problem. I had never seen any reason to doubt that our drawing was by Ruskin; but the Huntingdon drawing is inscribed by Ruskin, and ours is not. Thus I was drawn to the inevitable conclusion that ours was the drawing referred to by Cook and Wedderburn as being a copy by 'Miss Harrison'.

I re-catalogued the Bembridge drawing, although it was too late to correct published errors because the drawing was, by now, on tour in my *John Ruskin and the Alps* exhibition. Indeed it is reproduced in colour in the Italian edition of the catalogue.[3] But there the matter rested. I had wondered about 'Miss Harrison' but had not done anything about her.

Earlier this year I was re-reading the American edition of *John Ruskin's Letters to William Ward* (1922). Ward, of course, was a member of Ruskin's art class at the Working Men's College and Ruskin considered him sufficiently competent to become his assistant. He taught at the College, and he also taught some of the people who applied to Ruskin for lessons. In March 1856 Ruskin wrote to Ward:

> Look out at the Architectural Museum, Canon Row, Westminster (where the fly-leaf of this note will get you admission) a pretty, not too difficult, cast of a leaf. Pack it nicely and send it to Miss Agnes Harrison, Elmhurst, Upton, Essex. With it send a copy, consisting of a little bit of cast, drawn with the brush, in *grey*, not in sepia, three times over. The first to show how to begin; the second, carried further; the third, finished. Explain, as well as you can in a letter, the mode of working. A *very little bit* will do. I have told Miss Harrison that she is to pay you two shillings a letter.[4]

The lessons presumably continued smoothly as there seems to be only one further reference to Miss Harrison in the Ruskin-Ward correspondence.

The same March 1856 letter is printed in the first volume of the T. J. Wise edition of *Letters from John Ruskin to William Ward* (1893), where there is a footnote explaining that

> Miss Agnes Harrison (now Mrs Agnes Harrison Macdonell) is a niece of the late Mary Howitt, and the authoress of *Martin's Vineyard*, *For the King's Dues*, *Quaker Cousins*, and various short stories and biographies which have appeared in English and American periodicals. She married Mr John Macdonell, of the American Bar.[5]

The same volume contains a further reference to Miss Harrison in a letter merely dated 'Wednesday' [1856]. 'I hope to see you at the meeting tomorrow night but please fetch some of Miss H[arrison]'s drawings with you, and I'll tell you what to do.'[6]

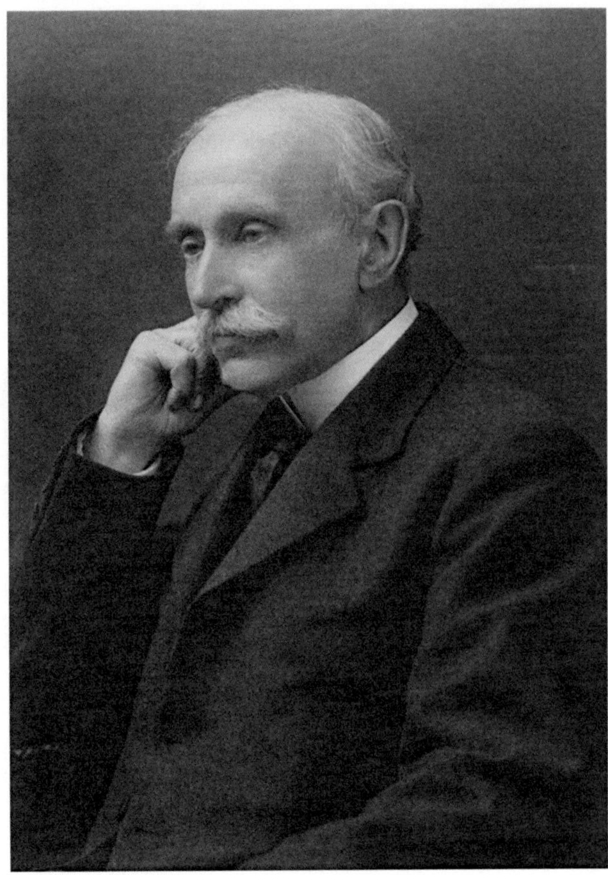

Sir John Macdonell, husband of Agnes Harrison, c. 1916, photographed by Walter Stoneman (National Portrait Gallery)

In the *Library Edition* Cook and Wedderburn reprinted the first letter[7] and the biographical footnote. The second letter only appears in the 'Bibliographical Appendix' to the Letters volumes.[8] But anyone searching the Index for Miss Harrison will not find her, and thus would be unlikely to stumble across the references to her in Ruskin's letters to Ward. I mentioned that Miss Harrison's copy of the Geneva drawing is referred to in the *Works* 'Catalogue of Ruskin's Drawings'. This entry too is not indexed. Neither are the other eight copies after Ruskin which a careful search of the Catalogue will reveal.[9] Miss Harrison's lessons probably only continued for two or three years because the nine dated Ruskin drawings which Miss Harrison copied range between 1841 and 1858.

It is unclear whether or not Cook and Wedderburn were directly in touch with 'Miss Harrison' when they were preparing their catalogue in 1912. Presumably they were not, since they refer to her by her maiden name. One supposes Ward must have kept a list of the drawings which she made, and communicated this to the editors of the *Library Edition*, because in the cases of numbers 1401 and 1404 they noted that the original Ruskin drawings were untraced but there were copies by Miss Harrison 'in her possession'. Because both Wedderburn and John Macdonell were very closely connected to the English Bar, it is surprising that the editors did not know that Miss Harrison had been Mrs Macdonell since 1873 – and Lady Macdonell since 1903.

Sir John Macdonell was described in his obituary[10] as a great jurist of vast knowledge and scholarship. 'He was a great teacher of men, for he had both wisdom and humanity'. He was called to the bar, Middle Temple, in 1873 (seven years before Wedderburn), knighted in 1903, and appointed a K.C.B. in 1914. He was a Master of the Supreme Court from 1889 to 1920, and the King's Remembrancer from 1912 to 1920. In addition to being occupied in the Law Courts throughout his life, he was also 'an honoured servant of *The Times*'.

From Lady Macdonell's obituary[11] and elsewhere, we discover that she was born in 1839 at Wavertree, Merseyside, and thus was seventeen years old when she applied to Ruskin for drawing lessons. We read that 'seven years of her youth were spent in America and during the Civil War (1861-5) she had talked with President Lincoln (d. 1865)'. It is possible that she originally met her husband during this visit to America, hence the strange reference in Ward's footnote to 'the American Bar'. However, they were not married until 1873. Perhaps they both visited America after their marriage.

Agnes Harrison was one of the daughters of Daniel Harrison, a Tea Merchant. She was the sixth of the surviving children. The Harrisons were a Quaker family who moved from Cumberland to Essex in the autumn of 1854. They settled at 'Marshall's', the old manor house of Romford. The birthplace of the poet Francis Quarles at the end of the sixteenth century, the house is now long gone. Harrison's wife, Anna, was the elder sister of the poet Mary Howitt. The Harrisons had a large family – five sons (two died in infancy) and five daughters. The eldest girl was Mary and the youngest, Lucy. Like her sister Agnes, Lucy became an author. She was also a teacher, and became the headmistress of Mount School, in York.

By the summer of 1855 Mary Harrison had become acquainted with Octavia Hill, and in that summer Octavia and a group of girls from her Toy Factory were invited to take tea at the Harrisons.[12] A long- standing friendship sprang up between artistic Mary Harrison and Octavia Hill. The latter had met John Ruskin, and indeed in the summer of 1855 had made her third visit to Denmark Hill. Towards the end of that year she applied to Ruskin for lessons and soon afterwards Ruskin appears to have begun employing her in illumination. Perhaps it was Octavia Hill who suggested to Agnes Harrison that she too should apply to Ruskin for instruction in drawing, and thus it was that her lessons with Ward began.

Ruskin told Ward to write to Agnes Harrison at Elmhurst, Upton. Upton at that time was a small hamlet just south of Forest Gate, and has now largely disappeared from maps, having been consumed by the sprawl of Greater London. At that time Elmhurst was the home of the Quaker, Smith Harrison, also a Tea Merchant. He had married Jane Lister, the sister of Joseph, later Lord Lister – the founder of antiseptic surgery. The Harrisons of Elmhurst had two children. Smith Harrison and Daniel (Agnes's father) were brothers. Certainly in March 1856, Agnes was staying at Elmhurst with her uncle and his family when Ward was instructed to write to her. However the situation is by no means clear, for on 23 June 1858 the *Essex Standard* reported the marriage of Ellis Yarnell of Philadelphia and 'Margaret Ann Harrison, daughter of Daniel Harrison, late of Elmhurst, Upton'. The house, Elmhurst, has now disappeared, and its site is occupied by the large Elmhurst Primary School, Upton Road, Forest Gate.

In searching Cook and Wedderburn's 'Catalogue of Ruskin's Drawings' for copies by 'Miss Harrison', I became aware that there was a number of drawings also shown as belonging to 'Miss Harrison'.[13] The more drawings I found to be owned by 'Miss Harrison', the more I wondered whether or not some of these could possibly be *by* 'Miss Harrison'. The revealing feature of this group of drawings is perhaps in the inscription by Ruskin on number 1939 which reads 'To W. H. Harrison Esq, With the workman's best regards. St Mark's, Venice. J. Ruskin, 1845'. Based on the inscription on this drawing, my conclusion – rightly or wrongly – was that all the drawings on *this* list were probably given by Ruskin to his 'first editor', W. H. Harrison. We know from a letter of 25 September [1847][14] from Ruskin to Harrison that Harrison had daughters – 'Kindest regards to Mrs Harrison and the young ladies'. Perhaps the 'Miss Harrison' shown as the owner of the drawings on my second list was one or both of the daughters of W. H. Harrison.

Thus it can be seen that Cook and Wedderburn were responsible for a significant lack of clarity in calling Agnes Harrison 'Miss Harrison' (when they must have known she was Lady Macdonell); and also in not differentiating between the first and second 'Miss Harrison', thus creating confusion.

ACKNOWLEDGEMENTS

I am indebted to Dr Sara Atwood and Dr Stuart Eagles for help in trying to understand the ramifications of the Harrison family.

REFERENCES

1. John Hayman, *John Ruskin and Switzerland* (Waterloo, Ontario: Wilfred Laurier, 1990), p. 81.
2. *Works*, XXXVIII, 215-306.
3. James S. Dearden, *John Ruskin e le Alpi* (Torino: Museo Nazionale della Montagna, 1991, 2nd ed.), p. 61.
4. *John Ruskin's Letters to William Ward, with a short biography by William C. Ward and an Introduction by Alfred Mansfield Brooks* (Boston: Marshall Jones Company, 1922), pp. 53-4.
5. *Letters from John Ruskin to William Ward*, ed. by Thomas J. Wise, 2 vols (London: Privately printed, 1893), I, pp. 13-14.
6. Ibid., p. 15.

7. *Works*, XXXVII, 233.

8. *Works*, XXXVII, 702.

9. The nine copies by Miss Harrison which Cook and Wedderburn list in their Catalogue are as follows. I cite their catalogue number first; the date of course is of Ruskin's drawing (dimensions in inches).

302 Old Buildings, 1854, pen and colour (6 x 6).

451 Mont Blanc de St Gervais, [?1849], watercolour (6 x 6).

761 Geneva, old town, [1846], watercolour (5 x 9).

762 Geneva, old town, [1846], watercolour on buff paper (13¼ x 17¾) [This was bought for J. H. Whitehouse at Christie's, 18 December 1942; now RF 1290.].

827 Guildford, watercolour on buff paper (5 x 9).

1379 Rheinfelden: view, [1858], watercolour (5 x 8).

1401 Rome: street with religious procession, 1841 (12½ x 18).

1404 Rome: view, 1841, pencil and wash, (13 x 18).

1624 Swiss scene: mountains and chapel, 1858, (8 x 11).

10. *The Times*, 19 March 1921.

11. *The Times*, 21 January 1925.

12. *Life of Octavia Hill as told in her letters*, ed. by C. Edmund Maurice (London: Macmillan, 1913). The developing friendship between Octavia Hill and the Harrison sisters begins with Ocatavia Hill's letter to Miss Harrison of 6 July 1855 [p. 47], 'We shall be very happy to see your friends and your uncle, who I think I have had the pleasure of meeting at Mrs Howitt's.' Letters of 16 and 19 October show that Octavia Hill was staying at Marshalls. Thereafter there are letters to Mrs Harrison, and Mary, Margaret, Annie, Emily, and Harriet, but strangely, not to Agnes.

13. These drawings, ten in all, are as follows (dimensions in inches):

482 Study of Chestnut, 1863, watercolour (9 x 5), repr. *Works*, XV, fig. 24.

966 Lausanne; chateau, moonrise, 1845, watercolour on buff paper (10 x 15), now RF 1342.

967 Lausanne; chateau, sunrise, 1845, watercolour on buff paper (10 x 15), now RF 1343.

1208 Normany, view on the coast, 1847, sepia (11 x 18), now RF 966 and retitled 'Avranches, looking towards Mont St Michel'.

1690 Trent, Tyrol, Fortress near, 1835, pencil and body colour on grey paper (10 x 8).

1702 Turin, view near, 1846, sepia (12½ x 18).

1765 Tyrol, sun rising above castle, 1838 [?], watercolour (10½ x 9).

1939 Venice, St Mark's, north west angle, 1845, pencil and watercolour (18 x 12).

2092 Vesuvius in eruption, 1840, watercolour (9 x 5), now RF 1080.

2125 Wellhorn and Wetterhorn from the Scheideck, 1835, pen and body colour (8 x 10), now RF 1087.

14. *Works*, XXXVII, 80.

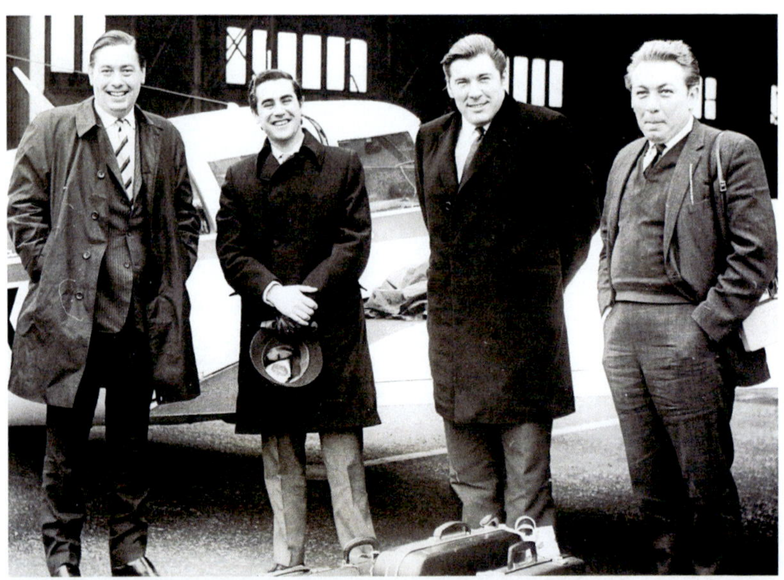

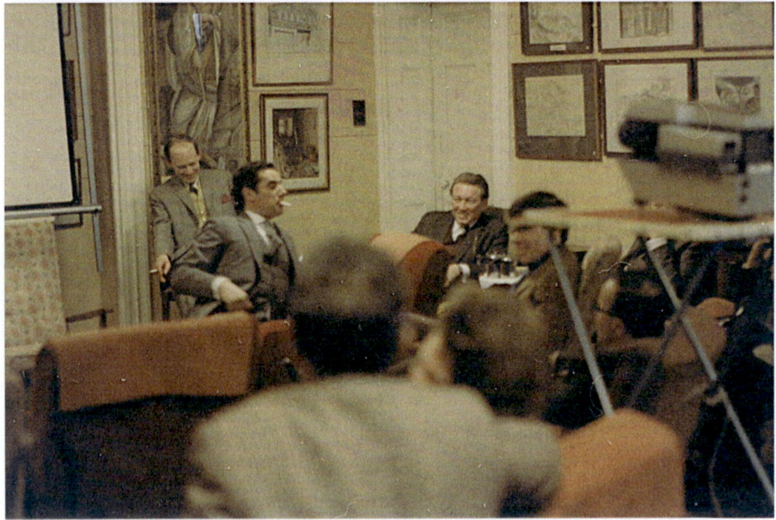

Top, Manuel Domecq (second from left) with directors of Luis Gordon Ltd, David Palengat, Charles Gordon, Luis Gordon Jnr, arriving at Walney airfield, Barrow-in-Furness, en route to the 1969 Brantwood conference; bottom, Manuel Domecq having a cigarette after reading his paper in 1969. J. S. Dearden is standing behind him; seated to the right is Luis Gordon Jnr, and Malcolm Hardman, later Chairman of the Ruskin Society

VI

DOMECQ AT BRANTWOOD

THE FRIENDS OF RUSKIN'S BRANTWOOD NEWSLETTER, AUTUMN 2008

❧

In my book *Ruskin, Bembridge and Brantwood* (Ryburn, 1994) I wrote of some of the Ruskin-related activities which happened in 1969, the year which saw the 150th anniversary of Ruskin's birth.

On 8 February in that year Luis Gordon, then the importers of Domecq sherry, held a reception and small exhibition at their offices in London. A number of the exhibits came from Bembridge, including the pen and ink drawing of Ruskin's birthplace, demolition of which had *just* taken place. Geoffrey Fletcher's drawing of the house appeared in *The Daily Telegraph* at the time. A shutter knob from one of the drawing room shutters, which I had rescued on New Year's Day, was loaned by Mary Lutyens. I lent a number of items from my own collection and Luis Gordon, himself a Ruskin collector, contributed John James Ruskin's silver wine taster, a wine glass used by Queen Victoria, and the grant of Ruskin arms which is now at Brantwood.

For presentation to the guests at the reception, Luis Gordon had bottled a special dry Oloroso sherry. The labels were numbered and I had No. 007. In *Ruskin, Bembridge and Brantwood* is a photograph of Manuel Domecq signing my bottle. Unhappily the bottle had disappeared when we returned from lunch – but fortunately there had been two editions of the label, so I ended up with an *unsigned* No. 001 of the cancelled edition! As a dedicated collector, of course, the unopened bottle – irreplaceable – is still in my collection.*

In March the Gordon brothers and Manuel Domecq came to

* Not Now! It was opened for lunch at my last directors meeting as Master of the Guild of St George on 21 October 2009.

Brantwood for part of the week-long Conference which I had arranged. While he was there Manuel signed the Ruskin Galleries Vistors' Book which I had taken to Brantwood for the Conference – 'At last! (a Domecq at Brantwood) – M. de Domecq. 25-III-69'.

In that week there were people staying at Brantwood from England, America, Spain, France and Japan.

During the February reception in London I had asked Manuel if he would read a paper on Ruskin and the Domecqs at the Conference. 'Yes', he said, 'if you write it for me' – which I did – and he did. It has never been published; perhaps one day...

The association which grew up between the Ruskin world and the Domecq organisation was fruitful. In September 1971 the Whitehouse Collection received the Adams Bequest of Ruskin material. On 15-16 September 1972 an exhibition of a selection from the Bequest was held at the Luis Gordon offices in Upper Belgrave Street, S.W.1, 'to commemorate the centenary of John Ruskin taking up residence at Brantwood, Coniston'. In fact the celebration was three days late! In the mid-1970s I was able to add three of Ruskin's portraits of Rose La Touche to the collection. Luis Gordon, the

The illuminated opening pages of Remembrance

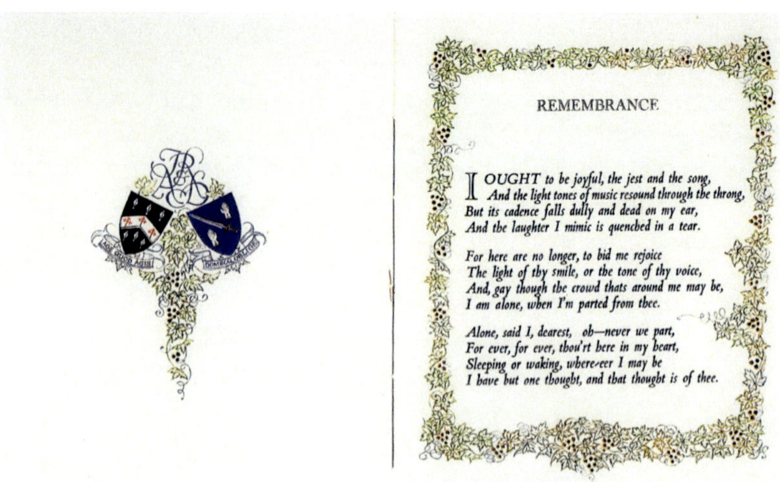

REMEMBRANCE

I OUGHT to be joyful, the jest and the song,
And the light tones of music resound through the throng,
But its cadence falls dully and dead on my ear,
And the laughter I mimic is quenched in a tear.

For here are no longer, to bid me rejoice
The light of thy smile, or the tone of thy voice,
And, gay though the crowd thats around me may be,
I am alone, when I'm parted from thee.

Alone, said I, dearest, oh—never we part,
For ever, for ever, thou'rt here in my heart,
Sleeping or waking, where-eer I may be
I have but one thought, and that thought is of thee.

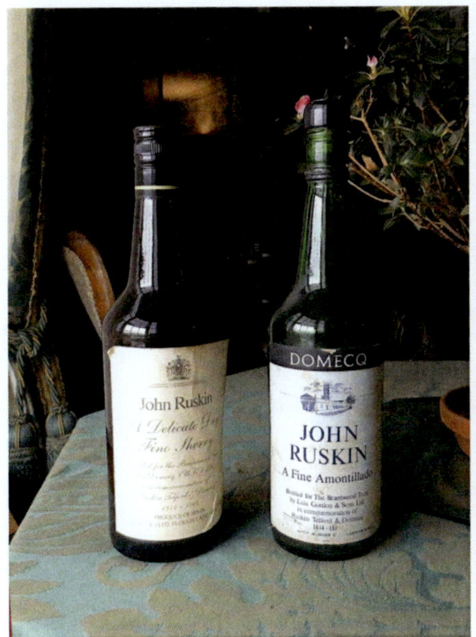

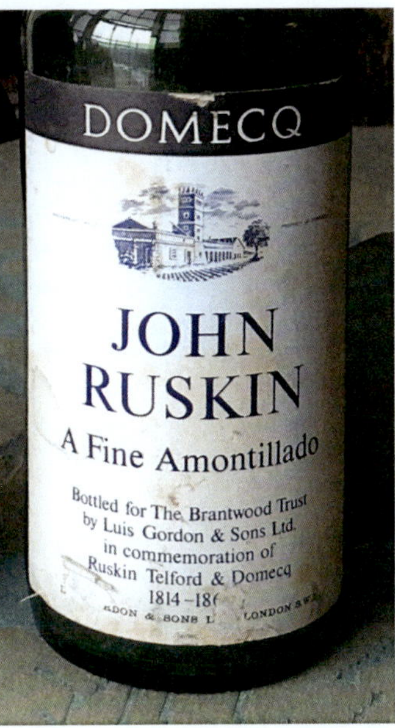

Sherry bottles from the collection at Brantwood

importers, contributed substantially to the cost. To mark this, I organised another small exhibition to be held in their offices. The theme was 'Ruskin in love' and the exhibition included material relating to Adèle Domecq, to Effie Gray, and of course, Rose. In 1970 I had printed, in a strictly limited edition, Ruskin's poem addressed to Adèle – *Remembrance.* At the exhibition Peter Egan read extracts from Ruskin's letters to Effie, and I presented a copy of *Remembrance* to Manuel, who had come especially from Spain for the exhibition.

Luis Gordon, for many years, supplied the Brantwood shop with sherry – fino and amontillado – specially labelled for us at their bottling plant in Kent. Unfortunately we were no longer able to have our own label after the sherry began to be bottled in Spain, but there are still specimens of the *empty* bottles in the collection at Brantwood.

John James Ruskin had his own barrel in the bodega in Jerez; the partners' barrels are still there, labelled Ruskin, Telford and Domecq.

John James's was taken out of the solera system in 1864 when he died. It still contains a little of his own blend of sherry. Several years ago I was given two bottles of this pre-1864 sherry. And very nice it is too. One of the two remains. I no longer have my contacts with the Domecq empire, so my remaining bottle, again, is irreplaceable!

[This final bottle was drunk with much appreciation at a lunch party I gave, for Ruskin friends, to celebrate my eightieth birthday!]

VII
THE PORTRAITS OF ROSE LA TOUCHE

BURLINGTON MAGAZINE, FEBRUARY 1978

In December 1968 I had a letter from France from an elderly lady living at St Jean-de-Luz. She told me that she had two portraits of Rose La Touche which she wished to sell. The lady was Mrs Feodora Ward-La Touche, and Rose La Touche had been her aunt by marriage. Naturally portraits of Rose La Touche are of extreme interest to a Ruskinian because of the long friendship between her and Ruskin and because of the dramatic influence which she had on his life. I took up the correspondence with enthusiasm, but several letters and six months later it stopped – but not before I had managed to obtain photographs of the two portraits in France. I heard nothing more from Mrs Ward-La Touche and I assumed that she had changed her mind about selling the portraits.

There matters rested until May 1976 when I received a letter from Mrs Sheila Taylor. Mrs Taylor told me that her great-aunt, Mrs Ward-La Touche, had died and that she now had the portraits. Correspondence revealed that there were in fact *three*, not two, portraits as I had originally been told. These have now been bought for the Ruskin Galleries at Bembridge School with generous grants from the Purchase Grant Fund, the National Art-Collections Fund, and Luis Gordon & Sons Ltd, the importers of Domecq sherry, the last organisation helping with the purchase because of the association between Ruskin's father and the Domecq family.

The re-appearance of these portraits has presented a new opportunity to examine all the known portraits of Rose, and the resultant catalogue and notes follow. But first perhaps a brief word on Rose La Touche herself would not be out of place.

Rose was born on 3rd January 1848, the youngest child of John and Maria La Touche of Harristown, Co. Kildare. Ten years later she met John Ruskin, thirty-nine years old and an established writer on art. Mrs La Touche hoped Ruskin would teach her children drawing. The friendship between Ruskin and Rose which sprang up at that time, deepened into love, but Rose who was almost fanatically religious was deeply upset by Ruskin's religious scepticism. 'How could one love you if you were a pagan' she wrote to him.

In a year or two Rose began to have serious and unexplained illnesses. But by 1865 she had temporarily recovered and on her seventeenth birthday Ruskin asked her to marry him. She told him to ask again in a year's time, but in any case she would answer when she was twenty-one. Not until now had the senior La Touches realized the feeling between Ruskin and their daughter. They determined that the couple should forget each other and forbad them to meet for a few years.

There were occasional meetings but the strain was telling on both of them and it may well have been the cause of Ruskin's illness at Matlock in 1871.

With the turn of 1874 Rose's physical and mental condition deteriorated rapidly. By December the last traces of sanity had left her and by January 1875 Ruskin knew she was dying. He was able to visit her, probably for the last time, on 25th February, and calm here during her illness. Ruskin later wrote of the occasion to Francesca Alexander:

> Of *course* she was out of her mind in the end; one evening in London she was raving violently till far into the night; they could not quiet her. At last they let me into her room, She was sitting up in bed; I got her to lie back on the pillow, and lay her head in my arms, as I knelt beside it. They left us, and she asked me if she should say a hymn. And I said yes, and she said, 'Jesus, lover of my soul', to the end, and then fell back tired and went to sleep. And I left her.

Rose died on 25th or 26th May 1875 (the date is uncertain) and Ruskin wrote to Carlyle '... the little story of my wild Rose is ended, and the hawthorn blossoms this year would fall – over her'.

Rose's influence had been strong on Ruskin in her lifetime and it was not to decrease with her death. In the early 1860s it was possibly because of Rose that he took an interest in the girls' school at Winnington and wrote *Ethics of the Dust* for the girls. After her death Ruskin began to identify Rose with St Ursula and this led to his detailed study of the Carpaccio series of paintings in Venice in 1876. Two years later it was undoubtedly the memory and unhappiness of Rose that brought on his own illness. Later, when he established his May Queen Festival at the Cork Girls High School, it was called a Rose Queen Festival, in honour of Rose.

During the seventeen years that Ruskin knew Rose La Touche he made a number of portraits of her. Most of Ruskin's drawings were done for his own use or pleasure and his large output contains no more than perhaps twenty portraits. Of these, six are self-portraits and the others are of close friends – his cousin Joan Severn, Lily Armstrong (one of the Winnington girls) and Connie Hilliard. Of Rose he made at least six portraits.

As is the case with much concerning Ruskin, classifying the various portraits of Rose is by no means as simple as it would at first appear.

Until 1954 only two portraits of Rose had appeared in books. Joan Evans's *John Ruskin*, 1954, contained a third, a miniature now in the collection of the Guild of St George which had previously been published by the Guild as a postcard. There was no further progress in the story of Rose portraits until I received the photographs of her two portraits from Mrs Ward-La Touche in 1968. It was immediately obvious that one was an unpublished water-colour (which subsequently appeared in V. A. Burd's *Winnington Letters* in 1969). The other appeared at first sight to be one of the already published drawings.

In the catalogue which follows the portraits are by Ruskin unless stated to the contrary and are arranged in *probable* date order. However, as none is actually dated, the order and dating of the portraits is tentative.

CATALOGUE

A Profile looking left, with floral headdress, ?March 1862, pencil and black and white washes, 19½ by 13 ins. oval mount 15½ by 11½. Inscribed by Ruskin below mount, 'Flos florum Rosa' – Rose, the flower of flowers (see opposite).
Exhibited: Ruskin in love, London 1976, no. 30.
Collections: J. Ruskin/Maria La Touche/Percy La Touche/E. Ward-La Touche/Fedora Ward-La Touche/Sheila Taylor/Ruskin Galleries, Bembridge School/Ruskin Foundation (RF ADD/P/62).

In company with the other two portraits then at Bembridge, B and D, this portrait was probably given by Joan Severn to Maria La Touche after Ruskin's death in 1900. They could not have passed to the La Touche family *before* 1872 because B and D have Ruskin's Brantwood visiting card, endorsed by Joan Severn, attached to them. Alternatively they could have been given to the La Touches when Rose died in 1875 or during one of the La Touche visits to Brantwood in the eighties. But I favour 1900 as the most likely date because of Joan Severn's writing on the visiting cards, rather than a Ruskin inscription.

At first this portrait appears to be the same as the well-known version – F – originally published in the Ruskin *Library Edition*, vol. xxxv, but a closer examination reveals several differences.

Ruskin saw a lot of the La Touches in the spring of 1862. On 3rd January he gave Rose a fourteenth-century Psalter, and on 15th March he gave her sister Emily a fifteenth-century Book of Hours. On 9th March his father noted in his diary that John had been 'every day at La Touches'. Professor Burd draws my attention to Ruskin's letter to Lady Waterford conjecturally dated by Virginia Surtees in *Sublime and Instructive* as 'April 1862' in which he says 'I was long in Switzerland this autumn – trying in vain – ah, so much in vain-er! to draw little Rosie La Touche …' I feel sure that this reference must be to the present portrait of Rose.

B Three-quarter head, looking right, ?late 1860's or early 1870s, pencil, water-colour and bodycolour, 15½ by 10½ in mount with oval aperture 12 by 10. Ruskin's Brantwood visiting card attached to old

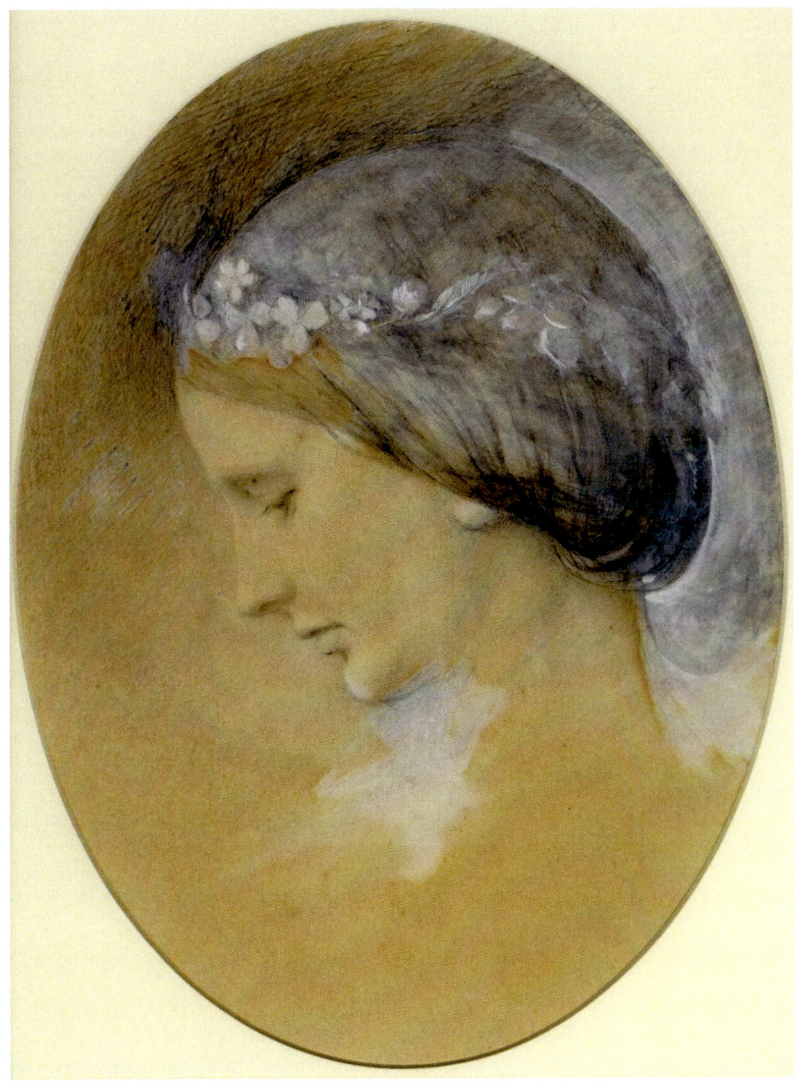

A: Portrait of Rose La Touche, by John Ruskin. ?March 1862. Pencil and black and white washes, 49.5 by 33 cm. (Ruskin Foundation)

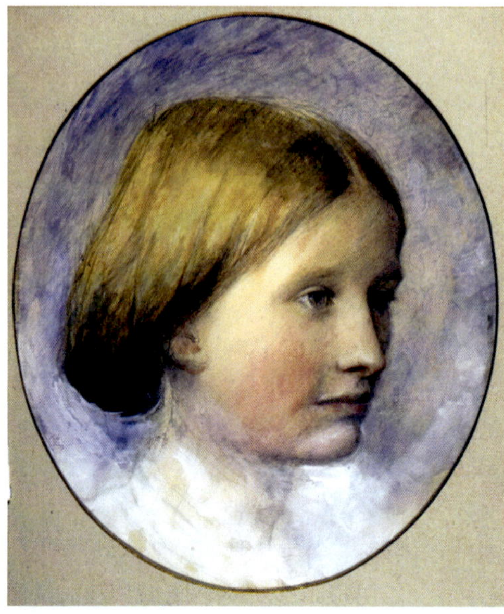

B: Portrait of Rose La Touche, by John Ruskin. ?Late 1860's or early 1870's. Pencil and water-colour and body-colour, 49.5 by 26.7 cm. (Ruskin Foundation)

mount inscribed by Joan Severn: 'By John Ruskin. Joan Severn' (see above).

Exhibited: Ruskin in love, London 1976, no. 37.

Reproduced: V. A. Burd (ed.): *The Winnington Letters*, p. 496, where dated about 1860.

Collections: J. Ruskin/Maria La Touche/Percy La Touche/E. Ward-La Touche/Sheila Taylor/Ruskin Galleries/Ruskin Foundaion (RF ADD/P/64).

C Miniature, 1872, water-colour 2¼ by 1¾ (oval) dated by engraving on back of frame, 'Rose La Touche, painted by John Ruskin in 1872. She died in 1875' (see opposite).

Exhibited: Ruskin & his circle 1964, no. 284.

Reproduced: as a postcard by the Guild; Joan Evans: *John Ruskin* [1954], p. 209; K. Clark: *Ruskin Today* [1964], p. 26; *Ruskin & his circle* catalogue [1964], pl. 14.

Collections: J. Ruskin/Juliet Morse/Guild of St George.

This portrait was apparently unknown to Cook and Wedderburn when they prepared their Catalogue of Drawings in 1912. Nevertheless

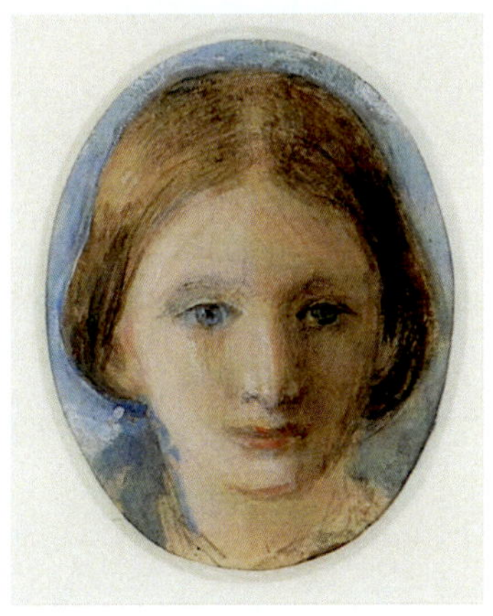

C: Portrait of Rose La Touche (miniature), by John Ruskin. (Collection of the Guild of St George)

it is the only portrait of Rose which can be dated with any reasonable degree of accuracy for the metal frame containing the miniature is dated 1872. The date may be relied upon with reasonable certainty because it probably came from Ruskin himself, whether the miniature was framed for him, or later for Mrs Morse by whom it was acquired on Ruskin's death. It remained in Ruskin's possession until 1900 when it was given as a keepsake to Mrs Morse. Juliet Morse's father, Alfred Tylor, F.G.S., of Carshalton, was a geologist and author of scientific papers. The friendship between Ruskin and the Tylor family was a long-standing one, and they were active for many years in St George's Guild business. Juliet, one of the three daughters, married Sydney Morse. In 1934 the miniature passed from the Morse collection into the Collection of the Guild of St George and it is now at the Guild's Gallery in Sheffield.

D Profile looking left, ?1874, pencil, 16½ by 13½, irregularly oval, in oval mount and frame. Ruskin's Brantwood visiting card attached to old mont and inscribed by Joan Severn: 'Rose' by [Mr Ruskin] (see p. 112, top).
Exhibited: Ruskin in love, London 1976, no. 40.
Works Catalogue of Drawings, no. 1350 (where dated 1874).
Collections: J. Ruskin/Maria La Touche/Percy La Touche/E. Ward-La Touche/Fedora Ward-La Touche/Sheila Taylor/Whitehouse Collection/Ruskin Foundation (RF ADD/P/63).

E Profile looking left, copied from Portrait D by Juliet Morse and E. R. Hughes for Mrs Hubert Burke (see p. 112, bottom).
Reproduced: M. F. Young: *Letters of a Noble Woman* [1908], p. 20; subsequent frequent reproductions of this profile must have been taken from the 1908 reproduction.

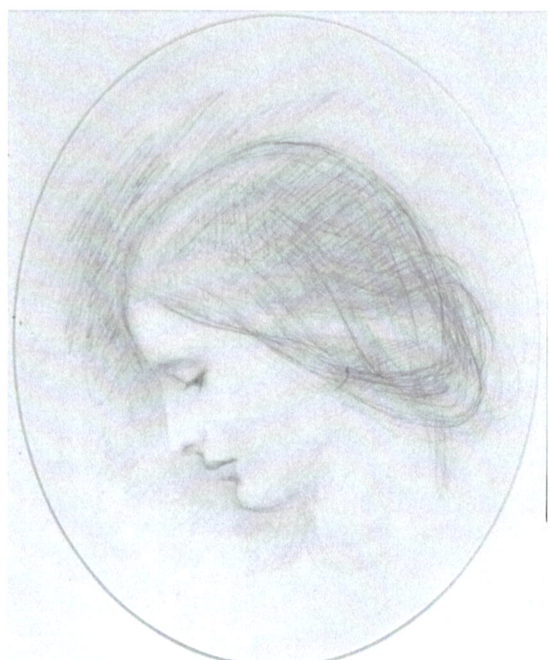

D: Portrait of Rose La Touche, by John Ruskin. ?1874. Pencil, 41.9 by 34.3 cm. (Ruskin Foundation)

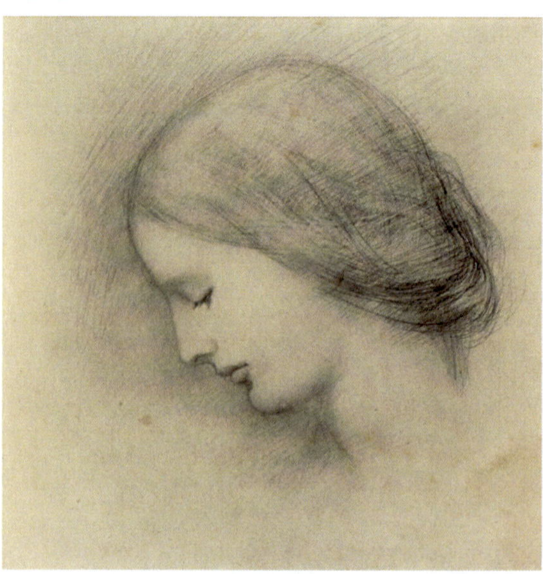

E: Portrait of Rose La Touche, by Juliet Morse and E. R. Hughes after the portrait illustrated in Fig. 48. (Present whereabouts unknown)

Collections: Mrs Hubert Burke/present whereabouts unknown.

Portraits D and E must be considered together. As far as can be traced Portrait D has never previously been reproduced. Although it is perhaps the best-known portrait of Rose, all reproductions appear to have been based on Portrait E. Although Portrait D was in the possession of the La Touche family at the time, when M. F. Young's biography of Mrs La Touche was published in 1908, the portrait of Rose which was reproduced was not D, the original Ruskin, but E, a copy which Juliet Morse and Edward Hughes had made for Mrs Hubert Burke, formerly Florence Bishop the daughter of Mrs La Touche's cousin. That the Morse/Hughes copy had been made from the original Ruskin for Mrs Burke is evident from a letter which she wrote to Mrs Morse:

> 'A few days ago there was published by George Allen and Sons *Letters of a noble woman, Mrs La Touche of Harristown*. You will ask for it at your library won't you. And in it you will find a facsimile of the exquisite drawing that you and Mr Hughes so kindly did for me – the head of Rose La Touche – I enclose for yourself an extra proof copy which Allen & Co have sent me – no one deserves this more than you do. Your drawing hangs on our wall in my little drawing room and any visitor worthy of the honour is allowed to see it …'[1]

F Profile looking left, with floral headdress, ?1874, pencil, 17 by 11 (see p. 114).

Exhibited: Manchester 1904, no. 338 (where catalogued as an example of Ruskin's 'pencil work in the 'sixties'); Fine Art Society, 1907, no. 29.

Reproduced: *Works*, vol. XXXV, pl. C [1908], and thereafter frequently and almost certainly from the 1908 reproduction.

Works Catalogue of Drawings, 1349 (where dated 1874).

Collections: J. Ruskin/Joan Severn/Arthur Severn/sold at Sotheby's, 20th May 1931, lot 99. Bought by Stevens and Brown for C. E. Goodspeed/Now presumed destroyed.

This portrait is very similar to Portrait A. A close examination shows the subject to be older in the present portrait for which she

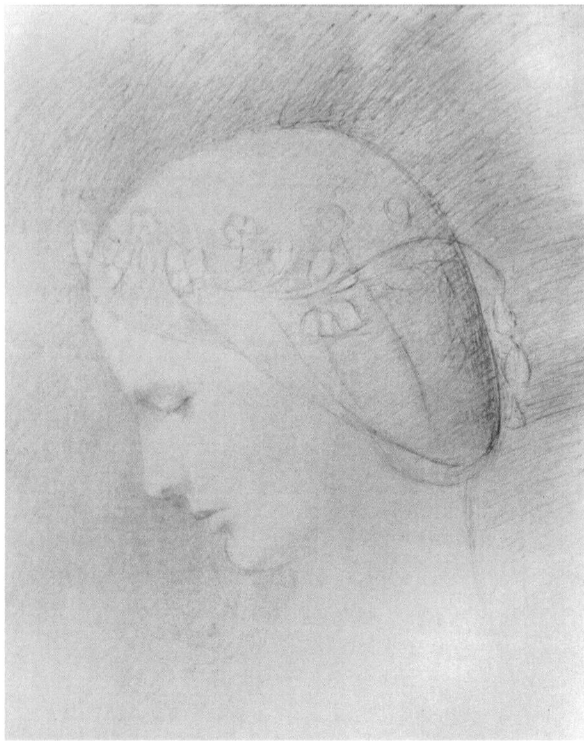

F: Portrait of Rose La Touche, by John Ruskin. ?1874. Pencil, 43.2 by 27.9 cm. (Presumed destroyed) (Ruskin Foundation)

was probably asked to adopt a similar pose. Whereas Portrait A almost certainly went to Ireland in 1900, the present portrait remained at Brantwood until it was sold at Sotheby's in 1931. At this sale it was bought for Charles E. Goodspeed, the Boston bookseller and Ruskin collector, as he recalled in his autobiography:

> '... a large number of all sorts of drawing by Ruskin [fell to me] and, of superlative interest, the pencil sketch of Miss Rose La Touche of whom I also secured another portrait, a coloured photograph on porcelain, at the sale of the contents of Arthur Severn's town house in the same month of July 1931'.[2]

Later Goodspeed had a serious fire in the study of his home; much of his important Ruskin collection was damaged and a number of items were destroyed, including, one must assume, the present portrait which is reproduced here from a photograph of the original in the Whitehouse Collection.

G Half length, lying in bed, ?1875, 25th February, pencil, 7 by 4 ¾ (see below).
Exhibited: Ruskin & his circle 1965, no. 285; Ruskin in love 1976, no. 43.
Reproduced: W. D. Amos: *Brantwood* (Lancashire Life [March 1976]); R. Hewison: *John Ruskin, The Argument of the eye* [1976], pl. 39.
Collections: Mrs Thorold/bought through K. Clark, February 1937 by J. H. Whitehouse/Ruskin Foundation (RF 976).

G: Portrait of Rose La Touche, by John Ruskin. ?1875. Pencil, 17.8 by 12 cm. (Ruskin Foundation)

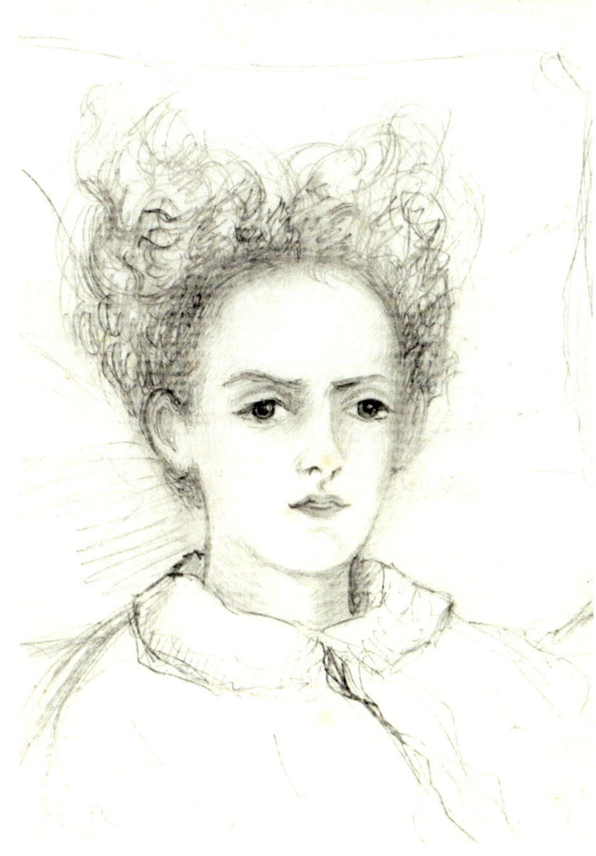

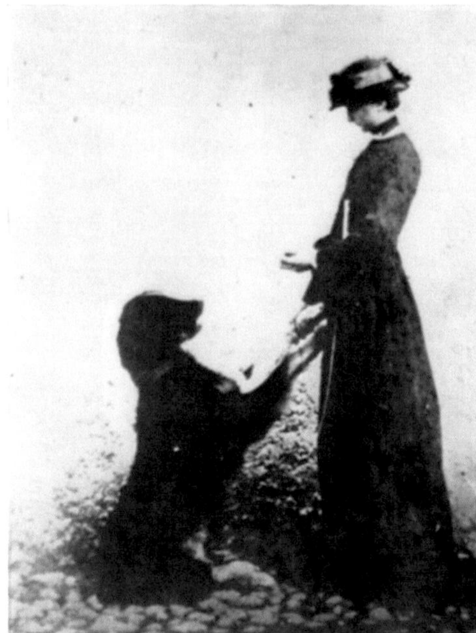

I: Photograph of Rose La Touche with Bruno. (Collection Mr Charles Balston)

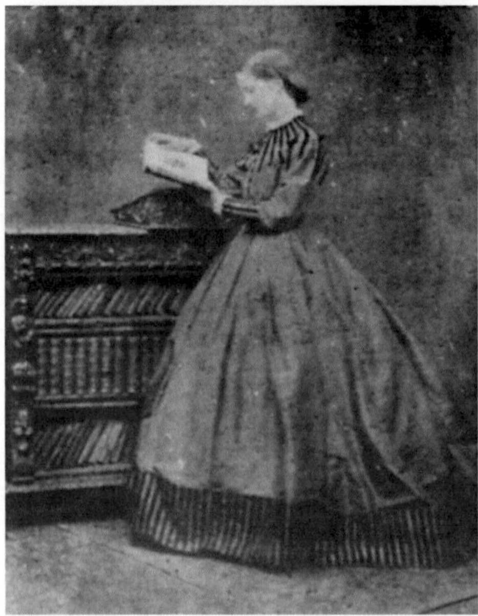

J: Photograph of Rose La Touche. (Collection Mr Charles Balston)

Almost beyond doubt, Rose drawn by Ruskin on the last occasion on which he saw her. In 1937 this drawing belonged to a Mrs Thorold. Through the good offices of the then Mr Kenneth Clark, J. H. Whitehouse was able to buy it for his collection at Brantwood. Writing to Whitehouse about the portrait, Lord Clark said:

> 'A Mrs Thorold has written saying that she is the possessor of a unique and pathetic Ruskin document, nothing less than the drawing that Ruskin did of Rose La Touche on her deathbed when he visited her in London ... I have seen the drawing, and although it is slight and obviously done under a feeling of strain which has rather cramped the painter's style, it has a touching simplicity, which makes it into a work of art as well as a document ...'.[3]

Unfortunately Mrs Thorold's letter to Lord Clark detailing the provenance of the drawing does not seem to have survived. However the content of it was clearly sufficient to convince both Whitehouse and Clark that the drawing was exactly what it purported to be – Ruskin's last portrait of Rose.

Robert Hewison has recently drawn attention[4] to the similarity between this portrait of Rose and an illustration of a young girl on her sick-bed in *The Story of Harry's Sad Christmas* which Ruskin was reading at the beginning of 1875. An even more remarkably similar drawing – by Francesca Alexander – forms the frontispiece to her *Story of Ida*, the first of her series of stories which Ruskin published in 1883.

H Other sketches in water-colour.
Works Catalogue of Drawings, no. 1351, lists 'Mrs Bishop has some other sketches in w.c.' These have not yet come to light.

I Photograph, with Bruno, reproduced in *Winnington Letters*, p. 496, where it is dated *c.*1866. Original in the possession of Mr Charles Balston (see opposite, top).

J Photograph, standing by a bookcase. Original in the possession of Mr Charles Balston (see opposite, bottom).

K Photograph in colour on porcelain; bought from Arthur Severn sale by C. E. Goodspeed; now presumed destroyed.

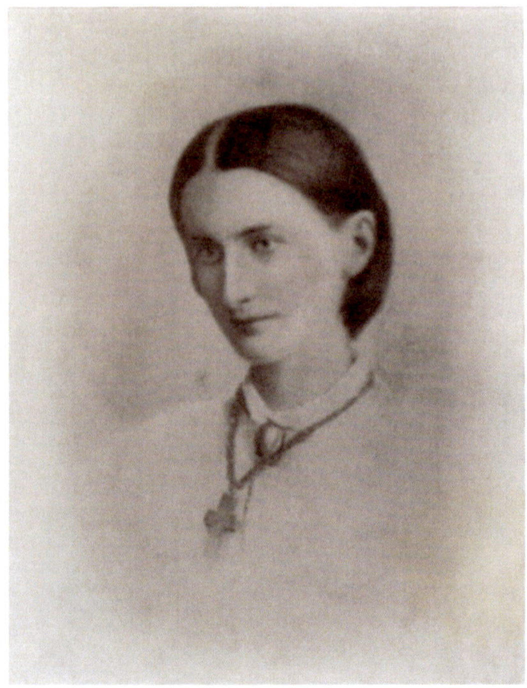

M: Photograph of Rose La Touche, ?1870

L Photograph, head and shoulders, said to have been hand-coloured by Rose, reproduced in J. G. MacNeill: *What I have seen and heard* [1925], p. 81.

M Photograph, head and shoulders, reproduced in Greville MacDonald: *Reminiscences of a Specialist* [1932], p. 96, where it is tentatively dated ?1870 (see above).

REFERENCES

1. Florence Burke to Juliet Morse, 11th December 1908, original in Whitehouse Collection, RF L 65.
2. C. F. Goodspeed: *Yankee Bookseller*, Houghton Mifflin Co. [1937], p. 268.
3. Kenneth Clark to J. H. Whitehouse, 10th February 1937, RF 80.
4. Robert Hewison: *John Ruskin, the argument of the eye*, Thames & Hudson [1976], p. 162 and pls. 38-39.

VIII

JOHN RUSKIN AND THE *SPLÜGEN*

TURNER SOCIETY NEWS, DECEMBER 1996

In his autobiography, *Præterita*, Ruskin wrote of Turner's *Splügen Pass*, 'I knew perfectly well that this drawing was the best Swiss landscape yet painted by man.'[1]

When Turner exhibited his Swiss sketches in the Spring of 1842 in order to solicit orders, he showed at the same time, four finished drawings as examples of what the finished works would look like. Among these four was the *Splügen*.

The Ruskins had begun to collect Turner watercolours just three years earlier, and by now they owned eight examples – *Richmond Bridge*, *Gosport*, *Winchelsea*, *Harlech Castle*, *Nottingham*, *Oxford*, *Warwick* and *Richmond*.

It appears that when the 1842 drawings were exhibited, John James Ruskin was travelling on business. His son saw the sketches and desperately wanted the *Splügen*. He could not act in his father's absence, and by the time his father was home, Munro of Novar had bought the drawing Ruskin so coveted. Instead, at this time they bought *Coblentz* and *Lucerne from the Walls*. Ruskin had said that they would take the latter 'if it turned out well;'[2] John James was sceptical, and said that his son would eventually have trouble in selling it. Both drawings appear in John James Ruskin's accounts in August 1842 at £84 each, the highest price they had yet paid. JJR had, in fact, weakened from his position regarding Turner's prices as stated to his son on 11 April in that year: 'I like him, Turner, after Roast & pudding & a few glasses of sherry which too many Turners would soon abridge us of!'[3]

Munro knew that the Ruskins wanted the *Splügen* drawing and periodically, Ruskin tells us, it was offered to them through dealers, at prices gradually increasing from the original 80 guineas to 400 guineas. On 13 April 1844 Ruskin noted in his diary, 'Into town to see Munro's collection, and made myself very unhappy for two of them – the Splügen and Zurich. Would give the world for them; I shall have them sometime however, if I live.'[4] Later Ruskin explained that his father would have bought the *Splügen* for him at 400 guineas, but he wouldn't let him, 'thinking it would too much pain my father'[5] to pay that much for a drawing.

Thus Ruskin had lost the *Splügen* for the *second* time. Just after Turner's death Ruskin had written to his father on 23 January 1852, dividing all Turner's drawings into four classes. The *Splügen* was in the first class, on which Ruskin commented, 'For these above, if at all time they came into the market, I should think no price I could afford too dear.'[6] Soon, he was very nearly to lose it again.

Ruskin spent the very beginning of 1878 writing the catalogue for the Turners which he was to put on exhibition at The Fine Art Society later in the year. But with the exhibition only partly completed, he was taken seriously ill at Brantwood on 23 February. At the time, he was not expected to survive, and it was not until early April that he was well enough to come downstairs again to his Brantwood study.

During his illness he had been attended not only by his local doctor, Dr Parsons, but also by Dr John Simon. John Simon and his wife Jane were old friends of both Ruskin and his parents, and during Ruskin's illness of 1878 Simon spent two long visits at Brantwood, attending his friend.

Meanwhile, although Ruskin was too ill to be told, the *Splügen* was to come on to the market again. It was advertised as lot 83 in Christie's sale on 4 April. One of those who didn't wish Ruskin to know about the sale was Mrs Alfred Hunt. She was in correspondence at this time with Joan Severn about the state of Ruskin's health. Joan was a distant cousin of Ruskin's ('the Coz'). She and her husband Arthur and their family spent much of their time living with Ruskin at Brantwood and she had taken charge there during his illness. As a postscript to an undated letter to Joan now in the John Rylands Library, Margaret Hunt added, 'Don't mention the Splugen to Mr R. Some of us are hoping to get it for him, but keep it secret.'[7]

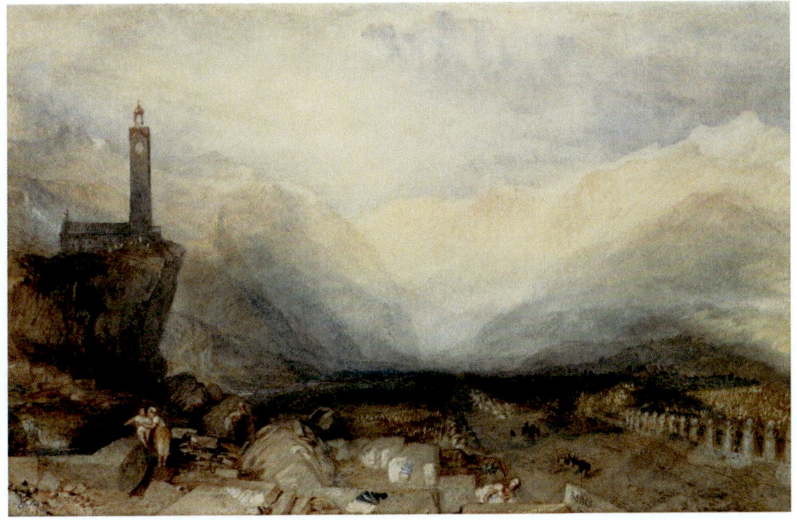

J. M. W. Turner: The Splügen Pass, 1842, watercolour, 292 x 451. (Bridgeman Images)

Margaret Hunt was not the only one who was interested in the *Splügen*. Among the groups of letters and other documents bought from Brantwood in 1931 by the Grasmere antique dealer T. H. Telford, was a collection relating to the fate of the *Splügen*. Telford was quite happy for material in his hands to be split up, and over 150 letters relating to the *Splügen* were bought by F. J. Sharp and are now in the Pierpont Morgan Library. Other material from this particular group of papers passed into another collection and was, a few years ago, acquired by the Ruskin Galleries at Bembridge.

In this second group of papers is a four-page statement written by Dr Simon's wife Jane. (This appears to be duplicated by a second copy among the Sharp Papers.) In her statement, Jane Simon tells what happened next:

> On Friday the 15th of March 1878 Mrs Arthur Severn called at Mrs Simon's, 40 Kensington Square. In the course of the conversation about Mr Ruskin, who was then ill, Mrs Severn spoke regretfully of the circumstance, that the 'Pass of the Splügen', a

drawing by Turner, should be about to be offered for sale at the dispersion of the Novar Collection, while Mr Ruskin was in a condition to render it impossible for him to make another effort to obtain it. Mrs J. Simon registered this remark in her mind; and having ascertained from Mr Simon that Mr Ruskin would have given 'carte blanche' to obtain it, she determined that Mr Ruskin's illness should be no bar, and that, if possible, it should be bought for him.

As Mr Ruskin's state of health at this time was very precarious, Mrs Simon concluded that should his illness end fatally, the alternative would be, to present the Drawing *in memoriam* to the National Gallery, and to make a further collection for a bust of Mr Ruskin to be placed (by permission) in the Turner Gallery of the National Gallery.

Without one word said to anyone (not even Mr Simon) Mrs Simon set to work and wrote to Mrs Cowper Temple, whose sympathies and those of Mr Cowper Temple, were of course most warmly elicited, and who entered most cordially into Mrs Simon's views; but they did not quite see their way (for reasons which need not here be stated) to doing exactly what Mrs Simon wished, viz; that the drawing should be bought and held in safety, by some wealthy and generous person, until the friends of Ruskin could be invited to subscribe for its purchase and presentation to him.

But Mrs Cowper Temple suggested Mr Graham, of 35 Grosvenor Place, as being very likely to see his way to do what Mrs Simon wished.

Happily Miss Graham had been very often calling, and a slight acquaintance having thus arisen between her and Mrs Simon, Mrs Simon invited Miss Graham to call upon her, which Miss Graham immediately did when Mrs Simon developed her plan, which was warmly received by Miss Graham to whom Mrs Simon gave a letter to be presented to Mr Graham.

[Frances Graham had sat to Burne-Jones on a number of occasions, and it was Burne-Jones who introduced her to Ruskin in the 1870s. A firm friendship grew between the two. In her autobiography[8] she recounts how she took Ruskin to the first Wagner concert in England. Her father was an India merchant and Member of Parliament for Glasgow. He was a Trustee of the National Gallery and an omnivorous collector, particularly liking Millais, Rossetti and Burne-Jones. They had several houses in Scotland, and theirs was described as a wealthy home where 'money was not much considered'.]

A correspondence followed, the result of which was, that on the 4th of April Mrs Simon received a note from Miss Graham saying 'My Father *is ready to do anything you wish about the drawing*'.

The Sale was fixed for Saturday the 6th April. Mrs Simon sent Miss Graham's note to Mr and Mrs Cowper Temple, and had arranged to go to Grosvenor Place the next morning to thank Mr Graham and settle all about the best way to proceed after the Drawing was secured.

On the *afternoon* of the 4th April Mrs Simon had the honour of a visit from Mrs A. W. Hunt (a stranger to *her* previously). Mrs Hunt said that Mr Hunt and herself and a few friends had felt a great wish not to let the Novar Pictures be sold without purchasing, by subscription, one of the drawings, to present to Mr Ruskin; as they considered he surely would have bought some had he been well enough to interest himself in it.

Mrs Simon heard Mrs Hunt to the end, and then asked on which drawing had Mr and Mrs Hunt and their friends fixed? Mrs Hunt replied 'The Fall of the Tees' [*Chain Bridge over the River Tees*, c.1836, Wilton 878]. Mrs Simon then told her story, and Mrs Hunt proposed they should unite, which Mrs Simon very gladly did, and wrote to Mr Arthur Severn to satisfy Mr and Mrs Hunt that the 'Pass of the Splugen' was the drawing for which Mr Ruskin said he would be willing to give 'carte blanche'. Mrs Simon then spoke of Mr Graham's kind intentions, but Mrs Hunt said *her husband* would pay and had arranged to do so – and Mrs Simon felt it would be most ungracious to oppose this wish of Mr Hunt's.

On Friday the 5th April Mrs Hunt and Mrs Simon accordingly went to Christie's and there Mrs Hunt settled with Mr Agnew to bid for the Drawing, giving carte blanche.

Mr Agnew *immediately* offered his commission as his contribution, saying, he owes all he knows to Mr Ruskin.

Since then Mrs Hunt, Mrs Simon and Mr and Mrs Cowper Temple have been gathering up the subscriptions and hope soon to be able to present the Drawing to Mr Ruskin, as a token of gratitude and affection to him and thankfulness for his recovery from severe illness, with the trust that it will be a pleasure to Mr Ruskin all his life, and may eventually be placed in the National Gallery – to perpetuate not only the Genius which made Turner's Genius more appreciated and more precious, but also to perpetuate the remembrance of those high qualities and aspirations, that fervour of devotion to all he believed to be *good* which won for Mr Ruskin the love and gratitude which this little gift sort to express.

April 24th 1878

After the sale a letter signed by eight of Ruskin's friends, including William Cowper Temple, John Simon, A. W. Hunt and Henry Acland, was printed and circulated.[9] It sought subscriptions to the presentation and concluded 'When one thousand guineas, the price of the Drawing, has been received, the Subscription List will be closed.' Donations came pouring in. Those made to Mrs Simon included 25 guineas from George Richmond, George Smith (of Smith Elder, formerly Ruskin's publisher) and Eliza Fall, £25 from Frances Graham, 10 guineas from Joan and Arthur Severn, and £10 each from Henry Acland and the Simons. Thirty-five art students at University College subscribed £5. Ruskin's Coniston doctor, Dr Parsons, sent £1, and William Agnew waived his commission of £52 10s. Mrs Hunt's collecting book, now in the Morgan Library, shows a similar wide range of donations. By late May Margaret Hunt was writing to Jane Simon saying that already 'I have refused a good many subscriptions.'

Meanwhile, arrangements were made to send the drawing to Brantwood where Ruskin was gradually recovering from his illness. Writing on 28 April to Mrs Simon, Arthur Severn said

> I am very glad that it will be sent *here* & soon – because I am sure that is the best way – I want it to come in its own little packing case, and for the Coz to wonder what it is, and to order Downs to open it very carefully, then I want to see his – or rather what *happens* when he becomes really aware of what it is!

About three weeks later, on 15 May, Severn wrote to Jane Simon again.

> The Splugen arrived last night – and everything happened just as we wished. Joan went and fetched it at the station and drove it home! picking me up on the way. She arranged to have it all ready for him to undo in the drawing room after dinner – he seemed quite taken by *surprise and awestricken* at first, and evidently had no idea about it. We read him the inscription on the back. He has written to you today on the subject, so perhaps the less I attempt to say the better .... It is a lovely drawing and grows upon one more and more.

Mrs Simon's account of how the drawing came to be bought, which I have printed above, was also sent to Brantwood, and the Severns read it to Ruskin. Joan Severn added a postcript to her husband's letter:

> Arthur has written this hurried line – to which I can't help adding a word just to say the Coz seemed astonished and touched beyond all words – & evidently hadn't the *faintest* idea about it. At first he thought it was a very good copy sent for him to look at – then he said what *can* [be] the meaning of people sending it here? Then I danced with joy and told him it was the real Splugen & his very own as a token of love & rejoicing from many friends on his recovery &c – & then read him carefully your note – & the narrative written by you about it – ever your loving and grateful Joan

On the same day that the Severns wrote to Mrs Simon, Ruskin also wrote to her.[10]

> The Splungen Pass – with all its mountains – was moved here by your faith in me and that of other dear friends last night. I could well be content to go through a worse illness than that in which John and Dr Parsons have carried me forth of the shade … I am, however, profoundly thankful both for the sweet gift, and that I have again eyes to see it, – for indeed, I am, as far as I can make out, quite myself again …

By way of public thanks, Ruskin added a second part to his Turner exhibition which was still running at The Fine Art Society's galleries in Bond Street, and he added the *Splügen* to the exhibition. In the Preface to Part II of his catalogue, he wrote:[11]

> The presentation to me by friends' kindness, of the long-coveted drawing of the Splugen, has given me much to think of, if, just now, I were able to think; – and would urge me to say much, – if I were able to speak. But I am shaken and stunned by this recent illness, – it has left me not a little frightened, and extremely dull.
>
> I cannot write a circular letter of thanks, of so wide a radius as to include all I feel, or ought to feel – on the matter; and besides, I do not usually find that any one worth pleasing is pleased by a circular letter. The recipients always, I think, 'speak disrespectfully of the Equator.' A parabolic letter, or even hyperbolic, might be more to the purpose, if it were possible to me; but on the whole I think it will be the best I can do in this surprised moment to show the importance of this Splugen drawing, in connection with the others in my collection, belonging to its series; by trusting in public indulgence for the exposition also of so much of my own hand-work in illustration of Turner, as may explain the somewhat secluded, and apparently ungrateful, life which I have always been forced to lead in the midst of a group – or as I now thankfully find, a crowd – of most faithful and affectionate friends. …
>
> Of the Splugen drawing, and of the collection which it in a manner consecrates finally to public service, I hope yet to make some practical uses, such as my friends will be glad to have

> strengthened me in: but recovery from such illness as struck me down last February, must be very slow at the best: and cannot be complete, at the completest.

When the drawing returned to Brantwood from The Fine Art Society, it was hung in Ruskin's study, where it joined the other favourite Turners in the room – *Farnley*, *Terni*, *Arona*, *Bonneville* and *Narni*. Ruskin often rearranged the pictures in the house, and by January 1884 the *Splügen* had moved to his bedroom, where it became one of the twenty Turner watercolours to hang there. He wrote:[12]

> Turners beautifully arranged in bedroom, with Constance and Coblentz beside Rouen and Goldau and St Gothard, with Splugen, at bedside. Bolton so bright in last night's sunset

The *Splügen* drawing continued to be one of Ruskin's favourites, and to occupy a favourite place at Brantwood until his death there in 1900. Brantwood and its contents were inherited by the Severns, who lent the drawing to the 1900 Fine Art Society's 'Ruskin's Turner Watercolours' exhibition. Throughout the next three decades the Severns sold off the more desirable contents of the house, in order to provide their income. In 1923 it was the *Splügen*'s turn to go. Despite Mrs Simon's expressed wish that the drawing should eventually be placed in the National Gallery to perpetrate the genius of Turner and Ruskin, the *Splügen* was consigned to Agnews – and it set out on its travels again.

REFERENCES

1. *Works*, XXXV, 309-10.
2. *Notes by Mr Ruskin … on his Drawings by J. M. W. Turner*, 1878; *Works* XIII, 481.
3. Van Akin Burd (ed.), *Ruskin Family Letters*, Cornell University Press, 1973, vol. 2, 725.
4. J. Evans and J. H. Whitehouse (ed.), *The Diaries of John Ruskin*, Clarendon Press, 1956, vol. 1, 273.
5. *Notes by Mr Ruskin …*; *Works* XIII, 482.
6. J. L. Bradley (ed.), *Ruskin's Letters from Venice 1851-1852*, Yale University Press, 1955, 146.
7. Robert Secor, *John Ruskin and Alfred Hunt: New Letters and the Record of a Friendship*,

English Literary Studies, University of Victoria, 1982, 91.

8. Frances Horner, *Time Remembered*, William Heinemann, 1933, 54.

9. *Works* XXXVII, 245n.

10. *Works* XXXVII, 245-6.

11. *Works* XIII, 487-8.

12. *Diaries*, vol. 3, 1072.

IX

WHY *DID* RUSKIN SELL *THE SLAVE SHIP* ?

TURNER SOCIETY NEWS, DECEMBER 2002

Over the years there have been many references to Ruskin and J. M. W. Turner's *The Slave Ship*. This painting was bought for Ruskin by his father as a New Year's present, and given to him on 1 January 1844, in gratitude for the success of the first volume of *Modern Painters*. It hung, for the next twenty-seven years, in the family's dining room at their home, 163 Denmark Hill. The dining room was a tall, spacious room, big enough to adequately accommodate the Ruskins' frequent dinner parties – 'never more than twelve for dinner'.

Just as frequent have been the references to Ruskin selling *The Slave Ship*; the most recent I have seen, by Jan Marsh in her interesting article in *Visual Culture*, vol. 2, no. 1. The general concensus of opinion seems to be that Ruskin parted with the painting because he found it – and its subject – too painful to live with, after having managed to live with it for more than quarter of a century.

But was it the *subject* of the picture which was too painful to live with, or did Ruskin wish to sell the painting because it reminded him too painfully of his often difficult relationship with his father?

That *may* have been the reason why he put it into Christie's where it was offered as lot 50 on 15 April 1869, just five years after the death of John James Ruskin. It did not sell, being bought in at 1,945 guineas, presumably not having reached the reserve.

Ruskin finally sold the painting in January 1872 to the New York collector John Johnson. Ruskin's American friend Charles Eliot Norton had a hand in the sale because on 28 January 1872 Ruskin wrote to him, 'I have the registered letter, and will pack the "Slaver" forthwith. It is right that it should be in America.'

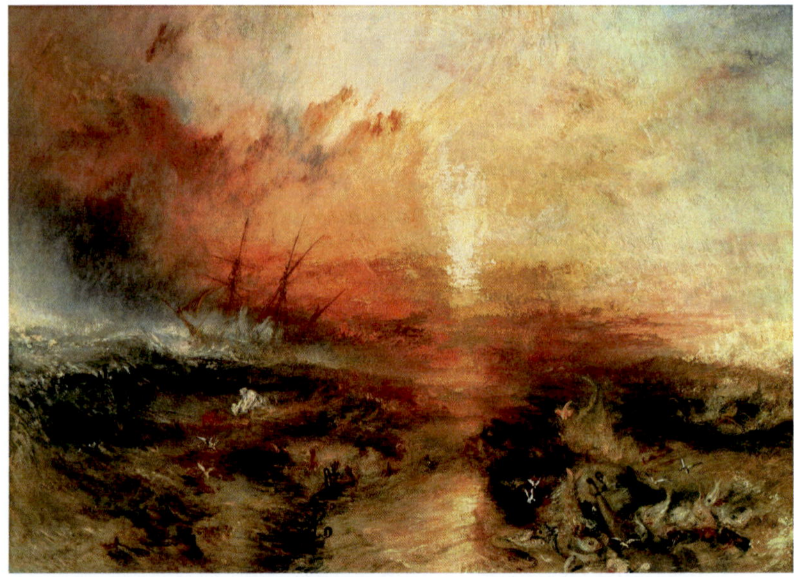

The Slave Ship, *by J. M. W. Turner (Bridgeman Images)*

I think that, to discover the reason why the painting *was* finally sold, one has to go back to the summer of 1871 for it was then that Ruskin bought a new home for himself. Brantwood overlooking Coniston Lake. In December of that same year his mother died and he decided to part with the family home at Denmark Hill. The contents which he wished to retain were sent either to Brantwood, or to his rooms at Corpus Christi College, Oxford, and he finally left Denmark Hill at the end of March 1872.

Brantwood at that time was a small house comprising four rooms on the ground floor in addition to the kitchens. For various structural reasons the walls of all these rooms had interruptions in them – doors, windows, recesses and curves. The largest uninterrupted wall in the house was in the hall, facing the front door. That space measures 8' 5" high by 12' wide. The painting seems to be still in its original frame, which measures 4' x 5'. It seems to me that the painting would, thus, be quite the wrong proportion for the space available, and it would have been hung too near the ceiling – or floor – in this dark hall. Had the picture been hung in this position, there would have been a lot of vacant space on the wall to left and right, but I doubt if Ruskin would have wanted to hang anything so near to *The Slave Ship*, and thus attract attention away from it. Added to this, the lower part of the picture would have been partly obscured by furniture in the centre of the hall floor.

I believe that Ruskin sold *The Slave Ship* in 1872, not because it was too painful to live with, but because he had nowhere to hang it in his new home. Confirmation of this supposition is perhaps provided by Ruskin writing to Norton on 31 March 1872 about his other Turner oil, 'I am going to sell my Venice Rialto by Turner. It

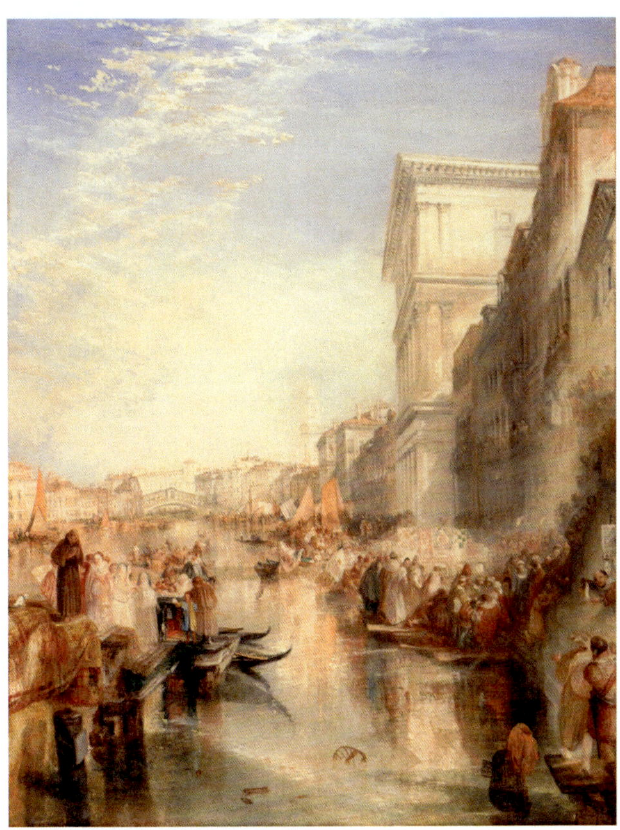

The Grand Canal, *by J. M. W. Turner (Bridgeman Images)*

is too large for Brantwood…'. In fact it was a little over a foot higher than *The Slave Ship* but not quite as wide. It sold at Christie's on 8 June 1872 for £4,000. John James Ruskin had bought it in April 1847 for £840.

There does not seem to be a record of the price Johnson paid Ruskin for *The Slave Ship*. We do not know what reserve Ruskin put on the painting when it was offered at Christie's in 1869, but we do know that it was higher than the bid of 1,945 guineas. I do not think that Ruskin would have sold an important Turner painting for less than he believed it was worth (too difficult to live with or not) – so whatever that was, Ruskin must have sold it in 1872 for more than 1,945 guineas. Let us assume he sold it for 2,000 guineas;* he made a handsome profit. His father had paid 250 guineas for it when he bought it in 1844 from Turner's dealer, Thomas Griffith. The pound at that time was worth much the same in 1872 as it had been twenty-eight years earlier. Thus, in real terms, Ruskin had made a profit of 1,750 guineas. In the previous year he had paid Linton £1,500 for Brantwood and its sixteen acres of ground.

Incidentally, John Taylor Johnson (who at the time was President of the Metropolitan Museum) only kept the painting for four years. It was sold at the American Art Association in New York (19-22 December 1876, lot 76) to Miss Alice Hooper of Boston for $10,000 (£2,062), the highest price for a European painting ever paid in America.

* I have subsequently discovered that Ruskin sold the painting for 2,500 guineas.

X

THE RUSKIN SOCIETY OF NEWPORT, ISLE OF WIGHT

THE FRIENDS OF RUSKIN'S BRANTWOOD NEWSLETTER, AUTUMN 2002

When I presented books to the May Queen and her attendants at Whitelands College on behalf of the Guild of St George on 11 May 2002, I spoke briefly about the Ruskin Society of Newport, using it as an example of how such organisations so often depend for their existence on the enthusiasm of one person.

As far as I can trace there is no archive in existence for the Newport Ruskin Society. Perhaps, indeed, they never kept minutes or otherwise generated paperwork. Were it not for the very full reporting by the *Isle of Wight County Press* at that period, we would not even know of the society's existence.

On 24 February 1900, the following letter was printed in the *County Press*:

> Sir, it may interest some of your readers to know that an attempt is being made to form a Ruskin Society for Newport. The object of this society is the study of Mr Ruskin's works, and to further this object it is proposed to hold fortnightly meetings on the second and fourth Wednesdays of each month, when readings from the great author's work will be given, explanations made when necessary, and the subject discussed. This will take about an hour.
>
> The first meeting of the society will be held in the school room of the Unitarian Church in the High Street, on Wednesday 28 February, and will begin at 7.30 p.m. Admission will be free. All who are interested in the subject will be welcomed. The society is entirely unsectarian.

The work chosen to begin with is the series of letters to working men entitled 'Fors Clavigera'.

Your contemporary, the *Pall Mall Gazette*, in commenting upon a similar society formed in London, said 'That it is good for us – for all of us who can – to study the works of the great masters of English prose and a devout lover and fervent apostle of the Beautiful, is indisputable', and 'The sort of genius that is Ruskin's ought to be the common treasure of everybody who can read English.'

To afford an opportunity for this study and to help others to get this treasure is the object of this Ruskin Society.

Faithfully yours, Clement E. Pike.

The Rev. Clement E. Pike, a Fellow of the Royal Historical Society, was the author of the *Constitutional History of the House of Lords*, in 1894, and became the minister of the Unitarian Church in Newport in 1899.

The idea of a Ruskin Society was not new, of course. The first society had been formed in Manchester in 1878; the following year saw the formation of a society in Glasgow. Thereafter, they proliferated rapidly – Sheffield, London, Birkenhead, (1881), Ambleside (1882), Liverpool (1883), Birmingham, Isle of Man (1896), Paisley (by 1899), Ruskin Union (1900). Additionally, the Ruskin Reading Guild which was formed in 1887, had branches in London, Birmingham, Liverpool, Bradford, Oxford, Edinburgh, Glasgow, Arbroath, Elgin, Dundee and Armagh. Thus, the Newport society was the youngest of a large group.

The new society's first meeting, on Wednesday 28 February 1900, attracted 'a very good and representative attendance at the Unitarian schoolroom. The Rev. Clement E. Pike, F.R. Hist. S., read the first letter in 'Fors Clavigera', and a discussion followed, chiefly concerning the author's remarks on a National Store and a National Debt, those taking part being Messrs L. Jordan, McPherson, H. Shepard, and W. H. Upton. Ruskin portraits were exhibited by the Rev. C. E. Pike and Messrs Shepard and Jordan, and the last named gentleman stated that the editor of the *Sphere* had kindly promised to send for the use of the society a special copy on art paper of the portrait which appeared in the first number of that periodical.'

The Ruskin portrait duly arrived and was framed and hung in the Schoolroom where it remained until it was rehung in the Vestry. It remained there until probably the 1970s when it was given to a later minister, The Rev. John Sturges, 'because he went to Ruskin College, Oxford'. I have been unable to trace its present whereabouts.

The society continued to meet regularly every other Wednesday until the end of its first session on 22 August 1900, reading and discussing one letter of *Fors Clavigera I* at each meeting. The second session opened on 14 November 1900 and continued until 22 May 1901. They devoted the fourteen meetings of this session to reading and discussing the twelve letters of *Fors II*.

Interestingly the *County Press* of 4 May 1901 reported at substantial length a lecture on Ruskin given in Ryde on 25 April by the Rev. W. Hudson Shaw, as the final lecture in a series of six which he had delivered on the Island. No doubt members of the Ruskin Society would have been in Shaw's audience to hear him describing Ruskin as 'the most splendidly endowed man of genius of whom England could lately boast, as the last of the prophets, the most eloquent voice that stirred the hearts of the nineteenth century, the most consummate master of the English language. His deprecators included Philistines, money worshipers, the devotees of art for art's sake, Mr McNeill Whistler, and *Blackwood's Magazine*.....he was not an author, he was a cyclopaedia.....by character and work he had a claim to be regarded as one of the chiefest men of genius of whom the nineteenth century could boast'.

Hudson Shaw was a member of the Oxford University Extension Scheme between 1886 and 1913, and on his retirement, according to an illuminated page in volume 1 'with gratitude and affection [his] colleagues, students and friends' presented him with a set of the Ruskin *Library Edition*, bound in half morocco. The set is now with the Ruskin Foundation and a label in each volume explains that the set was 'Bequeathed to the Brantwood Library by Rev. W. Hudson Shaw who gave a great part of his life and strength, both in this country and the United States of America to teaching the principles proclaimed by one whom he was proud to call his Master, John Ruskin.'

Meanwhile, in the Ruskin Society of Newport, perhaps there had been whispers of dissent because when their third session opened on 13 November 1901, they had abandoned the remaining six volumes of *Fors Clavigera*. In a letter to the editor of the *County Press* on the previous Saturday Mr Pike announced that in the new session they proposed 'to go through *The Crown of Wild Olive, four series of lectures on work, traffic, war, and the future of England*, which contains some of Mr Ruskin's most direct and powerful teaching. This session the experiment of devoting one evening to the lecture and the next evening to a discussion of it will be tried'. And so the session progressed, with 'Work' being read on 13 November and discussed on the 27th; 'Traffic' being read on 11 December and discussed on 8 January (they had the day off on 25 December!), and so on throughout the session, when finally on 26 March they had a social evening.

The next session did not begin until 3 January 1902, when they began by reading the first chapter of *Unto This Last*. They continued with the alternate reading and discussion of the four chapters until 25 March and the end of the session.

The final session opened on 17th December 1903 with a change of pattern. The evening was changed to Thursday because 'two other organisations meet on [Wednesday] night'. The book chosen for study was *Mornings in Florence*, and Mr Pike announced that he proposed to open the session with a preliminary lecture on the work, 'illustrated with lantern views of Florence'.

However, their announced scheme was abandoned, and at the meeting in early January 1904 (according to the *County Press* report which was headed 'Fiscalities') 'The I.W. Ruskin Society departed from their customary theme....when the fiscal question was the subject of a debate. The debate was adjourned until another meeting a month hence.'

Whether or not they held their next month's meeting, or indeed *any* further meetings, is not known. There the *County Press* chronicling of the Ruskin Society of Newport ends.

There was one further reference. On 21 January 1905 the paper carried a notice of the 'Unitarian Pastor's Resignation'. Mr Pike was moving on to a church in Hampstead because of 'a desire for a wider field and greater facilities for pursuing his literary labours.' The report continued, 'He has rendered splendid service in reviving in the town the Oxford University Extension Movement, of which he is the present hon. secretary, as well as in the promotion and giving of a series of "Ruskin lectures"....'.

And with the departure from the Island of the Rev. Clement E. Pike, the Ruskin Society appears to have vanished without trace.

XI

THE CASE OF THE GROCER OF WALKLEY: A STUDY IN RUSKIN DETECTION

THE FRIENDS OF RUSKIN'S BRANTWOOD NEWSLETTER, AUTUMN 2001

ↄ

In Letter 88 (March 1880) of *Fors Clavigera*, John Ruskin's monthly 'Letters to the Workmen and Labourers of Great Britain', he wrote:

> Here, for instance (Sheffield, 12th February), I am lodging at an honest and hospitable grocer's, who has lent me his own bedroom, of which the principal ornament is a card printed in black and gold, sacred to the memory of his infant son, who died aged fourteen months, and whose tomb is represented under the figure of a broken Corinthian column, with two graceful-winged ladies putting garlands on it.

Fors Clavigera is a fascinating publication containing Ruskin's thoughts on anything and everything that interested him; Tim Hilton has described it as his most important publication. Including the Index, it runs to eight volumes, and it has not been readily available for many years. A volume of selections from *Fors* was, therefore, an obvious volume to include in the Whitehouse Series of Ruskin reprints when it was planned several years ago, and Dinah Birch was invited to edit that particular volume.

As Joint General Editor of the series, Dr Birch was one of 'my' editors, and we were in regular communication in that connection.

One day in April 1999 I had a card from DB with the question, 'Do you happen to know anything about the Sheffield grocer Ruskin stayed with on 12 February 1880?'

The simple answer was that I didn't, but Ruskin's life is so well documented that it must be a relatively simple task to answer the question.

Central to Ruskin's activities in Sheffield was Henry Swan, the curator of the St George's Guild Museum at Walkley. A group of Ruskin's admirers and Swan's friends had urged Ruskin, in 1877, to let them have some land to rent from the Guild where they could put Ruskin's teaching into practice and spend their spare hours in useful labour. A smallholding of thirteen acres in Mickley Lane, Totley, was found. Ruskin bought it for £2,200 and it was leased to the group to work. But there was almost immediate internal dissent about its running.

Meanwhile, by 1873, William Harrison Riley, a socialist and Republican, had got to know Ruskin; it was he who introduced Ruskin to Walt Whitman. Riley had been trying to interest Ruskin in co-operative ventures for some time, and by the end of 1877 he had settled in Sheffield. Before long he seems to have taken charge of affairs at St George's Farm. But things went from bad to worse and early in 1880 Riley returned to America.

In February 1880 Ruskin may have gone to Sheffield to try and unravel the situation following Riley's emigration – or indeed Riley may have emigrated as a *result* of Ruskin's visit. However, whichever was the case, the arrangement of Ruskin's accommodation was probably left in the hands of Swan. It merely remained to look up the address.

The first reference was to Ruskin's diary, but unhelpfully there were no entries between 10 February and 13 April. However, reference to the *Library Edition* (XXX, xliv) confirmed that the search should not be too complicated. The editors had written: 'On these occasions Ruskin used to stay at the little grocer's shop in the village of Walkley… and a young friend who visited him there found him drawing the cottage and trees on the windows of his bedroom in illustration of the laws of perspective.' The friend was Swan, thus adding weight to the idea that he would have arranged the accommodation.

However, the idea that identifying the 'little grocer's shop in Walkley' would be easy was a little dashed when DB said that a local census showed there were several grocers in Walkley in 1880. She also confirmed that she had checked everything that she could think of without finding any trace of our man. I too had checked all the volumes of the published letters in my own collection without success.

The best source of biographical information on Ruskin is the series of letters that he wrote – almost daily – to Joan Severn. Before too long, I had to go to Lancaster to examine the various editions of *Fors Clavigera* in connection with the bibliography for DB's volume. Having done *that* research I decided to pursue the dreaded grocer, and I asked for the 1880 box of Severn correspondence – to find there *were* no letters before August!

I knew that several volumes of Ruskin's diaries included in their early pages, lists of names and addresses not included by Joan Evans in her edition. Assuming that Ruskin would want to have with him a note of the address to which he was travelling, I asked for the appropriate manuscript volume. My memory had not failed me – there were addresses in the volume, but nothing to throw light on where Ruskin stayed.

Inexplicably I had omitted to look in Helen Viljoen's edition of the Brantwood Diary. This is a volume which, unlike his other diary volumes, did *not* travel with Ruskin but remained at Brantwood for use there. I had a look in the published copy at Lancaster and found on page 224 the first reference I had discovered to the visit – not that it was very helpful. On 18 February Ruskin wrote, 'Have been at Sheffield since the 10th and am more glad to get back than ever yet. The days not diaried were overwhelmed in doing new Fors…' And did *this* volume contain a list of addresses? I remembered my almost daily correspondence thirty years ago with Helen Viljoen when she was editing the diary and I felt certain that if there were addresses, then I would find them at the beginning of her volume; but all there was, was a disappointing note, 'The volume begins with twelve alphabetized pages on which Ruskin wrote the addresses of friends.' But had she transcribed them?

I mentioned my disappointment to Stephen Wildman who said that Ray Haslam had transcribed the address list when he was last at the Pierpont Morgan Library, thinking that it may be useful. I asked him if he could possibly follow up the trail for me and that evening he wrote to say that the list had been checked and three Sheffield addresses had been found: Benjamin Creswick, the sculptor, a Michael

Beal of Market Place, Sheffield, and a Mr Toger or Tozer, of Lawton Road, Sheffield – but no grocer. Meanwhile, SW had also asked me if I had checked Peter Morgan's list. No, I hadn't. I did remember Peter Morgan coming to Bembridge once or twice, but I had never known what his particular field of research was, and I *did* remember that I couldn't see any logic to the files of letters for which he had asked.

SW produced a print-out of part of Peter Morgan's list from the internet. Here, arranged chronologically, was a list of letters written by Ruskin with a note of the location of the originals, and listed between 10 and 18 February were eleven letters which must have been written from Sheffield. Surely *one* of these would have his address on it, or contain some clue to the identity of his host! And here was the ball going firmly back into DB's court – ten of the letters listed were in the Bodleian. I was determined that the grocer wasn't going to defeat us!

I sent the Morgan list to DB only to hear from her on 1 July that all the manuscripts in the Bodleian were completely inaccessible until at least 19 July because Duke Humfrey's Library was closed while they attended to its Death Watch Beetles. Then DB was going away for ten days; meanwhile she had e-mailed to Peter Morgan to ask if *he* could find the answer to our problem in *his* transcripts, but hadn't had a reply.

I had contemplated an approach to the Sheffield City Archivist, but then I remembered that fellow-Companion Eric Mackerness had both an interest in Ruskin and a knowledge of Sheffield history, so I wrote to ask if he could help. He very kindly went through the Sheffield directories for the period and sent me a list of the thirty three grocers in Sheffield, indicating on it the *ten* which could be considered to be in the Walkley area! When I sent this list on to DB I suggested it might be easier to tour Sheffield graveyards looking for a broken column and two graceful ladies!

Eventually DB wrote to say that her Scottish holiday being over and Bodley's beetles having been eradicated, she had been pursuing matters in Oxford. She had consulted with Bodley's librarians but unfortunately the reference system on the Morgan list bore no resemblance to Bodley's catalogue, and we can only surmise that the references which he cites are to his own transcripts, rather than to the originals – which the Bodleian staff were unable to trace. A further e-mail was sent seeking elucidation, but there has been no response.

Clutching at straws, I told DB that I hadn't kept a copy of the Morgan list and so couldn't check – but could his references possibly be to the Cook and Wedderburn letter transcripts in the Bodleian, but not unexpectedly DB had also thought of this, and had already checked this line without success.

It finally did look as if the only route to the answer was a physical graveyard check. I asked Eric Mackerness where anyone dying in Walkley would have been buried; if only one possible location was involved, I planned to check this when I was next in Sheffield.

However, I re-read what Ruskin had written in *Fors* about the decoration of his Walkley bedroom. *Nothing* was simple in this inquiry. What exactly *was* Ruskin saying? Did the card with the name of the grocer's dead son incorporate a picture of the tomb with its broken Corinthian column and two decorative ladies – or was it merely that the card bearing his name was in a *mount* thus decorated?

I put the question to DB, and on balance she thought that it was unlikely that the grocer could have afforded such an elaborate memorial, and that the ladies and the column were merely printed on the card's mount. In fact she put it more eloquently than that, but either way we decided that a graveyard search would probably be fruitless.

One possible alternative was a Parish Register search, and knowing that so many Parish Registers these days are deposited in Records Offices, I phoned Ruth Harman at the Sheffield City Archives, and explained the problem to her. First, the bad news: although St Mary's Parish, Walkley, was created in 1869, it didn't have its own graveyard until May 1880! Parishioners would have been buried in St Philip's. But the good news: the Registers were in the Archives Office, *and* they were indexed. I was due in Sheffield soon and I arranged to call and see them.

I checked the index to St Philip's Registers for all of the grocers' names which had been on Eric Mackerness's list (sadly, I learned that he had died just a few days before I went to Sheffield). Of all the names on the list, only three appeared in the Index – which was not just for the 1870s but for all time; I then checked the microfiches of the Registers for those three names to see if any of them were fourteen months old – but of course they weren't. Clearly most Walkley grocers were immortal.

Ruth Harman, the archivist, had really got her teeth into the inquiry and made a couple of helpful suggestions. She thought it entirely probable that Ruskin's visit might very well be recorded in one or other of the local newspapers, and secondly, she knew that there had been a Sheffield Ruskin Society and she wondered if the newspaper reports of its inaugural meeting might throw up the names of a few enthusiasts, including, perhaps, a grocer or two.

So the following morning I had an appointment in the Library's Local Studies Department, where my name had gone before, and they already had waiting for me xeroxes of the Ruskin Society press reports – but no grocers. I went through the *Sheffield Local Register* which is, as it were, a digest of the local information in the *Sheffield Independent*. While there were frequent references to Ruskin, there were none in 1880. By this time the *Sheffield Independent* and the *Sheffield Telegraph* were daily newspapers of some substance. I read them both, on film, from 10 February 1880 till three days after Ruskin had left the city. Not a whisper; it looked as if local sources were not going to produce the answer.

So where do we go from here? It looked as if we had to fall back on the Morgan list, and the largest group of letters of the right date, in the Bodleian. I put this to DB, but she said that she *had* tried again to find the letters, with the help of the assembled staff of Duke Humfrey's – but to no avail.

What of the other letters on the Morgan list? Well, they are all in America, and libraries are not as pleased to receive postal inquiries as they used to be. But all was not lost. A new Ruskin acquaintance living in New York had asked me if there was anything he could do to help me in the city. I suggested that perhaps he could look at the letter which Ruskin wrote to George Allen from Sheffield which is now in the library at Columbia University. In no time at all came his reply with a photocopy of the letter. In the light of the success of this inquiry to date, it came as no surprise that Ruskin's letter was merely headed 'Sheffield

16th Feb', with no contextual reference to his host or his house.

I had always suspected that Henry Swan had been responsible for making Ruskin's domestic arrangements in Sheffield. (What arrangements were made for Ruskin's valet Peter Baxter, who was undoubtedly there too, I can't even contemplate.) In a final attempt to answer DB's original inquiry, I wrote to the Rosenbach Library in Philadelphia where are kept the Ruskin–Swan letters. I told them of my problem and they very kindly sent xeroxes of the only two letters bearing on the subject.

Ruskin's 31 December 1879 letter to Swan shows that he was then planning to visit Sheffield about the 18 or 20 January, and, as I suspected, Swan did make the arrangements. Ruskin wrote initially about his previous visit to Sheffield, '...much as I liked my good host and hostess I do wish I could get lodged nearer the Museum. How about that little tavern close to you? My special dislike is to that penitentiary opposite to my old lodgings – I should like, ultimately, to try to find some farmhouse further afield – but just in the mid winter it would be better in the town with little way to walk.'

This was followed by a postscript in a letter of 9 February 1880 to Mrs Swan, 'Have the lodgings comfortable. I've a most provoking threatening of cold coming on, but shall come anyhow. D.V.'

By now, of course, it is too late for the footnote in the new edition of *Fors Clavigera*; the inquiry had taken on a life of its own – and I fear it is not likely to get any nearer than the ground rules which Ruskin laid down for his lodgings. But to show would-be Ruskin inquirers that the field is not always plain sailing, it seemed that the inquiry was worth writing up in some form – and DB opined that I should be the one to do it!

SEQUEL TO 'THE GROCER OF WALKLEY'[1]

It is thanks to the eagle-eyed Rebecca Patterson of the Ruskin Library at Lancaster that I am able to add extra information in this case. Unfortunately we have not yet discovered where Ruskin stayed in Sheffield in 1880, but we *do* know where he lodged during his previous visit of 1879.

In my original report on the case I quoted a letter from Ruskin to

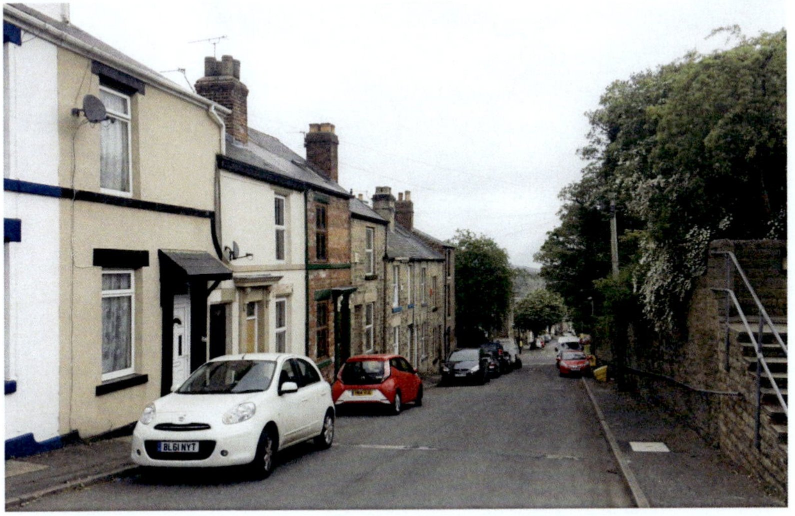

158 Fulton Road, Sheffield, where Ruskin lodged in 1879

Henry Swan in which he said that he liked his host and hostess in 1879 but he took a special dislike 'to that penitentiary opposite to my old lodgings.'

We now know that Ruskin's 'old lodgings' were at 158 Fulton Road, Walkley. His host was Joseph William Cook, a 39 years old foreman carpenter, who was married to Annie (41) and they had one son, Frank, aged ten.

Ruth Harman, of Sheffield Archives, tells me that the 'penitentiary' opposite the lodgings was the North of England Catholic Girls' Reformatory School which had been opened in 1861 to provide accommodation for about a hundred girls from the northern half of England. By the 1950s it had become St Joseph's Roman Catholic Home for Mentally Deficient Girls. Although closed and demolished in the 1970s Ruth Harman remembers the 'penitentiary' as plain three or four storey stone buildings with large sash windows, typical of an institution of the 1860s.

According to Ruskin's Brantwood Diary of 18 December 1879 he arrived 'Back here on the 16th having been three months away – a fortnight at Canterbury, ten days in Sheffield, a week at Broadlands and the rest London.'

There are three letters from Ruskin to Joan Severn in the Whitehouse Collection at Lancaster, written from 158 Fulton Road. In them Ruskin describes his lodgings and in one there is a particular emphasis on food which is reminiscent of his 'Little Pig' letters written to Joan in 1867-69 and printed by me in *The Pigwiggian Chaunts of John Ruskin*, 1960.

On 17 October 1879 he wrote to Joan, 'And I'm in such funny wee lodgings di ma, with a nice carpenter and his wife (only I never see the carpenter) and was rather taken aback when his wife sate down at the fireside while I had my dinner – she was by way of waiting – but sate down quietly like an old fashioned landlady – in her own house and talked as serenely as if she'd been the Princess Louise – without the least impudence. [Four days later Ruskin was to conduct Princess Louise's brother, Prince Leopold, around the Guild of St George's Museum at Walkley.] Everything beautifully clean – but too much *china* di ma – and things on tables – and and everywhere – a little Swiss cottage as good as can be – and pics and photos –...'

On the following day '...me's to have Wiltshire bacon for bek – oo dee-di, wee piggy-wiggie – Bacon as pink as salmon! – di ma with balmy fat – and it's *toasted* before the fire on a fork like real toast – and it makes me think of the Hernehill bacon – as of so much dead oak-leaves frizzled with greasy cinders. And they've got *such* Cheshire cheese – just the colour of one of Arfie's fiery sunsets – and all crumbly – Crumbles Roy all to nothing! ...'

Three days later he told Joan, '...I have got a kitten to play with at breakfast – and a hard day before me.'

But we have still to discover where he stayed in 1880!

REFERENCES

1. 'The Case of the Grocer' was reprinted as a separate pamphlet in 2001. The 'Sequel' was printed as a separate leaflet in 2002.

XII
LOST BRANTWOOD

THE FRIENDS OF RUSKIN'S BRANTWOOD NEWSLETTER, SPRING 2011

❧

Many changes have taken place to the house and grounds at Brantwood since I first knew them some sixty-five years ago. It seems worthwhile, and possibly of interest, to record some of these changes. Some of them may be evident from reading my *Brantwood: The story of John Ruskin's Coniston home*; others will not have been mentioned there.

For the benefit of visitors arriving at Brantwood by water, the long wooden jetty was built more than thirty years ago so that the lake's various ferries could call here. The harbour breakwater itself was lengthened rather longer ago, in an attempt to stop the harbour entrance silting up. At one time the inner harbour was roofed over to form a little boathouse. I remember this in its final stages of decay. The stone path from the wooden jetty was built at the same time to accommodate ferry visitors, but was later improved. Before that, access to the harbour was by way of a set of rustic steps immediately below the gate onto the Harbour Walk. J. Howard Whitehouse – we always knew him as Warden – had been told that the large sycamore tree near these steps was unsafe and should be cut down. I remember my mother pleading with him not to do this. She was successful, and that must be more than sixty years ago. [Since writing this, I am saddened to learn that the upper part of this old tree came down in a July gale.]

But let us begin in the car park, where most visits begin. In the time of Ruskin and the Severns this was the kitchen garden. The wall between the garden and the road was the same as the present wall on the other side of the road. There was a field gate round about the

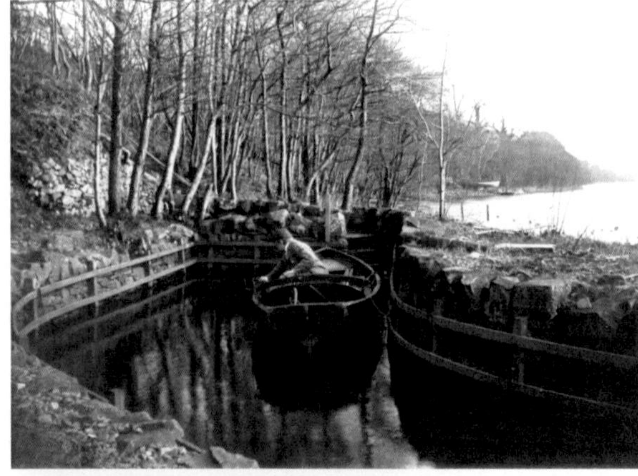

The inner harbour in the 1890s, subsequently roofed over to form a boat house

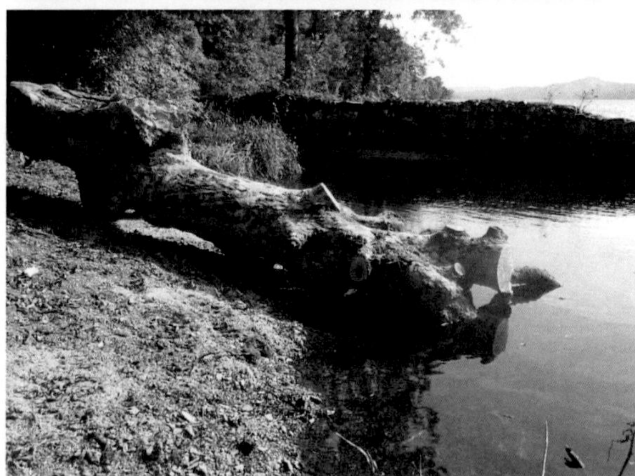

The fallen section of the Sycamore, July 2010

centre. Towards the northern end, where the greenhouses stood, the wall must have been higher, because I remember entering this little area from the road through a door.

The path and the steps leading up to the 'Jumping Jenny' café weren't there, but I seem to remember a rough path through the bushes bordering the road. The area around the stable block was not paved, just hard earth, as were both drives to the house. The area at the side of the stables had a low wall – not the present one – to prevent horses and others from falling into the garden, but towards the back of the block, there was a gap in the wall to enable the groom, having completed his mucking-out, to tip his wheelbarrow over the edge onto the midden in the garden below. The gate across the entrance to the stable yard can be seen in the photograph on page 29 of my book *Brantwood: The Story of John Ruskin's Coniston Home* (2009).

Let us return to the coach house. The partition splitting this into two is recent. On my occasional visits to the Lodge I remember asking Miss Wilkinson if I could borrow the coach house key. It was the same large key that fitted the lock on one of the outbuildings immediately adjacent to the Lodge. These outbuildings are all that remain of the original stables, pulled down when the Lodge was built in 1872. So the lock must have been changed when the new stable block was built.

There are two doors into the stables, now 'The Jumping Jenny'. The first went directly into the stables; the second entered the Tack

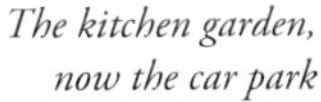

The kitchen garden, now the car park

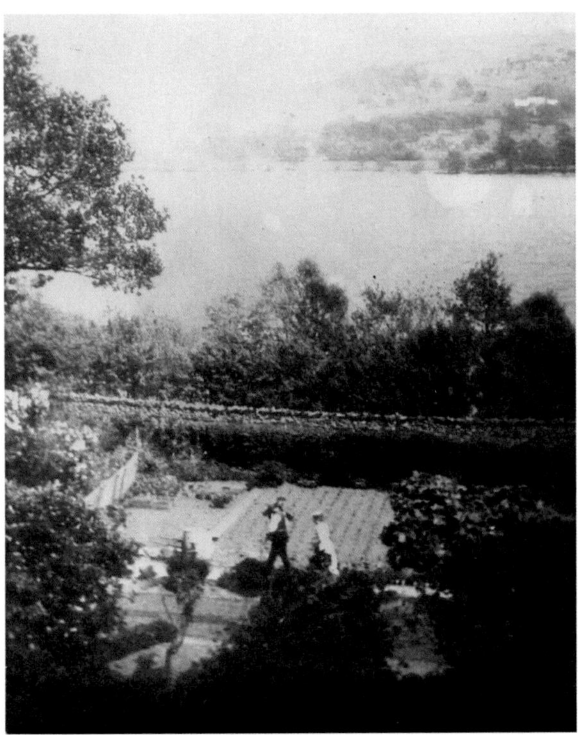

Room, with its own door into the stables. I remember the Tack Room when it was still entirely fitted with its harness brackets. The step up into the 'Jumping Jenny' is onto a wooden floor. When the stables were converted I persuaded the then manager to put in this false floor so that the original stable floor could be retained beneath it.

The stalls to the left are still evident. Facing you, as you entered from the Tack Room were two loose boxes. Above there was a trap door, as I remember it, between the stalls and the loose boxes, so that hay and straw could be lowered from the room above. The kitchen was originally a third loose box with its own outside entrance and at the very end of the building was a lavatory for the outdoor staff.

The configuration of the upstairs was different. There was no paved path leading up to it – just a hard earth path, then a short flight of steps up to the door – in the side of the building at the very corner – not where the present door is. This led into a short passage which ran across the front of the building. From it you could enter the storage space behind, or go into the room where the groom had his living quarters.

In the days when Twickenham College of Technology and the Council for Nature sent courses to Brantwood, I think this loft was used for student accommodation. Later, in the 1970s, my wife and daughter and I would bring an exhibition from the Ruskin Galleries at Bembridge to this room for a few weeks each summer – 'History of Brantwood' in 1975, 'Ruskin and Turner' in 1976, 'Ruskin in Love' in 1978. Driving the exhibitions from Bembridge to Brantwood in the School mini-bus was a dreary business. Because of insurance requirements there always had to be one person left in the bus during stops at motorway service stations. But it was trouble-free motorway driving; no overtaking problems. Foot hard down and we sat in the inside lane all the way going flat out at about 40 m.p.h. letting everything else overtake *us*! Bembridge to Brantwood was a *very long* journey.

The wooden platform (it can be seen on page 29 of my Brantwood book) outside the first floor door of the Lodge – the entrance to Lily Severn's sitting room – was reached by a wooden staircase. I remember it, but I don't ever remember ascending it. The stone gate post, seen in the same photograph, has been moved nearer to the road in order to make a wider entrance, and while the present gate is of similar design to the original, it was made to fit the wider entrance. On either side of the gateway stood two tall lime trees. I don't think I remember them; perhaps they were cut down just before my time, but they form one of the illustrations in *Drawings at Brantwood* by Graham Binns, published in 1942.

Going up the drive you reach the Linton Building. This was structurally altered a number of years ago when it was restored. If you look at the photograph of the pre-restoration building on page 11 of my book, you can see the skylight in the roof, there to give light to Linton's type cases below. The approach, *then*, to the upper room, was up short flight of steps through the narrow opening on the right. On the right, half way up these steps, was another outdoor lavatory. One of the other two doors gave access to the coal and coke store – I don't remember which. When electricity was laid on to Brantwood in the late 1940s, one of these rooms – I think the left (with its white notice on the door) housed a transformer sub-station, subsequently moved down to the end of the drive.

Near to that door can be seen a small square opening in the wall. On one of his visits to Italy Ruskin returned with a carved stone rose, which was set into the wall here. I suggested to Warden, on one of my visits, that it would be nice to have the rose set into the wall above the entrance to the New House at Bembridge School and it was duly

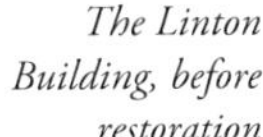
The Linton Building, before restoration

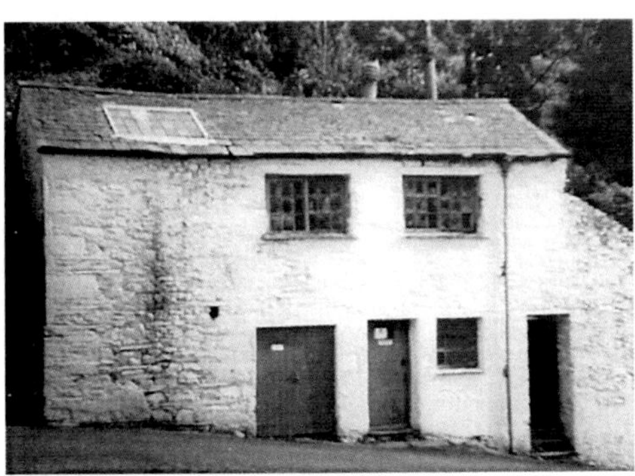

moved, leaving the hole in the wall, which was sub-sequently adapted to its current use! When the Whitehouse Collection left Bembridge, the rose, as part of the collection, was moved back to Brantwood – but since that house at Bembridge was a listed building, planning permission had to be obtained for its removal! Finally, higher on this wall of the Linton Building was a large wooden pigeon coop.

Continuing up the drive, the visitor enters the house by what *was* the back door. This reception area is completely changed. Immediately inside the door a passage faced you. To the right was the door into the kitchen – the video room – and to your left was a doorway (I don't think there was a door) which gave access to another of the kitchen rooms. This had a wooden wall with windows high up, near the ceiling. On this wall, either just above or immediately below these windows was a long range of bells, with their name plates – Dining Room, Study, Mr Ruskin's bedroom, etc. I was able to save two or three of the bells, which are now in the Whitehouse Collection. Unhappily only one of the name plates has survived

This wooden wall continued for a little way, and then turned left to form a passage to the green baize door that led to the front of the house – the doorway which opens to face onto the staircase. The doorway, which now leads into the hall, used to be a cupboard built into the thickness of the wall. On the other side of this passage was a door into the room which now forms the inner part of the shop. This was the Lamp Room, where the paraffin lamps were stored, cleaned, trimmed and filled. If you didn't turn left down this passage, but went straight on, you passed under the back stairs (there was a cupboard under them) and arrived at a door into the old dining room. The deep built-in showcase in this room has been created out of the under-stairs cupboard.

The other doorway into the old dining room – from the hall – used to have a door in which were patterned frosted glass windows. The room needed all the light it could get. This door (it is still stored at Brantwood) was removed at the time that the house was used for student accommodation. In those days Brantwood had a drinks license and a stone bar counter with a wooden top was built in the hall in front of this doorway. The room itself was divided down the middle; the left, window side, was the office and the other side was a bottle and barrel store. That was in the mid-'60s. When I first knew Brantwood, the farther end of the old dining room was partitioned off. It is shown thus on the plan in my *Brantwood* book. I guess this was either done in the late 1890s, or more probably after Ruskin's time. This partition provided a small cloakroom. There was a doorway in the right hand corner into a room which had two wash basins. The basins themselves were set into a wooden fitting and were pivotted at either side. To empty them you lifted them by a lip under the front edge and the basin swivelled upwards, tipping the water into some form of drain beneath. Leading off this wash room was another room wherein was a loo – I remember it was called 'The Furness' – against the outside wall; it had a high wooden cistern.

Many temporary changes to the house have been made over the years, to adapt it for its current usage. Once, during its occupancy by students, visitors to the house entered through the external door in the small room off the drawing room. In passing from the drawing room into the hall, there was a wooden partition built across the hall, separating off most of the hall, but allowing the visitor to go to the study, and *I think* on to the dining room. Presumably with that arrangement, residents used the rest of the hall and the old dining room as a refectory.

Mention of the drawing room reminds me that the edge of the small terrace outside the windows used to be flanked by rose arches. There is a watercolour of them by Arthur Severn in the collection. I remember the rusty iron arches set into the stonework edging to the grass terrace but by then there were no roses. The metal bases of the arches can still be seen embedded into the stonework.

I have already mentioned loos several times. Looking at my plans of the original eighteenth century cottage I realise that it is devoid of both loos and bathrooms. When it was built, there would have been an outside privy, and no doubt when or if bathing ever took place, it would have been in a hip bath in one of the bedrooms – or even the kitchen.

The first rooms for a loo and a bath were incorporated into Anne Copley's extension to the house in the 1830s. The bathroom, on the first floor – the first room you reach in the extension – was just *that*, a room containing a bath and I believe the present mahogany-cased bath is probably the original Copley fitting. The present loo and wash-basin, of course, are new. There was *one* other thing in the room, now long gone. On the floor in the corner behind the door was a lead-lined quarter circle space with a raised rim and a drain in the centre. Here would have been emptied the slop pails from the bedrooms.

Next door was the original loo. This was a water closet, probably a valve closet of the type originally patented by Joseph Bramah in 1778. Since this was in a room clearly built for the purpose, it was possibly the original Copley loo. However, this type of closet was still being manufactured by Thomas Crapper until the 1930s, so it could have replaced the original loo when the house was being restored for Ruskin in 1871. It was encased in a panelled mahogany fitting which occupied the entire width of the room. The panelling extended above the casing onto the walls on all three sides. The wall panelling has survived. Adjacent to you in the mahogany seat was a depression in which was a plunger handle. When this was pulled upwards, the loo was flushed. Thinking of the awful warning in some railway trains today – 'Do not flush while seated' – I'm sure this arrangement must have been an awful temptation to the Severn boys!

One thing which happily *has* survived, is the small triangular shelf at about shoulder height, to the right just inside the door. This was where you put your candle-stick. Today, it still has a use!

The next room along the landing, originally a bedroom, had been converted into a modern bathroom, with bath, loo and washbasin, when I first knew the house. They have now gone, and the room has been divided into two – a book store, and the Accounts Office.

Still farther along this landing still, and up the steps, the broom cupboard on the right of the staircase leading to the second floor has been converted into the entrance to a newly-created staff room beneath the Studio. The bedroom to the right of the staircase I remember as Nos. 8 and 8a. No. 8 a few years ago was the Friends' Library. In the 1940s there was a Friends' Library in a room on the second floor. On several of our long summer visits to Brantwood we occupied No 8, and our small daughter was in 8a. No. 8a had previously been a linen

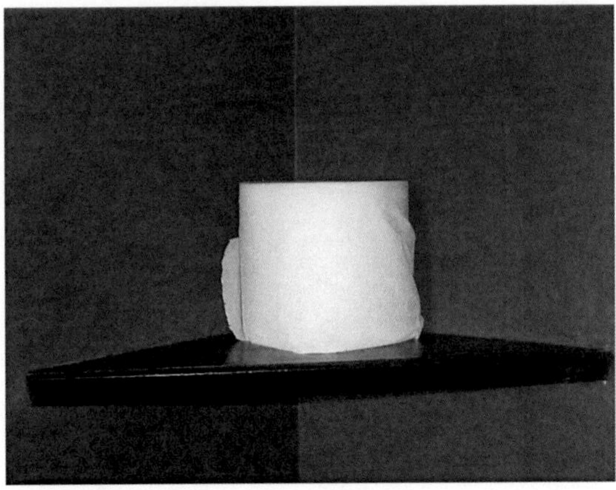

The triangular candle shelf still performs a vital, but different function today

room, with a large tank and wall pipes, all heated from the same hot water system which supplied the central heating system in the Studio above.

It is now Howard Hull's office, containing Warden's desk from his study at Bembridge, which I also used there for forty years.

At the beginning of this article I mentioned the car park. This reminds me of parking forty years ago. There was no car park then, except at the front door. Coaches were not allowed on that side of the lake without special police permission and a police escort. Eventually this prohibition was lifted as far as Brantwood when we provided rudimentary coach-turning space.

Coaches were few and far between, as indeed were visitors. An ageing population and increased leisure time means that there are now many more visitors to Brantwood than of yore. There are more now in the depths of winter than there were in the 1960s and '70s on a peak Saturday in August. Then, before the council banned parking on the lake side of the road, charging for car parking on our land at Beck Leven was a vital source of income.

Happily for Brantwood, times have changed. It is possible that the very occasional car passed Brantwood before 1900. It is just possible that Ruskin saw one. One thing it sure, we almost certainly will never know. Now there is a constant stream of visitors arriving by car and ferry.

XIII
MARGARET'S WELL

THE COMPANION, VOL. 1, NO. 4, 2008

Ruskin entitled the first chapter of his autobiography 'The Springs of Wandel'. Despite this the only reference to the river Wandel is limited to the final three lines of the chapter in which Ruskin refers to 'the cress-set rivulets in which the sand danced and minnows darted above the Springs of Wandel'.

The river Wandle – but let us use Ruskin's way – Wandel – has two main sources. The geological formation at the foot of the North Downs near Croydon means that there are a number of natural springs of water bubbling to the surface. Some of these form the Waddon ponds of the western edge of Croydon. From here the emergent Wandel flows west for about a mile and three quarters to Carshalton. At Carshalton are more ponds and the outflow from these merge with the water coming from Croydon to form the river Wandel. From this confluence the river turns north west and runs through Morden, Wimbledon and Earlsfield to a point between Putney and Wandsworth Bridges where it flows into the Thames.

In the early part of the nineteenth century the area was largely rural; along the Wandel's banks were large houses set in park land – Nelson lived at Merton Place on the Wandel. Most of these houses have gone, but some of the parks remain. Being quite fast-flowing, the lower reaches of the river powered many mills grinding corn, snuff, copper, oil and drugs. Water-wheels also powered paper mills, gunpowder mills; there were leather and skinning mills, breweries and firework and cattle-feed factories. In the summer of 1881 William Morris moved his textile weaving, dyeing and printing to Merton Abbey on the river. One of his chintz papers was called 'Wandle', to honour our helpful stream'.

By now the character of the river was changing as buildings spread along its banks. On 15 April 1883 Morris wrote to Ruskin[1] 'I should be very glad to see you at our place at Merton Abbey: though I fear it would be a grief to you to see the banks of the pretty Wandle so beset with horrors of Jerry-building: there is still some beauty left about the place however; & the stream is not much befouled'. May Morris remembered that 'there were ducks on the river and the stream was thick with trout'. The last trout recorded at Carshalton was in 1915 and one of the few sections of the river which still has a natural appearance is at Hackbridge, just below Carshalton, where the two branches of the river merge. Most of the old mills have disappeared, to be replaced by modern industrial estates and factories making paint, chemicals, plastics and electrical components.

There are many references in Ruskin's juvenile writings and memories reflecting his love of water. Indeed in his 'Springs of Wandel' chapter he writes about the waters of the *Tay* at the end of the garden of his Perth aunt – 'an infinite thing for a child to look down into'. It was not until 1874 when he was writing *Fors Clavigera* that Ruskin referred to his youthful delight in the Wandel – 'the stream to which my mother took me when a child to play beside'. This fascination with water continued throughout his life. Forty or fifty years later he was engineering harbours and waterfalls at Brantwood.

The river, and Carshalton, often drew Ruskin back to themselves. There are a number of references in his diaries in the late 1860s and early '70s to visiting Carshalton, and indeed his friends the Tylors lived there, as did his father's friend Mr Gassiot, and the author and journalist William Hale White. In 1866 Ruskin wrote about the pools at Carshalton in his introduction to *The Crown of Wild Olive*:

> Twenty years ago, there was no lovelier piece of lowland scenery in South England, nor any more pathetic, in the world, by its expression of sweet human character and life, than that immediately bordering the sources of the Wandel, and including the low moors of Addington, and the villages of Beddington and Carshalton, with all their pools and streams. No clearer or diviner waters ever sang with constant lips of the hand which 'giveth rain

from heaven'; no pastures ever lightened in spring-time with more passionate blossoming; no sweeter homes ever hallowed the heart of the passer-by with their pride of peaceful gladness, – fain-hidden – yet full-confessed. The place remains, or until a few months ago, remained nearly unchanged in its larger features; but with deliberate mind I say, that I have never seen anything so ghastly in its inner tragic meaning, – not in Pisan Maremma, – not by Campagna tomb, – not by the sand-isles of the Torcellan shore, – as the slow stealing of aspects of reckless, indolent, animal neglect, over the delicate sweetness of that English scene: nor is any blasphemy or impiety, any frantic saying, or godless thought, more appalling to me, using the best powers of judgement I have to discern its sense and scope, than the insolent defiling of those springs by the human herds that drink of them. Just where the welling of stainless water, trembling and pure, like a body of light, enters the pool of Carshalton, cutting itself a radiant channel down to the gravel, through warp of feathery weeds, all waving, which it traverses with its deep threads of clearness, like the chalcedony in moss-agate, starred here and there with the white grenouillette; just in the very rush and murmur of the first spreading currents, the human wretches of the place cast their street and house foulness; heaps of dust and slime, and broken shreds of old metal, and rags of putrid clothes; which, having neither energy to cart away, nor decency enough to dig into the ground, they thus shed into the stream, to diffuse what venom of it will float and melt, far away, in all places where God meant those waters to bring joy and health. And, in a little pool behind some houses farther in the village, where another spring rises, the shattered stones of the well, and of the little fretted channel which was long ago built and traced for it by gentler hands, lie scattered, each from each, under a ragged bank of mortar, and scoria, and bricklayer's refuse, on one side, which the clean water nevertheless chastises to purity; but it cannot conquer the dead earth beyond: and there, circled and coiled under festering scum, the stagnant edge of the pool effaces itself into a slope of black slime, the accumulation of indolent years. Half-a-dozen

> men, with one day's work could cleanse those pools, and trim the flowers about their banks, and make every breath of summer air above them rich with cool balm; and every glittering wave medicinal, as if it ran, troubled only of angels, from the porch of Bethesda. But that day's work is never given, nor, I suppose, will be; nor will any joy be possible to heart of man, for evermore, about those wells of English waters.[2]

From Carshalton, after this visit, Ruskin 'walked up slowly through the back streets of Croydon' where in the High Street he saw a newly-built public house with a narrow, useless area in front of it fenced by 'an imposing iron railing, having four or five spearheads to the yard of it' and he speculated that this stretch of railings represented a quantity of work which would have 'cleansed the Carshalton pools three times over'.[3] Ruskin was at Croydon and Carshalton again on 9 January 1870 and he noted in his diary that he 'saw Carshalton spring'.

Margaret Ruskin died on 5 December 1871 and four days later, just after her funeral at Shirley, the Tylors drove over from Carshalton to visit Ruskin at Denmark Hill. Juliet Tylor recalled 'Ruskin talked a great deal about Carshalton & Springs of Wandel… my father offered to help him about the Spring, which was polluted by being used as a washing place for various cabs and flys'. Tylor, whose academic subject was geology, was well suited to help Ruskin's developing pattern of social awareness and his attempts to help people. 1865 had seen the beginning of his housing scheme, 1871 his Seven Dials street-sweeping experiment, and the same year saw the very beginning of the Guild of St George, while 1874 saw the establishment of his Tea Shop and his providing useful employment for undergraduates – as well as another water/drainage scheme in the Hinksey Road.

Following the Tylors' visit to Denmark Hill, Ruskin wrote to his friend on 4 January 1872:[4]

> You will be wondering at my delay to put before you, in clear form, the request I have to ask you to present for me at Croydon. I wish to engage such workmen as may be recommended to me, resident at or near Croydon, and to pay them a fixed salary on condition

> of their keeping the pond and spring we looked at perfectly clean in every sense of the word; with daily watchfulness to remove any offensive substance thrown into it. Also, I wish to be allowed to plant the edge of it, at the side of the road, with grass and flowers – not intrerfering with the roadway nor with the present access to the spring – and to keep this flower border as pretty as the passers-by will let me keep it, at my own cost. Also, I desire to erect a low arch of marble, slightly sculptured in the manner of Pisan-Gothic, over the larger of the two springs, and to inscribe it to my mother's memory. I can come to Croydon to represent any matter farther to the proper authorities any day before the 20th of this month …

The Carshalton pond in question was behind the Police Station, on the corner of the now very busy West Street and Pound Street.

A. E. Jones, in his *Illustrated Directory of Old Carshalton* (*c.* 1970), explains that the pond's water, strictly speaking, was a manorial 'waste' and Ruskin could not do work on it without permission from the Manorial Court. The 1872 Court Rolls show that he was formally given 'liberty to make improvements in the rear of the Police Station by forming a dipping Well with Pathway thereto, and outlet from the pond, and, in so doing, to give the same facilities for the use of the Water as now exist, and to clean out the Pond at his own expense and continue to do so, and to plant Shrubs and Flowers by the Paths'.

Ruskin appears to have been helped in the initial stages of his project by George Brightling who was a Carshalton church warden. Perhaps the introduction was effected by Alfred Tylor.

Although called 'Margaret's Well', it is *really* a pool. Originally it was oval, and led into a sluice at the further point from the road, to allow the overflowing water to run on into the larger pond nearer to the village. According to Jones, the bottom of the pool was cemented and 'the seven tons of Cumberland boulders which [Ruskin] sent [from Coniston] to adorn the site are still there'. William Hale White, the journalist and author 'Mark Rutherford' who also lived at Carshalton, was a long-term correspondent with Ruskin. He wrote several pieces on the Well. In a short column in *The Nonconformist*

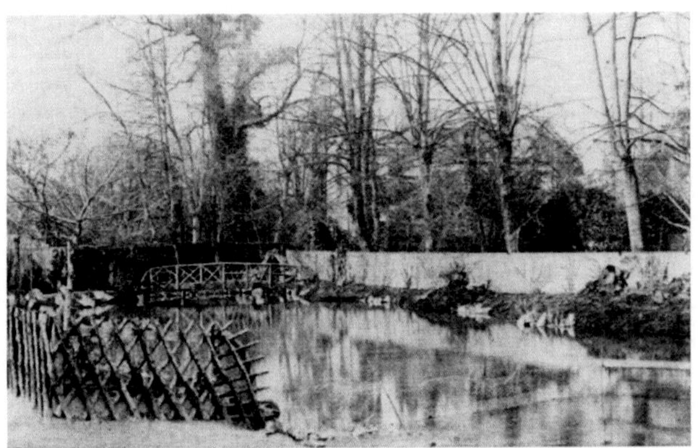

'Margaret's Well' at Carshalton, photographed about 1880. There is little resemblance to the Well as it is today

(11 September 1872) he mentioned that one of the ponds was still in a very neglected state and 'Mr Ruskin has determined to restore it at his own expense. It has been lined with flints, paved with sea-shore pebbles, fenced from the intrusion of cattle [the NFU is unable to tell me how far away the nearest cows *now* are!]; at once protected and developed. It is not yet finished but when it is complete it will be a worthy and characteristic monument to Mrs Ruskin's memory.' In another article in *The Norfolk News* (7 September 1872) Hale White adds that he understood that Ruskin intended 'to put a fountain in the middle'. This idea presumably had grown from Ruskin's 'low arch of marble … in the Pisan-Gothic manner' but never happened.

An inscribed tablet was erected at the Well by Brightling, presumably acting for Ruskin, which bears the words:

In obedience to the Giver of Life,
of the brooks and fruits that feed it, of the peace that ends it,
may this Well be kept sacred for the service of men,
flocks, and flowers,
and be by kindness called
MARGARET'S WELL.
This pool was beautified and endowed by
John Ruskin, Esq., M.A., LL.D.

Again, according to Jones, Brightling re-drafted Ruskin's original wording, and this, coupled with some mis-management of the operation of the sluice, led to Ruskin relieving Brightling of his responsibility. William Hale White then accepted responsibility for the Well until 1889 when he moved from the district. The inscription on the tablet may well have been changed from Ruskin's original draft because in his diary on 30 November 1880 he was working on a new draft which does not ever seem to have been used.

This Spring
In memory of a maid's life as pure
And a mother's love as ceaseless,
Dedicated to a spirit in peace
Is called by Croydon people,
Margaret's Well.
Matris animæ Joannes Ruskin
1880

Ruskin's ventures into hydraulic engineering were seldom successful, and Margaret's Well was no exception. Writing in December 1874 in *Fors Clavigera*,[5] Ruskin explained:

> At Carsalton, in Surrey, I have indeed had the satisfaction of cleaning out one of the springs of the Wandel, and making it pleasantly habitable by trout; but find that the fountain, instead of taking care of itself when once pure, as I expected it to do, requires continual looking after, like a child getting into a mess; and involves me besides in continual debate with the surveyors of the parish, who insist on letting all the road-washings run into it For the present, however, I persevere at Carshalton, against the wilfulness of the spring and the carelessness of the parish; and hope to conquer both; ...

Because of the constant care which was required, we find in Ruskin's accounts in *Fors*[6] on 20 January 1876 an entry 'Gift to Carshalton, for care of spring, £110'. He must have been disappointed with what he saw in early April of that year when he visited his father's old friend Mr Gassiot, and recorded in his diary 'I never saw such ghastly ruin of spring'. Perhaps it was about this time when Ruskin transferred its care to Hale White.

When Hale White left the district in 1889 the care of the pond was transferred to the Local Board, and about this time *Pile's Directory* described the site as 'a sylvan-like spot'.

The Police Station was demolished about 1899 and the Council then extended the pond forward towards Pound Street, making it rather more kidney-shaped. It was perhaps at this time that the engraved stone was removed, because writing in 1910 Cook & Wedderburn[7] explained that 'the tablet was at one time re-erected by a purchaser in a neighbouring garden'. It went through a chequered history. It was subsequently recovered by the Council, and put into one of their stores. Later, it was set into a pavement – inscribed side uppermost – leading to much wear. Eventually the council removed it, re-engraved it, set it into an iron framework, and restored it to the site where it can still be seen, together with a much more recent bronze plaque reading:

Heritage in Sutton
Margaret's Pool
This is one of Carshalton's ancient spring sites.
In the 1870s it was beautified by
The Art Critic John Ruskin
who had stone brought from Coniston to decorate the edges.
He named it in memory of his mother.
The inscribed stone was erected by George Brightling,
his local agent.

Today there are one or two large chestnut trees near the pool, which the Assistant Parks Manager tells me 'is maintained generally as a wild area with the grass and hydrangea bed maintained to a higher standard. The woodland part is allowed to develop fairly naturally, with the occasional clearance of Ash seedlings, and has large areas of ivy and wild garlic.'

The water table in the area must have changed since Ruskin's time and the pool is now usually dry and only tends to fill when other spring-fed water courses in Carshalton are full. The Environment Agency now controls part of the system by pumping water back upstream to ensure a constant flow to the main ponds. I am sure both this, and the iron railings which now surround the area, would not be entirely to Ruskin's mind! However, at least his mother's name is still remembered through 'Margaret's Pool'.

REFERENCES

1. N. Kelvin (ed.), *The Collected Letters of William Morris*, Princeton University Press, 1987, vol. II, pp. 186-7.
2. J. Ruskin, *The Crown of Wild Olive*, London: Smith Elder & Co, 1866, pp. [iii]-viii.
3. Ibid.
4. *Works* XXXVII, 47-48.
5. *Works* XXVIII, 204.
6. *Works* XXVIII, 531.
7. *Works* XXII, xxiv.

XIV

A LATE RUSKIN LETTER?

RUSKIN REVIEW AND BULLETIN, VOL. 4, NO. 1, 2007

My attention has been drawn recently to a 'Shorter Notice' in the *Burlington Magazine* of 1983,[1] entitled *'No old man's sorrow'; a new Ruskin letter*, by Matthew Levinger, when it was originally published.

The article relates to a letter purportedly written by Ruskin to one Clarence G. Hoag, on 22 December 1894. Clarence Hoag (1873-1968) graduated from Haverford College in 1893 and in the following year was studying in Germany. As the article points out, Hoag was a professor of English at several American colleges between 1898 and 1908. He later became an author and social reformer.

The inference drawn from the letter is that the young Hoag had met or corresponded with Ruskin prior to 1894 when, with this letter, Ruskin sent him a Dürer print from his collection – perhaps *Knight, Death and the Devil.* In the letter, which occupies four whole pages of a folded sheet, the engraving is described and discussed at length. As Matthew Levinger points out, Ruskin's analysis of the engraving had appeared in an almost identical form in *Modern Painters* v.

John Ruskin experienced a number of serious illnesses in the 1870s and '80s. The illness which overtook him in the latter half of 1889 left him incapable of further work and he remained at Brantwood from then until his death in January 1900. On many days during this period he was able to walk in his grounds, go out in his boat on Coniston Lake, visit neighbours or receive guests. But he undertook no further literary work.

Ruskin did, however, write a number of letters in his final eleven years. But from writing a dozen or more letters daily before his final illness, his letter-writing became dramatically curtailed. Between

1864 and early 1889 he wrote nearly 3000 letters to Joan Severn alone.[2] Following his breakdown and return to Brantwood from Seascale in 1889 he wrote only a further eight letters to her. Admittedly she spent more time at Brantwood with him, but by no means did she devote the entire eleven years to him.

Following his final retirement to Brantwood his letters can be charted with reasonable certainty. About 20 October 1893 he wrote to Susan Beever who was on her death-bed. This has been misleadingly described 3 as his 'last' letter; in fact it is his last letter to *Susan Beever*.[3] On 3 March 1894 he wrote nine lines to Lady Simon.[4] On 11 June 1894 he managed a half a page to Joan Severn.[5] What was probably his last letter to Joan, who was in London, was written nearly a year later, on 22 May 1895:

> Please come back quickly. Find I can't write letters now, and I don't like anything that's going on. all kinds of bother – but the weather's nice – come back & stop the plaguing trippers from everywhere.[6]

Probably his final letter sent to anyone, a faltering five lines, was written on 12 October 1895 to his old friend Sir John Simon.[7]

Possibly on 21 May 1898 he made two attempts to write to Mary Drew on the death of her father, W. E. Gladstone, but he could manage no more than: 'Dear Mary', and one barely legible line, 'I am very grieved at your having lost your father.'[8]

I do not think either of these attempts were posted. Probably Joan Severn wrote in his stead and the two attempts were kept at Brantwood. In addition to these letters there are twenty-four sheets of Brantwood notepaper bearing his very shaky autograph and dated between 1895 and 1898.[9]

In my opinion the Hoag letter is a clumsy fake. At the date in question – 1894 – I do not believe that Ruskin could have composed such a letter. In Frederick Hollyer's photograph of Ruskin sitting at Brantwood with Holman Hunt in September 1894, he is looking at Hunt in a bemused way, perhaps wondering who he was.

The Hoag letter is written on paper with a Vienna watermark. All

BRANTWOOD,
CONISTON LAKE,
R.S.O.

May 22nd 1895.

Dearest Joanie

J Ruskin

John Ruskin's letter to Joan Severn, 22 May 1895 (Ruskin Foundation)

135

My dear young friend:-

There is no old man's sorrow greater than the feeling that his life-work has been in vain. And now, when the critics see fit to class me with the "pilers of words on words" who "darken counsel", when the cause of Truth in which I have unceasingly laboured seems now no more prosperous than sixty years ago, it is no small comfort and delight to me to know that I have still fast friends among the young men, - young men to whom life and art are earnest. From them I hope all things.

To you, as to one of them who are to work after me in the cause, - not of "Ruskinism," but of Truth - I send this little reminder of an old man's regard. I must tell you that the good Knight has been a friend to me

The Hoag Letter, '22 December 1894', first page.
(Charles Roberts Collection, Haverford College)

through life, as Dürer's word of encouragement, and answer to those questions which must come to us all, especially in youth: and as such I give it to you now, trusting that what I tell you of it will be no mere mist of fine words, but will seem to you, as, in truth it is, justified by long and earnest living, and experience.

This Fortitude, then, commonly known as the "Knight and Death" represents a knight riding through a dark valley overhung by leafless trees, and with a great castle on a hill beyond. Beside him, but a little in advance, rides Death on a pale horse. Death is grey-haired, and crowned: — serpents wreathed about his crown; (the sting of Death involved in the kingly power). He holds up the hour-glass, and looks earnestly into the knight's face. Behind him follows Sin; but Sin powerless; he has been conquered and passed by, but follows yet, watching if any

The Hoag Letter, '22 December 1894', second page.
(Charles Roberts Collection, Haverford College)

way of assault remains. On his forehead are two horns, – I think, of sea-shell – to indicate his insatiableness and instability. He has also the twisted horns of the ram, for stubbornness, the ears of an ass, the snout of a swine, the hoofs of a goat. Torn wings hang useless from his shoulders, and he carries a spear with two hooks, for catching, as well as wounding. The knight does not heed him, nor even Death, though he is conscious of the presence of the last.

He rides quietly, his bridle firm in his hand, and his lips set close in a slight, sorrowful smile, for he hears what Death is saying; and he hears it as the word of a messenger who brings pleasant tidings, thinking to bring evil ones. A little branch of delicate heath is twisted round his helmet. His horse trots proudly and straight; its head high, and with a cluster of oak on the brow, where on the fiend's brow is the sea-shell horn. But the horse of Death stoops its head; and its rein catches the

The Hoag Letter, '22 December 1894', third page.
(Charles Roberts Collection, Haverford College)

little bell which hangs from the knight's horse-bridle, making it toll, as a passing bell. This was first pointed out to me by a friend — Mr. Robin Allen; it is a beautiful thought; yet, possibly, an after thought. I have some suspicion that there is an alteration in the plate at that place, and that the rope to which the bell hangs was originally the line of the chest of the nearer horse, as the grass-blades about the lifted hind-leg conceal the lines which cannot, in Dürer's way of work, be effaced, indicating its first intended position. But you may look for yourself when you are in Nürnberg in the Spring.

And now it only remains to wish you a 'Merry Christmas!' — I think my last on earth.

Your friend

J Ruskin

Brantwood, 22 December, 1894.
– To Mr. Clarence G. Hoag.

The Hoag Letter, '22 December 1894', fourth page.
(Charles Roberts Collection, Haverford College)

of Ruskin's letters of this period are written on a grey-green silurian paper with the die-stamped address, BRANTWOOD, / CONISTON LAKE, / R.S.O. This paper was certainly in use by 1893. Even in earlier letters written on unprinted paper, I have never known Ruskin put his address at the *end* of the letter, as in the Hoag letter, although the date does sometimes appear at the end. And I do not believe, in adding his correspondent's name, Ruskin would have prefixed it with the word 'To'.

The text of the letter was certainly not written by Ruskin. I have to admit that I do not recognise the hand. However, I *can* say that the letter was not written by Joan Severn, nor is it in the hand of her husband, Arthur. Sara Anderson acted as a secretary at Brantwood during this period, but the letter is not written by her. Neither is it in the hand of W. G. Collingwood, who also dealt with some of Ruskin's correspondence at this time.

I would suggest that the signature, 'J. Ruskin' is inexpertly copied from a letter written in the 1860s or 1870s. It will be noticed that the final stroke of the 'n' at the end of the name travels in an upward direction. In Ruskin's signature this stroke is invariably in a downward direction. And a cursory glance at Ruskin's late signature reproduced here will show that the signature on the Hoag letter bears little resemblance to Ruskin's writing in 1894.

The Hoag letter was given by Clarence Hoag to Haverford College Library, Pennsylvania, in 1949.[10] The Dürer engraving was not given to Haverford with the letter, and according to Mr Levinger,[11] Hoag's son did not recall ever having seen it.

Much work remains to be done on Ruskin's collection of Dürer engravings. We are not exactly sure of how many, or indeed, which engravings Ruskin owned, nor yet what precisely became of them all. There are references to Dürer in *Modern Painters* and *The Elements of Drawing*. He urged his Working Mens College drawing class to study Dürer engravings (presumably his). But we have no definite information about the total extent of his collection.

In December 1854 Ruskin made a list[12] – 'Albert [sic] Dürers. Value of – in my possession'. The list comprises twenty six engravings. Included in that number were three prints of *Melancholy*; there were three *Helmet* (one torn, one torn but fine), two *Adam and Eve* (one fine but torn, one poor), three *St Hubert* (one fine, one torn, one poor). There was one *Knight and Death*, which, valued at fourteen guineas, was the most valuable in the collection; a second torn print was valued at £3.

He continued to collect Dürer prints. In 1875 he bought a group of five prints and in Venice in March 1877 he was particularly pleased to find a print of *Venice*. But while he continued to collect, he had already begun to give prints away. In the 1870s he deposited a number of prints in his Oxford Drawing School Collection,[13] although some of these appear to have been subsequently withdrawn – apparently only leaving a *St Hubert*.

In the 1870s Ruskin gave six large and six small prints to the Guild of St George Collection.[14] A further fifteen were given to Whitelands College,[15] at the end of 1881. But Ruskin had not given away all of his Dürers for in the 1882 description of his painting of Ruskin in his study W. G. Collingwood refers to the chest with the velvet-cushioned top 'for framed Dürers'.[16]

But by the time of the Brantwood dispersal sales in 1930-31 the remaining Dürers seem to have disappeared. I find no trace of them in any of the sale catalogues. Because of our imperfect knowledge of Ruskin's Dürer collection we cannot tell whether or not an engraving was given to Professor Hoag.

REFERENCES

1. *Burlington Magazine*, vol. 125, no. 960, pp. 158-159, March 1983.
2. Ruskin Library, Lancaster University, RF L 33-54.
3. *Works*, XXXVII, 614. The original letter is in the Guild of St George Collection.
4. H. G. Viljoen, *Ruskin's Scottish Heritage*, Urbana: University of Illinois Press, 1956. fig. 15. Original: F. J. Sharp; H. G. Viljoen Pierpont Morgan Library.
5. RF L 53.
6. ibid.
7. H. G. Viljoen *op. cit.* Fig.16
8. RF L 29; Reproduced, J. S. Dearden, 'The Ruskin Galleries at Bembridge School, Isle of Wight', *Bulletin of the John Rylands Library*, vol. 51, No 2, Spring 1969, p. I.III – Chapter 1, above.
9. RF L 29.
10. Haverford College Library, Charles Roberts Autograph Collection, MS 135.

11. *Burlington Magazine*, *op. cit.*, p. 159, n. 13.
12. In his Diary, RF MS 8, p. 105.
13. *Works* XXI, 308.
14. *Works* XXX, 251.
15. *Works* XXX, 351.
16. J. S. Dearden, *John Ruskin. A Life in Pictures*, Sheffield: Sheffield Academic Press, 1999, p. 132.

XV

A TALE OF TWO CHURCHES: JOHN RUSKIN BUYS A PORCH, OR HISTORY REPEATS ITSELF

RUSKIN REVIEW AND BULLETIN, VOL. 10, NO. 2, 2014

In 1868 John Ruskin spent the late summer and early autumn in France, staying principally in Abbeville. He arrived there on 24 August and returned home on 21 October. A few days were spent in Paris with Charles Eliot Norton. There they met with Longfellow on several occasions, and the three men travelled together as far as Amiens, from where Ruskin returned to Abbeville. At Abbeville Ruskin was working on his lecture on 'The Flamboyant Architecture of the Valley of the Somme' and making an important series of drawings of the town, principally of the church of St Wulfran. Here too he wrote his paper *First Notes on the General Principles of Employment for the Destitute and Criminal Classes* – some of his ideas ultimately being put into practice with the Guild of St George.

Ruskin never travelled alone. With him in France this year was his valet, Frederick Crawley; he also took David Downs, his head gardener, who returned briefly to London on 30 September, perhaps taking with him to the printer the manuscript of the *Criminal Classes* paper. Both William Ward and Arthur Burgess, both artists and photographers, joined to help Ruskin with his work. On the day before he travelled to France, Ruskin had visited his friend Norton who was staying at Keston in Kent, and on 31 August he wrote to him, urging him to come to France: 'For it is dull here, somewhat – among the grey stones and ghastliness of Catholicism in decadence'.[1]

When Ruskin wasn't working on his series of drawings, he frequently took long walks in the area. In his diary for 1 September he recorded a number of wild flowers he had noticed, larkspur and

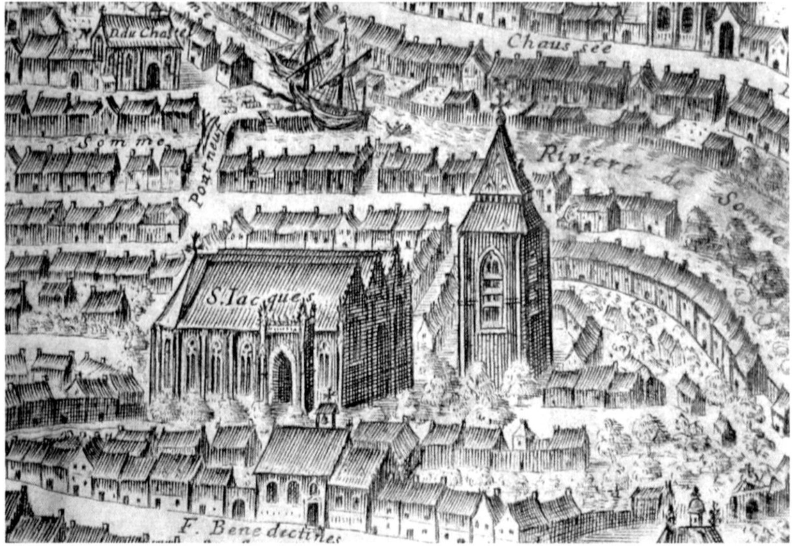

The church of St Jacques and its neighbouring bell tower. An enlarged detail from Robert Cordier's 1653 engraved panorama of Abbeville. (Courtesy of Bibliothèque d'Abbeville, coll. Macqueron)

yellow toadflax, which 'Downs says is a spring plant'. On another day he 'Took Crawley walk over hills to south, to high summit'.[2] On yet another day he 'Helped some boys to get their kite out of a tree'.[3] Ruskin was quite happy with the progress of his drawings, although he frequently had to contend with rain. On 27 September he noted: 'Everything round me horrible – my work good'.[4]

Ruskin was always disheartened to see old buildings being 'restored', or even worse, demolished. The old church of St Jacques (above), a short distance northwest from the centre of Abbeville, was in a state of decay, and work had just begun – or was about to begin – on its demolition, to make way for a replacement building for which the town had agreed to pay 150,000 francs over a period of ten years.[5]

Most of the municipal archives were destroyed during the war, so, largely, one must rely on published sources. Prarond maintains that St Jacques was originally built before 1136. Certainly there is a charter dated 1205 where St Jacques appears among the possessions of the collegiate church of St Wulfran.[6] So it was clearly built by that date.

There is reference again to the church being rebuilt, or possibly considerably extended, in 1482. The old church of St Jacques was a substantial building. Interestingly, a *separate* church tower was built in 1542. Perhaps this Italianate feature was an added attraction for Ruskin. He clearly regretted the imminent destruction of the church, which may have just begun before he arrived in the town. Paul de Motort, who was born on 22 July 1868, was – if not the last – then the penultimate child to be baptised in the old church when the removal of the floor flagstones was beginning.[7]

On 29 September Ruskin noted in his diary[8] that on the previous day he had 'photographed porch of St Jacques'. From there he went on to 'draw well, in colour, on Fishmarket'. Then he returned in the rain to St Jacques. The porch in question was probably that on the north side of the church (below). At this time a tributary of the

The porch of the church of St Jacques, from a lithograph by Delpech after Rouarge, n.d. (Courtesy of Abbeville Archives Municipales)

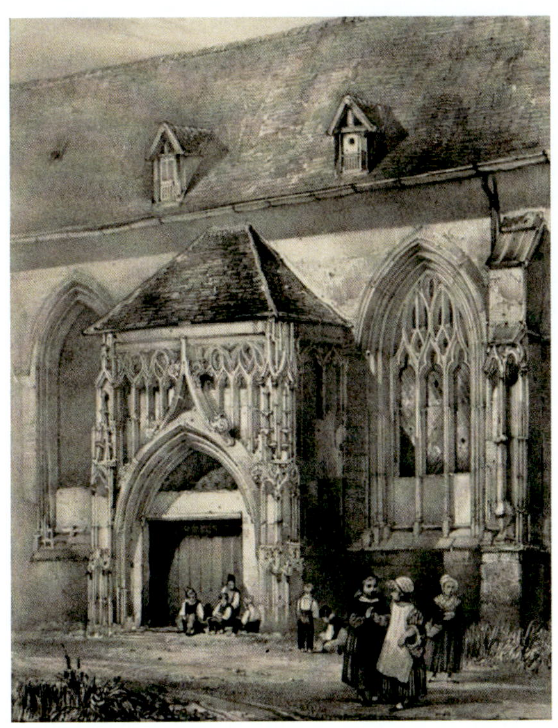

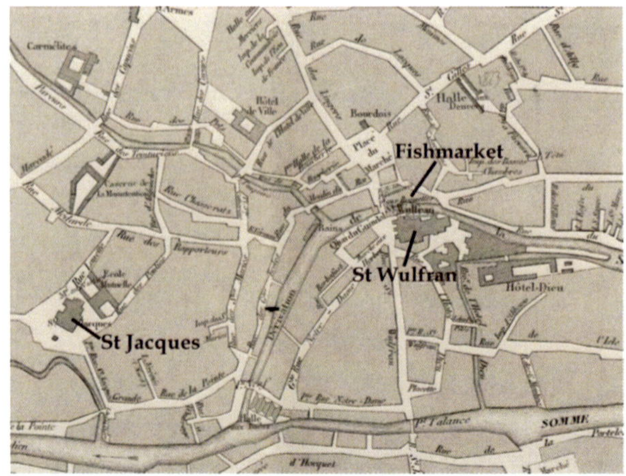

A map showing the relative positions of St Jacques, St Wulfran, and the Fishmarket. (Courtesy of Bibliothèque d'Abbeville)

River Somme looped through the town, skirting the north side of the church of St Wulfran. This waterway has now been covered over by a road (Avenue du Rivage), but in 1968 La Pouissonnerie – Ruskin's 'Fishmarket' – was on the opposite side of this tributary to St Wulfran (above).[9] On Ruskin's visits to the Fishmarket, when he 'drew well, in colour', he was almost certainly working on his beautiful watercolour of the north side of St Wulfran, which is now RF 1100 in the collection at Lancaster, and one of my favourite Ruskin watercolours (opposite).

When Ruskin says he photographed subjects it is not always quite clear what he actually means. Certainly on some occasions he probably did operate the camera himself, but on many other occasions the actual photography was done by his valet – at this time, Frederick Crawley. William Ward, who by now was also with Ruskin at Abbeville, was also a photographer. However on this occasion, judging from a reference in his diary, I think Ruskin employed a professional photographer. On 19 September he had noted: 'Y[esterday] worked disturbedly, photograph man getting his things run over'.[10]

On the same day that the porch was photographed, Ruskin wrote to Dora Livesey:

Well, what *am* I doing here? Drawing as well as I can, what will

> be destroyed next year of my favourite old flamboyant church – to justify my fancies of 1848 as far as they deserve or require, justification, and much more than that, to have some record of things that shall never more be, nor ever more seen by human sight in their present guise again.[11]

Ruskin was drawing again at the Fishmarket on 1 October 'after trying St Jacques'.[12]

> On the day before he had written to his mother: I have bought today, for five pounds, the front of the porch of the Church of St James. It was going to be entirely destroyed. It is worn away, and has little of its old beauty, but as a remnant of the Gothic of Abbeville – as I happen to be here, and as the church was dedicated to my father's patron saint (as distinct from mine) – I'm glad to have got it. It is a low arch, with tracery and niches and the Erbe della Madonna will grow over beautifully, wherever I rebuild it.[13]

Church of St Wulfran from the west with the river, by John Ruskin, 1868. (Ruskin Foundation)

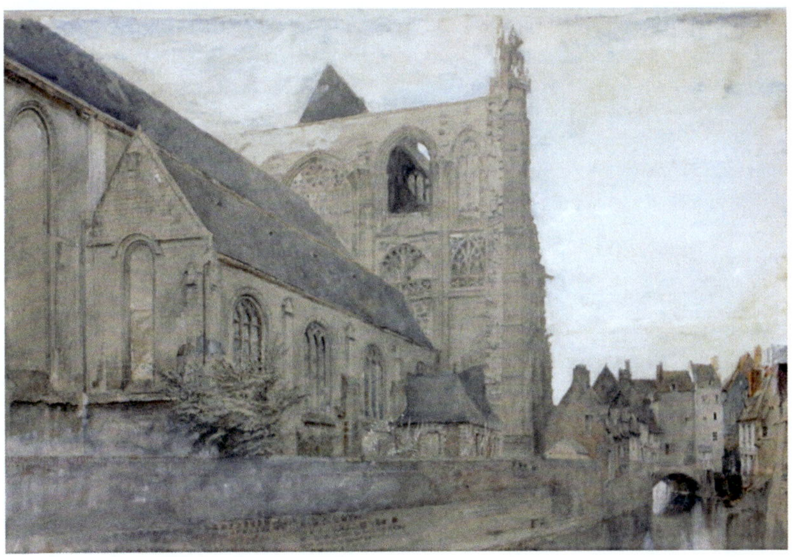

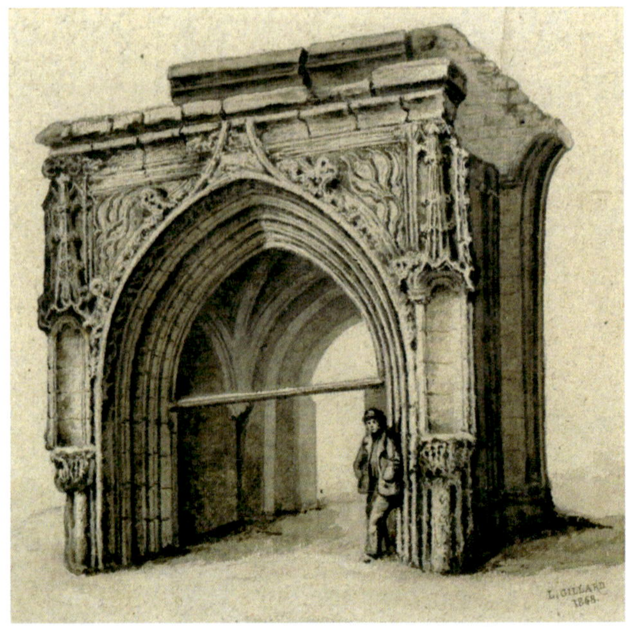

The porch of St Jacques by L. Gillard, 1868. (Courtesy of Abbeville Archives Municipales)

Writing later in the year to his friend Lady Mount-Temple, Ruskin explained why he had spent so much time in Abbeville:

> I worked hard during my two months in Abbeville – staying there, not going on to Verona, because I found the church there was to be destroyed this coming winter. I drew – for the first time in my life – as well as I could – and people like what I have done, & it will be of some value.[14]

As Ruskin explained to his mother, the porch is 'worn away'. As may be seen from the 1868 watercolour[15] by the Abbeville artist, Leon Gillard (above), it had suffered somewhat, perhaps during the actual demolition of the church itself. Perhaps soon after Gillard had painted the porch it was carefully pulled down, each stone being marked, packed, and dispatched to Denmark Hill. Clearly Ruskin intended to rebuild it somewhere – but what ultimately happened to it has long remained a mystery to me. My attempts to locate the porch have thus far remained unsuccessful. Perhaps it was never rebuilt. Many of the early plaster casts of architectural details which Ruskin had commissioned were given to the Architectural Museum in Westminster. Had the porch gone there too? This collection eventually passed to the Victoria & Albert Museum, but enquiries eventually revealed that the porch was not there. Many other enquiries were equally fruitless.

I knew from correspondence with the Abbeville Municipal Archivist that most of the town records had been destroyed. I thought perhaps the present church may have a record of the firm which demolished the church in 1868. Perhaps the firm was still in existence and had records to show what happened to the porch. Not knowing specifically to whom I should address my enquiry at St Jacques, I sought the advice of Cynthia Gamble. What *this* enquiry revealed was amazing! There was no one to whom I could write at St Jacques because the

The 'new' church of St Jacques, demolished in 2013, the spire having been long gone. (Courtesy of Abbeville Archives Municipales)

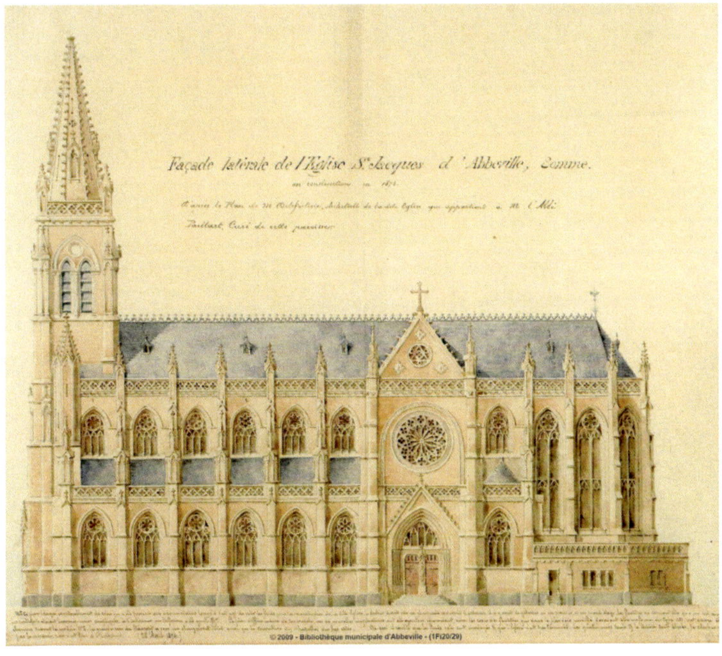

new, 1868, church (see p.181) had been demolished between February and April 2013. History had repeated itself. The large church had fallen into disrepair – and probably largely into disuse – and it was now proposed to turn the vacant space into a square, or perhaps even a car park.

Just as Ruskin had tried to preserve at least the porch of the medieval church, so some parts of its successor have been preserved. The font is now in the Musée Boucher de Perthes together with a crucifix; the organ and an old bell were also saved. An auction had been planned but did not take place. All of this was happening during the period when I was in correspondence with various Abbeville authorities regarding the 1868 demolition!

Meanwhile my attempts to discover what happened to the medieval porch have failed. Perhaps a future Ruskinian will succeed.

REFERENCES

1. *The Correspondence of John Ruskin and Charles Eliot Norton*, ed. by J. Bradley and I. Ousby (Cambridge: C.U.P., 1987), p. 113.

2. *The Diaries of John Ruskin*, ed. by J. Evans and J.H. Whitehouse (Oxford: Clarendon, 1956, 3 vols), pp. 652-3. Hereafter referred to as *Diaries*.

3. *Diaries*, p. 655.

4. *Diaries*, p. 656.

5. E. Prarond, *La Topographie Historique et Archaeologique d'Abbeville* (Paris: Dumoulin, 1830), vol. 2, p. 362.

6. Clovis Brunel, *Receuil des actes des comtes de Ponthieu*, 1062-1279 (Paris: Impr. Nationale, 1930), p. 268.

7. F.-C. Louandre, *Histoire ancienne et moderne d'Abbeville* (Abbeville: Boulanfer, 1834), pp. 534-4.

8. *Diaries*, p. 657.

9. Information from the Abbeville Archives Municipales.

10. *Diaries*, p. 655.

11. *My Dearest Dora*, ed. by O. Wilson (Privately published, 1984), p. 60.

12. *Diaries*, p. 658.

13. *Works*, XIX, xliii. The original letter is in the Whitehouse Collection at Lancaster, RF B VI.

14. *The Letters of John Ruskin to Lord and Lady Mount-Temple* (Ohio: Ohio State University Press. 1964), p. 176.

15. In the Abbeville Archives Municipales.

XVI

'THEY CAUGHT THE CAP OFF OF HIS HEAD':[1] WHAT HAPPENED TO CHARLES RICHARDSON?

RUSKIN REVIEW AND BULLETIN, VOL. 7, NO. 2, 2011

Some little time ago I was re-reading *Praeterita*. You will remember that in the seventh chapter of volume one – 'Papa and Mama' – Ruskin wrote about the death of his Croydon cousin, Charles Richardson.[2] Charles, only eight years his senior, was possibly the young Ruskin's favourite cousin. He had found employment with Smith, Elder & Co., the city firm which would ultimately become Ruskin's publisher. Charles often joined the Ruskins for Sunday dinner at 28 Herne Hill.

Charles's eldest brother, John, had emigrated to Australia and was building a successful career as a general trader. Seeing no real prospect of advancement with the publishers, Charles determined to join his brother in the Antipodes. Ruskin tells us that Charles joined his ship at Portsmouth, but she was anchored in the Solent for ten days to a fortnight, unable to sail because of adverse westerly winds. One day a small boat was going ashore for water and provisions, and Charles asked if he could go along for the trip. Five yards from the ship there was a sudden squall and the boat was capsized. One of the crew managed to snatch Charles's cap, but he 'went down like a stone'.[3] In *Praeterita* Ruskin tells us 'at last came word that his body had been thrown ashore at Cowes: and his father went down to see him buried'.[4]

Having known of this event for many years, I was surprised that I hadn't already sought Charles's grave. The summer weather being fine for a short while, I determined to seek out Charles. The first stage was easy. I telephoned the Assistant Curate of St Mary's Church at Cowes, the Rev. Kirsteen Morris; I had known her from her youth and in fact she is my daughter's god-mother. She put me onto her churchwarden, James Jones, who agreed to meet me at an appointed hour in the church.

In the church was a framed plan of the graveyard with the names of all of the graves marked. More or less in the same area were two Richardson graves, and we set out to find them. They were located in an area of the churchyard which in the past had been 'improved'. Many of the old headstones had been taken away in order that the area could be mown tidily. We found one Richardson tomb – but it was clearly not the right one because there was a whole family of Richardsons here; the other stone was not evident and must have gone in the tidying.

So there was no evidence of poor Charles here. The next stop was the County Records Office in Newport where lay deposited the Cowes Parish Registers. Archivist Richard Smout produced these for me – but there was no record of Charles's drowning on 22 January 1834. The next nearest church, albeit a mile or so inland, was at Northwood. These registers were also in the Records Office and were examined – but still no Charles. Knowing that Ruskin was frequently autobiographically inaccurate, I wondered for a moment if the story of poor Charles had been a figment of his imagination! Ruskin said that Charles's body had come ashore at Cowes and that his father had gone there to bury him. But there was neither physical nor documentary evidence to substantiate Ruskin's story. However, if Charles *hadn't* been drowned and buried at Cowes, then what *had* become of him?

The scent had gone cold, and there I let the matter rest, until a little while ago when Francis O'Gorman told me that he was preparing a new scholarly edition of *Praeterita* for the Oxford University Press. I asked him what he was doing about Charles Richardson, and told him my story. And this set me on the trail again.

Any maritime accident must be recorded in a Note of Protest at the office of the locally-appointed solicitor. It occurred to me that the drowning of a passenger would probably have to be recorded and I telephoned the Records Office to ask if they had Notes of Protest. They had several volumes, but of course not the period covering 1834, nor did they know where they would be, even if they had survived. I told

Simon Dear, to whom I was speaking, the reason for my enquiry. 'Have you checked our card index?' I was asked. I hadn't. Mr Dear checked and reported that they had a card for a 'B. Richardson' who died in 1834 and was buried at Wootton. Wootton parish is some four miles east of Cowes.

This was neither the right village nor the right Richardson. But since Charles was still missing, I thought I ought to see this entry in the registers of St Edmund's Church at Wootton. I sent off my cheque and a photocopy of the entry duly arrived. Intriguingly, it read:

> A man unknown supposed from the name engraved on the knife in his pocket and written in his boot to have been B. Richardson. Found on the shore of Wotton [*sic*] Parish. May 22nd 1834.

Now here was a coincidence; C. Richardson, drowned on 22 January and B. Richardson found drowned on 22 May. Were *two* Richardsons likely to have been drowned in the Solent within four months of each other? On the other hand, I asked myself, was it possible for Charles to have been in the water for four months and still be wearing his clothes? Remember, he was identified from the name engraved on his pocket knife; this presupposed that he still had a pocket with him. And of course Charles wasn't 'B. Richardson'. However, I supposed that the vicar or sexton could have misread the engraved inscription – or the knife could have belonged to Charles's mother, Bridget, and been given to him as a leaving present.

Bembridge, where I live, is another seaside village. I consulted my friendly neighbourhood undertaker. I told him the story and expressed my worry about Charles still having a pocket about his person after four months in the water. I was assured that this was indeed possible. So 'B. Richardson' of Wootton was worth following up. A phone call to the vicar, the Rev. Cath. Abbott, led to an appointment with her Archivist, Mrs Doreen Gazey, and we met by appointment at the church. Happily, Mrs Gazey was interested in my quest, and she had an old list of all the gravestones, their numbers, and their inscriptions.

She took me to the grave, located on the north (seaward) side of the church, near the boundary wall. The limestone headstone is

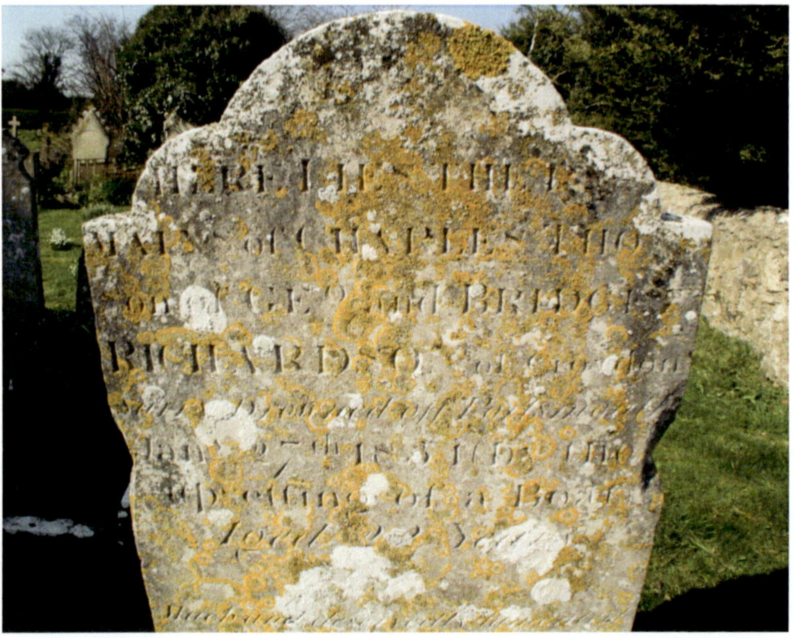

The headstone of the grave of Charles Richardson at Wootton. (Photograph by kind permission of Mrs Doreen Gazey.)

much eroded and lichen-covered, with its inscription barely legible. However, happily, a transcript had been made when it was less eroded, showing that this was the grave of:

> Charles Thos. Son of George and Bridget Richardson of Croydon, Surrey. Drowned off Portsmouth. January 27th [*sic*] 1831 [*sic*] (by the upsetting of a boat) aged 22 years.

The inscription was undoubtedly already weathered when the old transcription was made, and a '7' could be mistaken for a '2', and a '1' for a '4'. This was undoubtedly our Charles, and since there was no other earlier entry in the parish register for our Charles, then he clearly *had* been in the Solent for four months. And Cowes, and 'off Portsmouth' are not too far from being equidistant from Wootton.

But Ruskin appears to have been inaccurate after all. I am indebted to Francis O'Gorman for drawing my attention to a death notice in the *Bristol Mercury* of – strangely – 8 February 1834: 'Drowned by the upsetting of a boat off Portsmouth, on the 27th ult. Charles Thomas Richardson, in the 27th year of his age, son of Mr George Richardson of Croydon.'

One outstanding problem remains, and is likely probably to remain so. What were the lines of communication? Presumably the Master of the ship must have had a record of Charles's home address, and informed the parents of his drowning. Local authorities must have also been alerted because four months later – the ship having long gone – the vicar of Wootton was able to notify George and Bridget Richardson that their son's body had been found.

REFERENCES

1. *Works*, XXXV, 137.
2. *Works*, XXXV, 135-137.
3. *Works*, XXXV, 137.
4. Ibid.

XVII
JOHN RUSKIN'S POTTERY

RUSKIN REVIEW AND BULLETIN, VOL. 4, NO. 3, 2008

Other than his own homes, John James Ruskin did not normally invest in real estate. Thus one is surprised to read in his Account Book the entry on 16 May 1853. 'By (*sic*) Freehold Pottery £1250', and wonder just what he was doing, buying a Pottery which turns out to have been in Deptford. He adds that his expenses were £17 4s. Other entries in his accounts do not throw further light on the property except to show that he received £13 quarterly in rent from Mr Jee.

John James Ruskin continued to own the property until his death in 1864 when with almost all of his other possessions it was inherited by his son. Curiously, neither Ruskin nor his solicitors appear to have been particularly anxious to tie up the loose ends relating to JJR's estate. In the 1890s W. G. Collingwood refers to a 'Conveyance of Pottery – Greenwich to J. Ruskin, 1867' as being among the papers at Brantwood. Ruskin also refers to this Conveyance in a note at the front of his 1875 Diary,[1] 'Deeds for Potteries Freehold in Deed Box at Brantwood with other deeds.'

Other than actually owning the Greenwich property Ruskin seemed to take little interest in it, although he *does* refer to it – for the first time I think – in *Fors Clavigera* Letter 4 (April 1871)[2] when discussing utility and wealth:

> I have a bit of low land at Greenwich, which, as far as I see anything of it, is not money at all, but only mud: and would be of as little use to me as my handful of gravel in the drawer, if it were not that an ingenious person has found out that he can make chimney-pots of it: and, every quarter, he brings me £15 off the price of his chimney-pots: so that I am always sympathetically glad

> when there's a high wind, because then I know my ingenious friend's business is thriving. But suppose it should come into his head, in any less windy month than this April, that he had better bring me none of the price of his chimneys? And even though he should go on, as I hope he will, patiently, – (and I always give him a glass of wine when he brings me the fifteen pounds), – is this really to be called money of mine? And is the country any richer because, when anybody's chimney-pot is blown down in Greenwich, he must pay something extra, to me, before he can put it on again?

Tim Hilton reports that Ruskin wrote to George Allen in the early 1870s, asking why the usually punctual Mr Jee 'has not come to pay the rent on my brickyard at Greenwich'. Later in the decade Mr Jee was having financial problems. In discussing his accounts in *Fors Clavigera* Letter 74 (February 1877)[3] Ruskin reported:

> My Greenwich property usually brings me in £60, but I remit most of the rent, this year, to the tenant, who has been forced into expenses by the Street Commissioners. He pays me £24 16s 9d.

Writing again in *Fors Clavigera* Letter 76 (April 1877)[4] Ruskin described what he had inherited from his father and how he was gradually parting with his inheritance. In listing his inheritance he refers to 'his [father's] freehold property at Greenwich' and a couple of pages farther on[5] he lists 'In funded cash something more than fifteen thousand pounds ... Greenwich freehold – twelve hundred...' 'The Greenwich property was my father's and I am sure he would like me to keep it. I shall keep *it** therefore ...'

Perhaps Thomas Carlyle noticed the Greenwich reference in the April *Fors* and asked Ruskin about it, for on his father's birthday, 10 May 1877,[6] he told Carlyle:

* In the previous paragraph he had said that he intended giving his Marylebone houses to the Guild of St George.

> That Pottery, field *chiefly*, the buildings very shabby I believe – I've never seen it!!! – is – and will be, mine.

However, despite Ruskin's protestations that he would keep the Pottery because it had been his father's, Cook & Wedderburn, in a footnote,[7] observe that Ruskin sold his properties 'when opportunity offered of increasing the Brantwood Estate'.

Ruskin appears to have sold the Greenwich property about 1879-80. This date would coincide with the first major extension to Brantwood after the 1871 Turret Room. In 1879 Ruskin gave up his rooms at Corpus Christi College, Oxford, and the pictures, books, bookcases, mineral cabinets and much other furniture was moved to Brantwood, thus presenting a housing problem. It was at this time that the new dining room was built at the southern end of the house, leaving the rather dreary old dining room to become a secondary library and store. Then in 1881 work began on the building of a new stable block, some of the second floor was added to the house, and in 1883 Jackson Low Wood – behind and above the stables – was bought. No doubt these are the additions to the estate to which Cook & Wedderburn referred. All of this would have help absorb the Pottery money!

So what do we know about Ruskin's pottery? Very little really. It was in existence from about 1838 until 1879-80. It occupied land on Blackheath Road, Greenwich, next door to a public house called the White Swan, and within a couple of doors of the Blackheath Road Police Station. Throughout its forty years the pottery had only one tenant, Thomas Pottle Jee. It probably went out of business on Jee's retirement. The Rate Books list Jee as occupier in 1879, but the whole entry was deleted in 1880 when the premises were empty, and it seems probable that this was when Ruskin sold the property, the pottery was demolished and the site re-developed. By 1903 there was a small grocery shop on the site.

Finally, why did John James Ruskin buy the pottery? The Rate Books for the early 1850s show that the property was owned by a 'Mr Ritchie'. Combining the name Ritchie with the knowledge that JJR did not normally invest in real estate, but had a clerk called Henry Ritchie, led me to evolve a nice theory.

Ritchie is a Scottish name and family correspondence[8] reveals that the Ruskins knew various Ritchies. But whether these Ritchies were related to Henry who became JJR's clerk in 1833[9] is unclear. He may well have been employing a family friend. Certainly the two clerks, Henry Ritchie and Henry Watson, dined regularly with the Ruskins.

My theory was that Henry Ritchie's father died, the family fell on hard times, and as an act of charity, John James Ruskin bought the pottery from them. Unfortunately I have been unable to prove this theory and it seems probable that I am wrong.

Julian Watson the Local History Librarian at Blackheath in 1978 (when this inquiry began) explains to me that the 'Mr Ritchie' of the Rate Books was probably Alfred Ritchie, who would have been forty one when JJR bought the Pottery. The 1851 census described him as a sand and stone merchant with six children – none of which was called Henry – and he didn't die until 1879 by which time his home was near Stroud. I am also indebted to Mr Watson for looking through the Greenwich Census Returns and telling me that he found no other Ritchie who had a son called Henry.

So there my research foundered. We know a *little* more about Ruskin's pottery, but we are no nearer knowing *why* John James Ruskin bought it.

But all was not entirely lost. My own visit to the Greenwich Archives Office added nothing further to the information I already had about the Pottery. However, interestingly, the Archives Office is now in a building within Woolwich Arsenal, bordering one side of the former parade ground and immediately adjacent to the former Royal Military Academy building where Ruskin delivered his lecture 'War' on 16 February 1866. And nearby was the Royal Artillery Institution where he lectured on 'the Future of England' on 14 December 1869.

REFERENCES

1. RF MS 20.
2. *Works* XXVII, 69.
3. *Works* XXIX, 50.

4. *Works* XXIX, 100.
5. *Works* XXIX, 102.
6. G. A. Cate (ed.), *Correspondence of Thomas Carlyle and John Ruskin*, 1982, 237.
7. *Works* XXIX, 102, n. 4.
8. V. A. Burd (ed.), *The Ruskin Family Letters*, 1973, 33. Catherine Ruskin to John Thomas Ruskin, 11 July 1809; p. 213, Margaret Ruskin to John James Ruskin, 8 December 1829.
9. M. Lutyens, *The Ruskins and the Grays*, 1972, 145. Writing to Mr Gray on 31 August 1848 JJR told him that Ritchie had been with him for fifteen years.

XVIII
THE BRANTWOOD BOOKS

THE FRIENDS OF RUSKIN'S BRANTWOOD NEWSLETTER, AUTUMN 2006

One of the presents my parents gave me at Christmas 1950 was a *Collins One Day Standard Diary 1951*. It is a hard-bound foolscap (for the young, that is 12¾" x 8") volume and you might wonder what use that might be to a nineteen years old chap presently engaged in doing his National Service – I see that it is signed on the fly-leaf 'James S. Dearden 2/Lt'.

I did not, of course, use it as a diary, but my parents knew it would be useful to me and in fact I have used it ever since. I must have first used it in 1952 – or possibly '53, because the first notes are on the exporting of Hereford cattle to America, in which subject I happened to be interested then.

At the back of the book I began a list called 'Suggestions for possible articles and research'. It was while idling through this list recently that I came across 'Brantwood Books (mine)' and it seemed to me that the opportunity had come to cross this off the list.

It must have been in the summer of 1957 that we were staying with my parents in the flat at Bridge House, Coniston, that the Wilsons then let to visitors. My parents had known the brothers and their mother for some time, and during the visit, knowing my interest, they gave me the 'Brantwood Books', together with the Log Book of Torver School, 1875-1927, which my mother had attended sporadically.

Strictly speaking there are two Brantwood Books, albums of card leaves bound in half green calf and oatmeal buckram, 10¾" x 14½", lettered in gilt on the front boards, Brantwood I and Brantwood II. There is a third volume of roughly the same size, containing photographs – principally groups of Exeter College, Oxford, undergraduates including young Arthur Severn. Here too are a number of good photographs of the Heythrop with which Arthur and his sister Lily used to hunt. (Lily, apparently was rather short-sighted, and thus a severe danger to anyone in the hunting field!) There are also a number of small photographs of Arthur, Lily and Violet Severn with horses outside the Brantwood coach house.

The first volume of the Brantwood Books is the more interesting. A note by Arthur Severn snr. on the first leaf, dated 1883-4, describes the contents.

> The Brantwood Book
>
> A collection of drawings & scraps, &&&, chiefly relating to the children and their doings at Brantwood, some by the children themselves, but the most part, by friends who came to tea in the 'cool 'oom' as Miss Violet aged 4 chooses to call that delightful room! And 'Mr Bussy', who started this book – hopes that in future years it will serve to remind them of the Happy days spent at Brantwood, and of their too kind 'Di Pa'. 1883-4

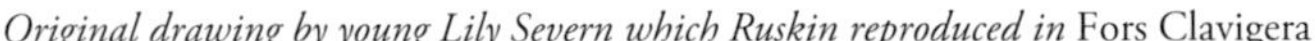
Original drawing by young Lily Severn which Ruskin reproduced in Fors Clavigera

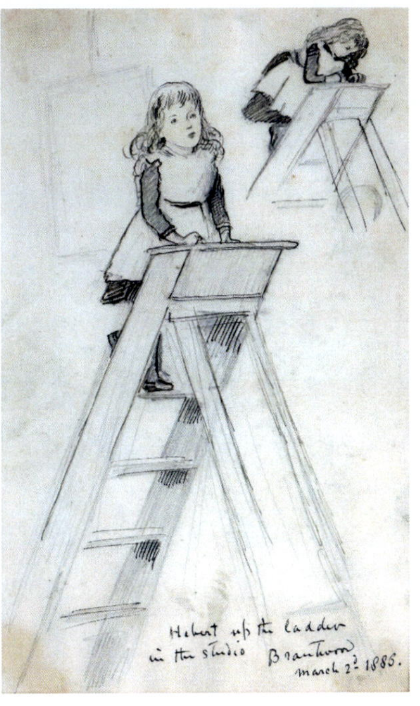

Arthur Severn's sketch of his youngest son Herbert, in the Studio

The content is primarily Severn, but there *are* Ruskin connections. For example, on the next page is an original drawing inscribed by Joan Severn 'By Lily 18th Jany 1880' (opposite). It is the drawing which Ruskin reproduced in *Fors Clavigera* Letter 95 (October 1884 – *Works* XXIX, 508) to illustrate the harmony between a child's way of teaching itself to draw and write. Accompanying it is a proof of the engraving, inscribed by Arthur, 'These drawings are by Lily. Jany 18th 1880. No 2 is a wood cut – Profr. Ruskin had it engraved for his 'Fors'. He was much interested in the original!'

The album contains many other childishly indifferent drawings preserved by their fond parents, most of them of little interest. The main interest lays in the drawings by Arthur Severn and Laurence Hilliard contained in the volume, although there *is* one Ruskin sketch – of a sailing boat in rough water, inscribed by Joan, '3 Feby by the Professor 1889' – just five days before his seventieth birthday and while he was still active.

On early pages are drawings of boats by Hilliard, a pencil head and shoulders portrait of Agnew Severn by his father, 17 September 1885, and a sketch of a young Arthur and Agnew fishing from a boat on the lake a few weeks earlier. Here too is the nice portrait sketch of Arthur Severn by Hilliard, which I reproduced in 1967 in *The Professor*.

There are portrait sketches by their father of the young Arthur and Agnew, about 1881, and drawings of Lily and Herbert on a stepladder in the Studio, dated 1886 (above). These are important in showing that the studio had been built by 1886. I had always assumed that the

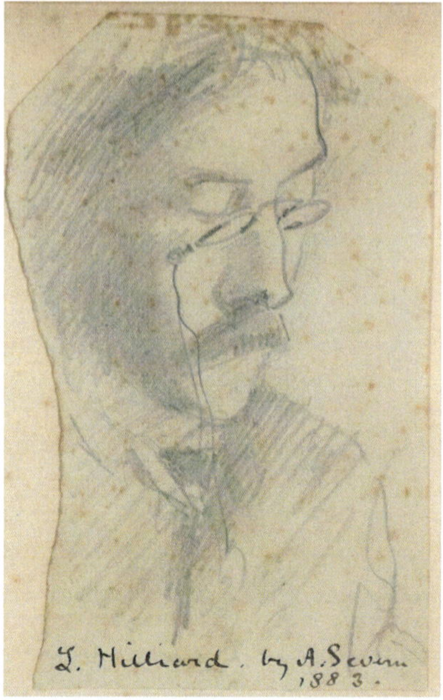

Laurence Hilliard by Arthur Severn, 1883

date 1892 cut into one of the roof window struts was the date of its building, but clearly I was wrong.

On one page are three little sketches of ladies who must be Joan, Mattie Gale and Alice Rathbone, sitting in the evening of 26 February 1880 listening to a reading by Ruskin from *The Antiquary*. Mattie Gale, a relation of the Severns, was already at Brantwood when Alice Rathbone arrived on the 21st and there was another reading from *The Antiquary* on that evening while, as Ruskin noted in his diary, Arthur and Hilliard drew serpents which Ruskin was later to exhibit when lecturing at The London Institution. This same page also has a portrait of Hilliard by Severn (left).

Another page has a watercolour and pencil sketch of a yacht sailing on the lake in 1883, and from the same year, three sketches of the Jumping Jenny, *sailing*, and inscribed by Severn, 'by L. Hilliard – a boat he started for the Professor!' Severn has dated these sketches 1883 but I believe them to be earlier. The Jump was designed by Hilliard and his model of her in the Coniston Museum is rigged to sail although the finished boat, launched at Easter 1879, was never so used.

Boats feature frequently. Another page has sketches of boats by Hilliard together with one by Severn of 'Kismet yawl 10 tons belonging to Q[uartus] Talbot Esq of Barmouth. I sailed with him to Carnarvon Castle, we had to beat all the way, much struck with the castle, want to go back and paint it. Aug 18th 1885.' And again, 'Mr Grafton's boat at Heysham. I hope to buy it some day for this lake.

1886.' On the same page is a not very flattering drawing of the very hirsute Rev. Charles Chapman, 'This is a portrait of our vicar, Coniston' (below).

Portraits abound – Agnew by Hilliard, Lily or Violet by Collingwood, 'Punchard' by Agnew, various musicians at the Ambleside Choral Society's performance of *Elijah*, 4 April 1893, a photograph of Sir Henry Acland 'in my boat', a slightly scurrilous tennis-playing Arthur by Reginald Barratt, and an ink drawing of a lady 'by AS 1884 drawn to amuse Norma Druce. Mr and Mrs Walter Druce stayed here for some weeks Aug-Sep 1884. We had great fun – especially about Wedderburn and "Dave", a sweet collie we brought here to Brantwood – the dog belonged to a Mr Alexander, an actor – who, at this time was away in America with Irving.' Ruskin had sold the lease of his Denmark Hill house to the Druces in 1872.

Towards the end of the first volume is a page of drawings, which I reproduced in an article for *Country Life* in 1978 of various scenes: walking, skating, a table and chairs laid for tea, on the frozen Coniston Lake on 4 March 1895. 'There has only been a winter like this – Lake District – once in the last 30 years'.

On the last page of this album are pasted two invitations, Arthur Severn's invitation to the Delhi Coronation Durbar, January 1903, and a card for Mr and Miss [Lily] Severn, the Viceroy's invitation to a Ball at the Diwan-i-Am, Delhi Fort, 6 January 1903, at 9.30 p.m.

Rev. Charles Chapman, by Arthur Severn

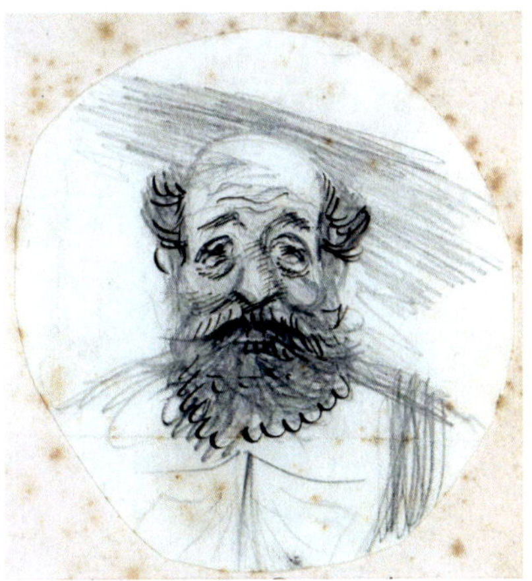

The second Brantwood Book contains more photographs than drawings, although there is a sketch of 'The Royal George on which Herbert [Severn] sailed to Canada 10 Sept 1910'. There is a sketch of Arthur Severn on the tennis court on 16 April 1911, and a rather nice pencil sketch by Severn of 'Miss Eva asleep over her sandbag [sewing] 21 October 1915'. Eva Walsh was a friend of the Severns and their children. I knew her many years later as Mrs Constantinesco. I had this sketch photographed for her, and in acknowledging it, her son, Richard Litton wrote on 24 June 1975 – sixty years later – saying that his mother 'vividly recalls the afternoon when she, Arthur and Joan Severn, were sitting after lunch and the memorable sleep took place'.

This second volume contains quite a lot of Eva Walsh's photographs, and photographs by others taken at Brantwood. There is a squirrel sitting on a chair in the study by an open window, a Victoria and a pair of bays on the road in front of the lodge, and various views of the elderly Joan and Arthur in the grounds – Joan sitting by

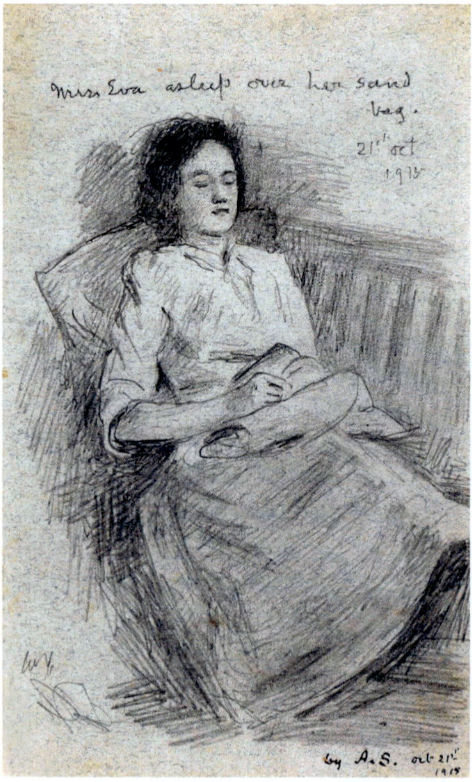

Miss Eva asleep over her sandbag [sewing] 21 October 1915, drawn by Arthur Severn

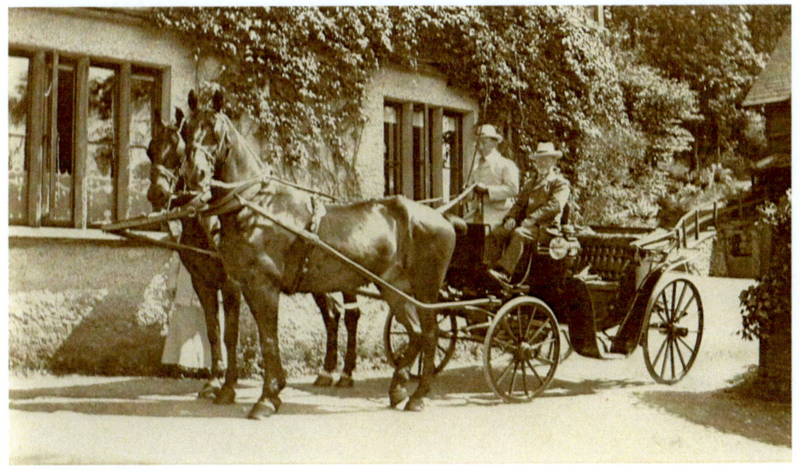

The Severns' Victoria outside the Brantwood Lodge

the side of the dining room, Arthur painting near the High Walk, Joan in the kitchen garden with the glasshouses behind her, groups on the new tennis court, and other interesting views.

Among the photographs is a series, with newspaper cuttings, of the first wedding in New College, Oxford, of Ellen, daughter of the Warden, Rev. W. A. Spooner, and Lt A. J. L. Murray, R.N. at which the Archbishop of Canterbury officiated. There is also similar coverage of the New College wedding of her sister Catherine to Campbell Dodgson of the British Museum. I assume the Severns had become friendly with the Spooners when young Arthur had been at Oxford. Apparently, during his four years at Oxford his only achievement has been to win a fly-casting competition!

And finally there is a newspaper cutting and photograph inscribed by Arthur Severn, 'My niece Margaret Smith whose husband is now Attorney General'.

The two Brantwood Books present an interesting view of life and activities at Brantwood during the last twenty years of Ruskin's life, and of how it continued almost to the end of Joan's life.

IXX

'OLD MAISIE'

THE FRIENDS OF RUSKIN'S BRANTWOOD NEWSLETTER, SPRING 2014

ఌ

Inevitable limitations on the space available to him in his admirable recent edition of *Præterita* meant that Francis O'Gorman was only able to devote five lines to 'Old Maisie,' the housekeeper at John James Ruskin's offices at 7 Billiter Street in the city of London. Perhaps I may re-print extracts from the seventh chapter of *Præterita* in which Ruskin described his father's office.

> My father's counting-house was in the centre of Billiter Street… His counting-house was a room about fifteen feet by twenty, including desks for two clerks, and a small cupboard for sherry samples, on the first floor, with a larger room opposite for private polite receptions of elegant visitors, or the serving of a chop for himself if he had to stay late in town. The ground floor was occupied by friendly Messrs Wardell and Co., a bottling retail firm, I believe. The only advertisement of the place of business was a brass plate under the bell-handle, inscribed 'Ruskin, Telford and Domecq,' brightly scrubbed by the single female servant in charge of the establishment, old Maisie – abbreviated or tenderly diminished into the 'sie' from I know not what Christian name – Marion, as Mary into Mause. The whole house, three-storied, with garrets, under her authority, with, doubtless, assistant morning charwoman – cooking, waiting, and answering the door to distinguished visitors, all done by Maisie…

In the first chapter of *Præterita* Ruskin had already explained that

No.7 Billiter Street belonged to Henry Telford, of Widmore near Bromley, one of the three partners in the business.

The national census of 1851 lists Elizabeth Skeane as being the housekeeper, or 'General Servant' at 7 Billiter Street. She had been born in 1808 at Headley Down, Surrey, and was forty three years of age at the time of the census. Headley is on the B2033 road some couple of miles south east of Leatherhead. Ten years later the census of 1861 lists Isabelle M. Skeen as the Housekeeper. She was then fifty years old and had been born in Kent at North Cray. Also staying there on the day of the census was the thirty four years old Angela Skeen, a 'Visitor' and perhaps a younger sister. Presumably it was this Isabelle M. Skeen of whom Ruskin wrote.

Judging by the slender evidence available, I assume that Elizabeth and Isabelle were sisters and the family had moved from Surrey to Kent after Elizabeth was born.

And if I may speculate further, since North Cray, the birthplace of Isabelle, is a very short distance from Bromley, near where Henry Telford lived, perhaps the Skeane/Skeen sisters were appointed by Telford. Indeed it would make sense if Telford actually employed the Housekeeper, since she was in charge of the building which also provided office space for Wardell and Co.

Unfortunately the account books of Ruskin, Telford and Domecq do not seem to have survived, and I know of no Telford accounts, to check these assumptions. Interestingly John James Ruskin's personal accounts for 1862 include an entry under the heading Charities and Gifts, 'Dec 25 Skene 20/-.'

So 'Old Maisie' was almost certainly Miss Isabelle M. Skeen, or Skeane, or Skene.

XX

A RUSKIN BOOK WITH AN INTERESTING BACKGROUND

THE FRIENDS OF RUSKIN'S BRANTWOOD NEWSLETTER, SPRING 2012

❧

In book collecting terms an 'association copy' is a book which has something which lifts it out of the ordinary. For example I have on my shelves a copy of the third edition of Ruskin's *Aratra Pentelici*, and they don't come much more ordinary than that! But what makes this a rather nice 'association copy' is the fact that it contains the bookplate of the great Victorian painter, G. F. Watts, and it is inscribed to him by his wife. A first edition of Ruskin's *Time and Tide* is a rather more collectable book, but what makes my copy an even more desirable 'association copy' is the inscription at the head of the title page from Ruskin to his valet Frederick Crawley.

Another rather nice 'association copy' which I acquired a little while ago is a copy of the first edition of *Hortus Inclusus*.

In 1827 William Beever and his family – his son John and his four daughters – moved from Manchester to Coniston where they settled at The Thwaite, the house on rising ground across the road from the present Waterhead Hotel. William Beever died four years later; his wife had already died some years earlier. The children continued to live at The Thwaite.

John Beever was a keen angler. He wrote a book called *Practical Fly Fishing*. At his house he had a fish pond where he regularly examined and studied its occupants. He also liked to experiment with different types of fishing rods. In these experiments he was helped by the seventeen years old carpenter William Bell. Probably also about now Bell built a printing press for Beever. His sister Susanna was a lady with artistic and literary interests, and on his press John printed some small volumes of his sister's verses, texts and tickets for the Sunday School, and other ephemeral work.

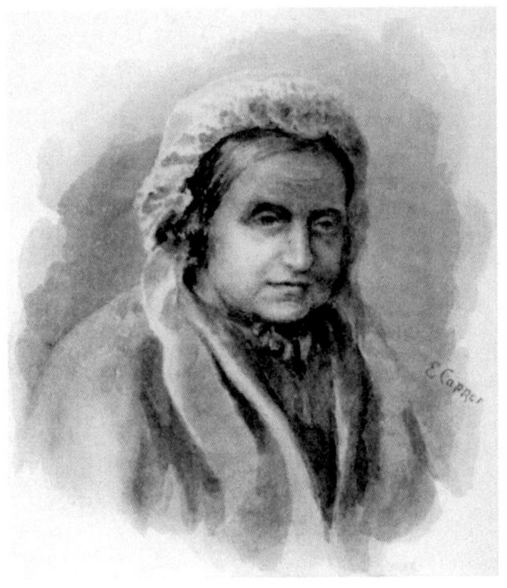

Susan Beever, after E. Capper

In the 1850s Susan Beever had published a couple of pamphlets supporting ragged schools and in 1870, the year before Ruskin bought Brantwood, she published her *References to Remarkable Passages in Shakespeare*. Ruskin owned a copy, but I don't know when he acquired it. He *seems* to have first met Susan Beever in 1873, but of course it could have been earlier. She was thirteen years Ruskin's senior, but a friendship developed between the two; they shared many common interests. During the next twenty years they corresponded on many varied subjects, Ruskin writing in excess of a thousand letters to her.

In 1875 George Allen published *Frondes Agrestes* which was Susan Beever's volume of selections from *Modern Painters*; it was a popular book and went through several editions.

William Bell became the leading carpenter in the district and one of Coniston's most respected residents. He was associated with the Coniston Foxhounds from his youth and for more than thirteen years he was Master. He was a dedicated Liberal and during Gladstone's administration he was appointed a Justice of the Peace. Ruskin met him soon after he moved to Coniston and the two men often had heated but friendly discussions. In 1879 Bell built the 'Jumping Jenny' for Ruskin in the boathouse at Coniston Hall. Ruskin also got to know Bell's son John and occasionally took tea with him and his wife. His diary for 6 September 1884 noted that on the previous day he had taken a 'heavy tea at Bells, with egg…' and on 16 January 1885 'Two large eggs and buttered cakes at the Bells'. John Bell himself was a local worthy, carrying on the family business and eventually becoming the Coniston Registrar of Births and Deaths.

In 1873 a London solicitor, Albert Fleming, sent Ruskin a copy of his book *In the House of Rimmon* which encapsulated many of the ideals and ideas which Ruskin had for the Guild of St George. Ten years later Fleming moved from London to Neaum Crag, at Loughrigg, near Ambleside. Once settled, he established the linen industry in the Lake District and his friendship with Ruskin developed. He also met Susan Beever, and in 1887 he edited *Hortus Inclusus*, a selection which he made from the extensive series of Ruskin's letters to Susan.

Hortus Inclusus was published on 29 September 1887 in an edition of 2000 copies with an extra run of 250 copies on hand-made paper. Susan Beever gave a copy of the general edition to her old friend William Bell, inscribing it on the fly leaf 'William Bell – from, S. Beever'. No doubt Bell was pleased to have the book, and on his death in 1896 it was inherited by his son John. In 1923 the book changed hands again. Tipped onto the first flyleaf is a folded sheet of notepaper recording its history:

> This book was presented to Mr Wm. Bell of Haws Bank, Coniston, Lanc[ashir]e by Miss S. Beever of The Thwaite – Coniston – (the 'Susie' of the letters) – and is so inscribed by her – in 1887. Mr Bell died in 1896 & his son Mr Jonathan Bell gave it to me when he sold his property in 1923.
> Edward G. Woolgar.

Edward Woolgar was a railwayman all of his working life. In 1888 he became the Coniston Stationmaster, a position which he held until 1902 when he moved to Grange, moving to Ulverston in 1912 and retiring from the Furness Railway in 1920. For many years he was a member of the Coniston Parish Council; he became a County Councillor, a magistrate and a County Alderman. When he was stationmaster at Coniston he met Ruskin and the Severns. A man of literary tastes and interests he built a large collection of Ruskin's books and relics, including watercolours by Ruskin, Severn, Collingwood and Kate Greenaway. He was very proud of his association with Ruskin, and it was to Woolgar, on his return from Seascale in

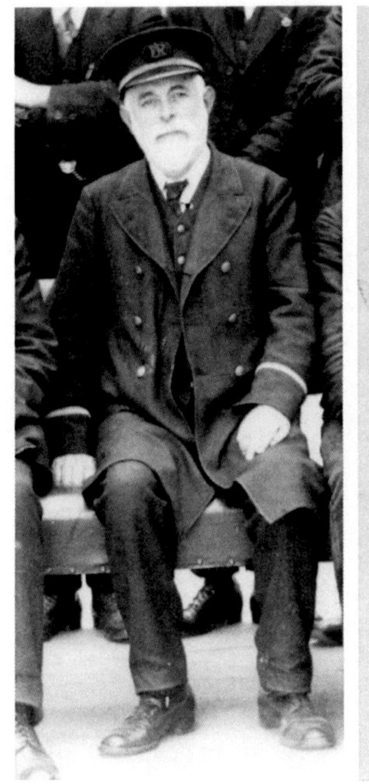

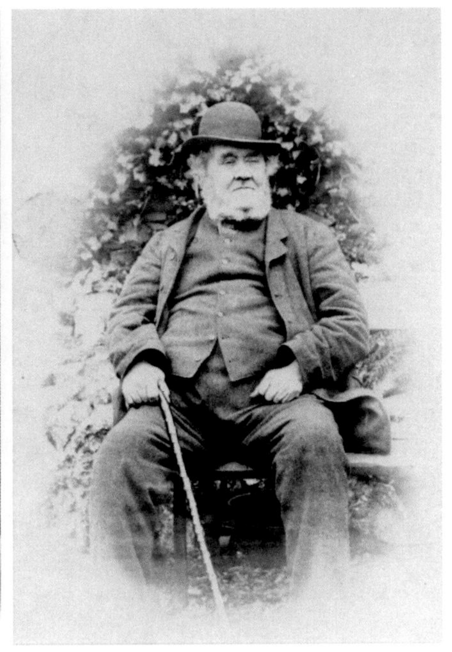

Left, Edward Woolgar; right, William Bell (by courtesy of Neil Salisbury Esq.)

June 1889 that Ruskin said 'I'm glad to be back. There's no place like Coniston – no place like Coniston.'

After Edward Woolgar died in 1950 his step-daughter gave a general part of his library to Brantwood for the use of students who were then attending residential courses. A number of years later she gave a small collection of books from the libraries of Ruskin and the Severns to Brantwood and at the same time she gave a collection of letters and other manuscripts to the Whitehouse Collection at Bembridge.

Some items clearly slipped through the net. The copy of *Hortus Inclusus* found its way into the library of John Hutchinson of York. He had put together an enviable collection of books from Ruskin's library. When he parted with his collection a couple of years ago I was able to add the Beever-Bell-Woolgar association copy of *Hortus* to my library.

XXI
YOUNG ARTHUR

THE FRIENDS OF RUSKIN'S BRANTWOOD NEWSLETTER, AUTUMN 2009

❧

Arthur Severn junior, known as 'Young Arthur' was the second child but eldest son of Joan and Arthur Severn. He was born on 16 August 1874 at Herne Hill and Ruskin would have seen him for the first time when he returned from a long continental tour on 22 October. As was the case with all the Severns, Brantwood was to become Young Arthur's second home. From an early age he enjoyed the lake – both messing about in boats and fishing. Both Young Arthur, and later his brother Agnew, enjoyed sailing with their father.

There is a pencil and ink sketch (see opposite) in one of my *Brantwood Books* by Arthur Severn of Arthur and Agnew fishing from a boat off Brantwood. This was drawn on 13 August 1885, just before Arthur's eleventh birthday.

Ruskin, no doubt, considered fishing for its own sake, a fairly worthless occupation for young boys, although he did note in *Dilecta* that 'Really useful fishing is not play; and to watch a trout is indeed, whether for a boy or girl, greater pleasure than to catch it, if they did but know!' But Ruskin had a more useful pleasure in mind for the boys.

As Arthur Severn recorded in his Memoir of Ruskin,

> When my children got old enough he [Ruskin] eventually thought he would try the experiment [of wood chopping] on them. He said to me one day, 'Now, Arthur, I am going to make those children do some nice useful work. I am sure they will be delighted.' I said, 'What is it?' 'They are to come up into the Moor with me and Jane Ann [who lived at Lawson Park] and as I chop the branches into lengths for firewood, they can tie them up in bundles, and

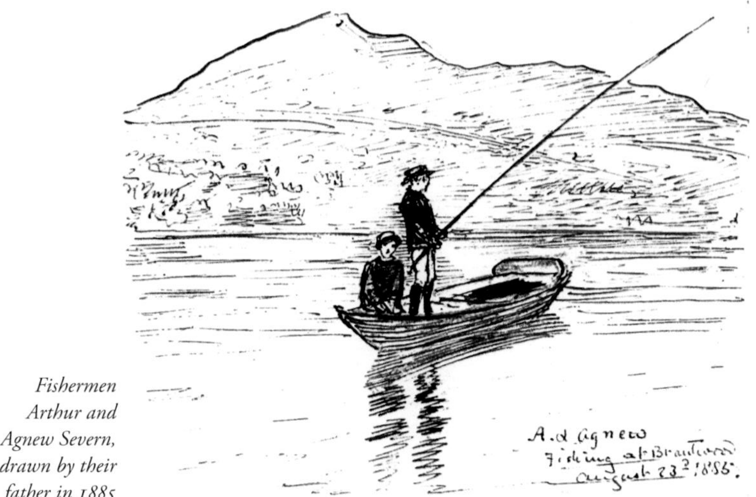

Fishermen Arthur and Agnew Severn, drawn by their father in 1885

we shall all be so happy.' 'My children', Severn explained, 'were delighted at first, but in four or five days they wanted to fish or be at something else...'

It was probably after this summer of 1885 that young Arthur and Agnew were sent off to boarding school. They went to St David's School at Reigate which was owned and run by the Rev. Harry Churchill, husband to Ruskin's and the Severns' old friend Connie Hilliard. The boys would have already met their new headmaster for he and his wife had visited Brantwood several times in the spring of 1883 when they were staying in Coniston with Laurence Hilliard and his sister Ethel. It was in this same year – 1883 – that Ruskin gave the school a large collection of minerals, for which he printed a special catalogue.

But fishing was not forgotten. On their first day home for the holidays in 1887 the boys were on the lake again and caught two pike.

From St David's Young Arthur went on, like his father and uncle Walter, to Westminster School where he began his first term on 25 September 1888. On that same day Ruskin was in Italy, at Bassano, where he visited Francesca Alexander and her mother, and wrote in his diary, 'It is no use any longer trying to keep a diary of days which fly like a weaver's shuttle.'

Arthur was no scholar. His sole interest was fishing. He left Westminster in December 1892 and his father had to have him specially coached, presumably in Latin, before he matriculated five years later, and finally entered Exeter College, Oxford, on 30 January 1897. His younger brother Agnew had gone up to Christ Church the year before.

Arthur Severn was at Oxford for five years during which time he seems to have been very popular. He played football and cricket for the college; he rowed, rode in point to points, and was a member of innumerable college and university clubs. Towards the end of his career at Oxford he entered a fly-casting competition, which he won. His father exclaimed that all his four years at Oxford had done was 'Simply taught him to throw a fly!' But it must have taught him a little more too, because he was finally awarded his B.A. on 20 November 1902.

Young Arthur at Exeter College, Oxford, standing left. (Author's collection)

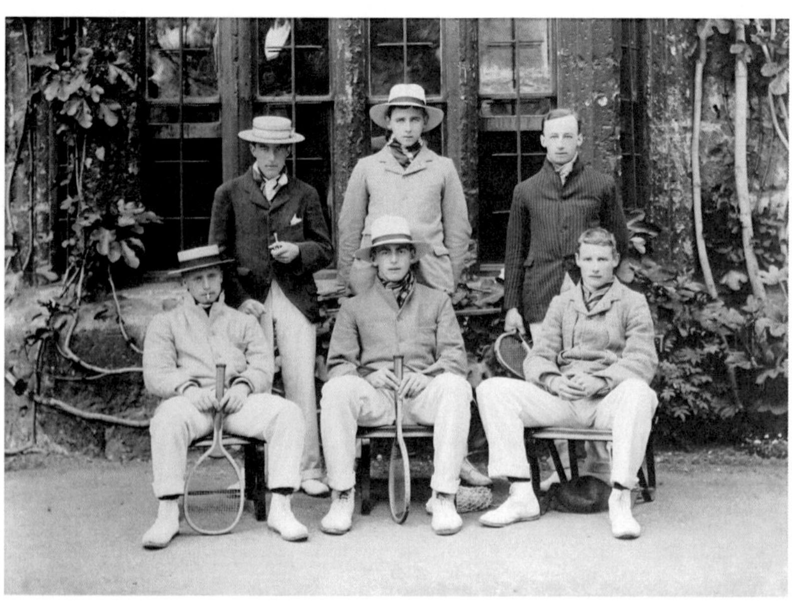

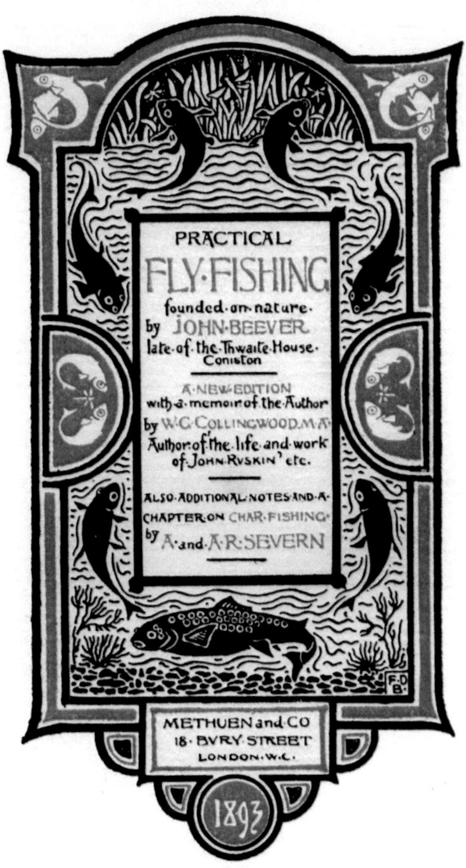

PRACTICAL
FLY·FISHING
founded·on·nature·
by JOHN·BEEVER
late·of·the·Thwaite·House·
Coniston

A·NEW·EDITION
with·a·memoir·of·the·Author
by W·G·COLLINGWOOD·M·A·
Author·of·the·life·and·work
of·JOHN·RUSKIN' etc.

ALSO·ADDITIONAL·NOTES·AND·A·
CHAPTER·ON CHAR·FISHING·
by A·and·A·R·SEVERN

F.D.B.

METHUEN and CO
18·BURY·STREET
LONDON·W.C.

1893

The new edition of Practical Fly-Fishing *with Arthur's appendix. (Author's collection)*

On coming down from Oxford his parents tried unsuccessfully to get Young Arthur into the Civil Service, like his uncle Walter. But no doubt he would have hated this. However he did have one scholarly achievement!

In 1849 John Beever, brother to Ruskin's friends Mary and Susan Beever of The Thwaite, had written a little book called *Practical Fly-Fishing*. It was highly regarded, and scarce, and in 1893 W. G. Collingwood prepared a reprint of the book for Methuen & Co. Added to this new edition was a long biographical account of the author by Collingwood, and as an Appendix, 'Additional Notes on Artificial Flies,' 'Fly-Rods and Landing Nets' and 'Char Fishing', contributed by Arthur and Agnew Severn (see p. 209).

Finally the Severns accepted that their son's only interest was in fish and at about the time he left Oxford they established him in a Fish Farm at Bibury in Gloucestershire. But they must have continued to support him financially. A year later, writing to C. E. Norton, Joan Severn was complaining that £1,000 per year from Ruskin's books did not nearly cover their annual expenses, what with 'Arthur at Fish Culture and Agnew with a wife', among many other expenses.

Once he was established at Bibury, Arthur's sister Lily spent a lot of time with him at his trout farm until her death after the war, and from there they hunted regularly with the Heythrop. But other than that, Arthur does not appear to have stirred far afield. In 1914, neighbouring Arlington Mill, both a fulling and corn mill, was closed

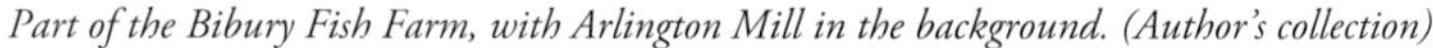

Part of the Bibury Fish Farm, with Arlington Mill in the background. (Author's collection)

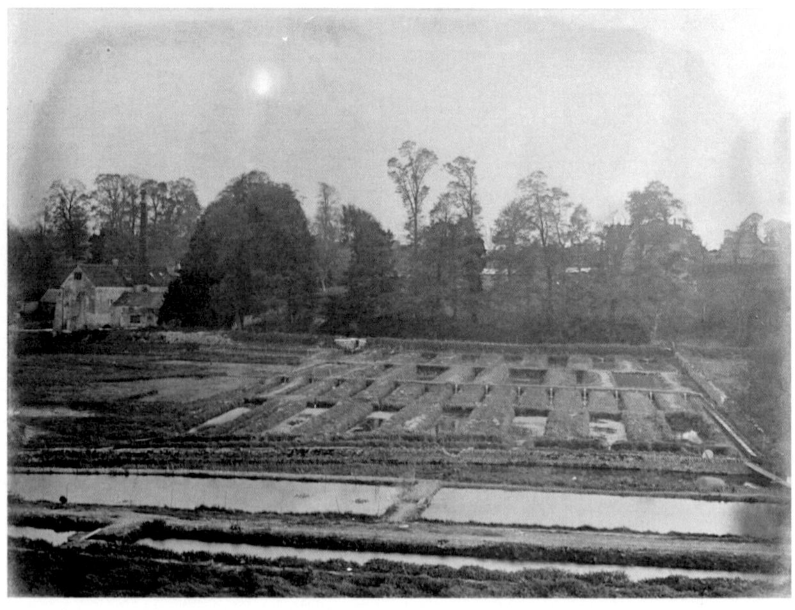

and the mill machinery was dismantled and sold as scrap. Arthur Severn appears to have bought the old mill building (or perhaps only the water rights) for use in connection with his fish farm.

He seems to have taken no interest in Brantwood and following the death of his father in 1931 and the sales of Brantwood and its contents, he left all of the arrangements in the hands of his youngest brother Herbert. Even his Exeter College photograph album was left at Coniston. Perhaps some of his father's artistic ability had been inherited. I remember seeing, hanging in the Swan Hotel at Bibury in the early 1950s several good watercolours of fish signed 'Arthur Severn' which presumably were the work of the son rather than the father.

Young Arthur continued to run his Fish Farm until his death in 1949. The mill has now been separated from the farm which itself covers 15 acres of the Coln valley. Here now are spawned up to six million trout ova annually, many of which are used to re-stock the local rivers and streams. Arthur Severn is now described by those running the farm as 'the famous naturalist'.

XXII

RUSKIN AND ST URSULA'S DISAPPEARING DOG

RUSKIN REVIEW AND BULLETIN, VOL. 1, NO. 3, 2005

One of the guide books which I bought on my first trip to Venice in 1966 noted that the wall above the rostrum of the Ducal Palace's Sala del Maggior Consiglio was painted by 'J. Tintoretto and assistants'. It also explains that elsewhere 'some repainting was entrusted to Tintoretto... his son Domenico and other collaborators'. Another guide explains that the ceiling decoration 'is the work of J. Tintoretto for which he made large use of assistants'. This really brought home to me the fact that J. Tintoretto and Partners was *the* firm of interior decorators to call in to do your redecoration in sixteenth century Venice.

When the members of the minor Scuola di Sant' Orsola decided to have their meeting house next door to the Basilica of SS. Giovanni e Paolo redecorated, they called in another interior decorator, the young Vittore Carpaccio. He had just appeared, at the age of 25, on the Venetian artistic scene and during the final decade of the fifteenth century he painted nine large canvases to cover the four walls of the Scuola's chapel.

Carpaccio's series of paintings illustrated the story of St Ursula, which is told in Voraigne's *Golden Legend*, 1475. The pictures were probably hung in an order to illustrate the sequence of events told by Voraigne, but the order seems to have changed over the centuries. One of the smallest of the cycle, *The Dream of St Ursula*, probably hung on the north wall above a small doorway leading to the albergo above the portico of the Scuola.

In 1504 a new floor to the room raised the pavement level by 40cm. Major remodelling of the building took place in 1646-7 and it is prob-

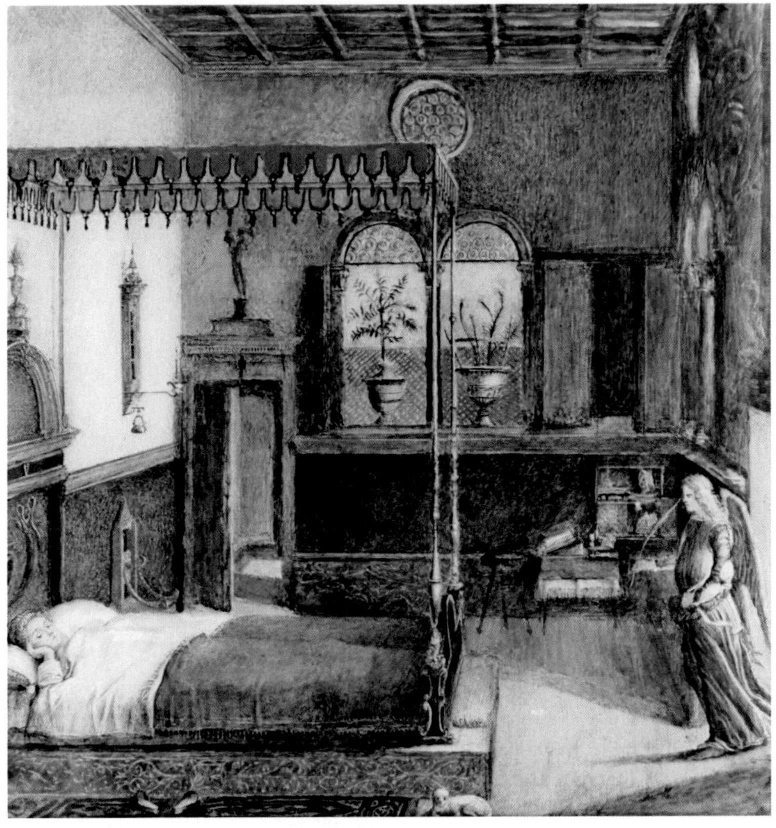

John Ruskin: Copy of Carpaccio's Dream of St Ursula, *1876. Watercolour, 11.5" x 10.5" (Ashmolean Museum, Oxford)*

able that the floor was again raised at this time. One of the largest paintings of the cycle, *The Arrival of the Ambassadors*, which hung above the doorway in the south wall, has indeed had a large section cut from it to accommodate the raised doorway. The lower part of *The Dream* may have been cut away at the same time, because of its position above the north door, and at other times the top and both sides of the painting have been trimmed. In any case, the picture's position certainly puts its lower part at risk.

I clearly remember, from my 1966 visit, seeing in the church of

San Zaccaria, the bottom part of Giovanni Bellini's great *Madonna and Child with four saints,* which Ruskin considered one of the two best pictures in the world, literally hanging in shreds, where shoulders in an adjacent pew had rubbed against it.

Carpaccio's paintings of the St Ursula cycle were still in the Scuola di Sant' Orsola until 1806 when the scuola was suppressed. In 1812 they were moved to the Gallerie dell' Accademia. However, the canvases were not finally safe just because they had arrived in a public gallery; they were again trimmed to adapt them to their new location.

When the series of paintings arrived at the Accademia in 1812, *The Dream* was the worst damaged of the whole cycle, and it was not hung until 1852, and then only for the sake of completeness.

Just where *The Dream* has been hung is difficult to determine. It has been moved on several occasions, and to compound the confusion, the numbers of the galleries have been changed too. Ruskin referred to it in the Notes to *Fors Clavigera* Letter 40 (*Works*, XXVIII, p. 75), describing it as 'High up and in an out- of-the way corner of the Academy of Venice, seen by no man – or woman either, - of all pictures in Europe the one I should choose for a gift, if a fairy queen gave me a choice'. At this time it was probably in Room IX, the Veronese Room, (now called Room X). Improbable though it may seem, by 1891 it was in Room XVI – part of Room VIII which is now the small bookshop. By 1906 it was in Room XVI – now part of Room 23, the former Church of S. Maria della Carita. The St Ursula cycle is now in Room 21 (at one time called Room XVII).

It seems possible that Burne-Jones first drew Ruskin's attention to Carpaccio. He and his wife travelled in Europe with Ruskin in 1862 and, as Ruskin noted in his diary, on 12 May he 'saw Carpaccio at Academy'. The next day, he wrote to Burne-Jones:

> There's nothing like Carpaccio! There's a little piece of humble pie for you! – I had never once looked at him... But this Carpaccio is a new world to me... I've only seen the Academy ones yet, and am going this morning to your St George of the Schiavoni. (*Works*, IV, p. 356)

Ruskin was in Venice again between 22 June and 13 July 1872, and it is evident from his diary that he revisited the Academy to refresh his memory of the painting of *The Dream of St Ursula* before writing a long description of it on 5 July for Letter 20 of *Fors Clavigera* (*Works*, XXVII, pp. 342-5). In his detailed description he mentions, on passing St Ursula's 'white dog' beside her little blue slippers. He had clearly fallen for the painting, and in his notes for his tenth Oxford lecture on 23 November 1875 he described two pictures by Bellini in the Frari as 'the best pure oil pictures in the world', but, 'the most delightful and covetable' he considered to be Carpaccio's *Vision of St Ursula* (*Works*, XXI, p. 501).

During this Venetian visit Ruskin was accompanied by Joan and Arthur Severn, Connie Hilliard and her mother, and Albert Goodwin. They had left home on 13 April. By the time they had reached Venice tempers were becoming a little frayed. Ruskin was in correspondence with George Macdonald, who thought that he could effect a reconciliation between Ruskin and Rose La Touche, but Ruskin and telegraphed that he would not return home unless he was *certain* of seeing Rose. Meanwhile, he seems to have quarrelled with the Severns, who returned to London. Finally, in the hope of being reunited with Rose, he left Venice with Goodwin and the Hilliards on 13 July, arriving in London thirteen days later.

Ruskin was briefly reunited with Rose for three days at the Macdonalds and later at Broadlands and again at the Leysters at Toft Hall in Cheshire. But despite all his hopes, Rose would not marry him, because, as he later told A. W. Hunt, 'I don't love God better than I do *her*'. Rose was to die on 25 May 1875. His love for Rose and her rejection of him affected the remainder of Ruskin's life and work.

In Venice again, in 1876, Ruskin visited the Carpaccios in the Academy once more. In his troubled mind, St Ursula became closely associated with Rose, and Professor Burd has written in detail of this Venetian visit in *The Christmas Story*.

Ruskin wished to examine *The Dream of St Ursula* in detail, and to copy it. But because of its skied position on the gallery wall, this was impractical. He was probably at the Academy on Tuesday 12 September and he described the room as being 'lighted like cellars', but three days later, on the Friday, he was 'seeing Carpaccio in sunlight'. The next day he was discouraged in his attempt to copy *The Dream* and on the following day, Sunday, he took C. H. Moore with him to show him the painting.

Ruskin was not without influence in Venice, and he persuaded the Gallery authorities of his need to examine the painting in more detail. On 18 September he noted in his diary 'Today St Ursula taken down for me, and began [copying it] properly'. On the next day he wrote to tell Joan Severn about the painting:

> ...It has been terribly injured, and wants securing to the canvas, and the Academy, like our own, can't get money from the Government – so I've offered to bear all the expenses of its repair, on condition it is brought down where can see it; and I think they'll do it! – at all events they're grateful for the offer.

Ruskin was of course aware that the painting had been much restored already, and all that he saw was not original Carpaccio. Writing in 1877 in 'The Shrine of the Slaves', the first supplement to *St Mark's Rest*, he said 'The picture itself has been more injured and repainted than any other [in the cycle] (the face of the recumbent figure entirely so); and though it is full of marvellous passages, I hope the general traveller will seal his memory of Carpaccio in the picture'.

But by now Rose and St Ursula had become so combined in his mind that Ruskin was not really copying *Carpaccio* but the image of Rose-St Ursula, and on 8 October he noted in his diary that he had been working on his copy of the painting 'three weeks yesterday... bring it near conclusion. Another week of courage on it, and I hope I shall be able to say that it has been done in the forenoons of four weeks'. On 20 October he noted that his copy was 'nearly done' but four days later 'I find I may still put in any quantity of work I choose [on St Ursula] – but I *must* stop, some day or other'.

To reduce a painting of 112"x 101" to an accurate watercolour of 11½"x 10¾" was no mean feat, and Ruskin was understandably irritated to find that the Venetian picture framer, to whom he entrusted it, had trimmed his picture. He probably only took off the unpainted margins from the sheet, but in so doing, he appears to have very slightly shaved the top and both sides. 'Horribly vexed and worried last night' wrote Ruskin in his diary on 19 December, 'with my own stupidity in getting Ursula left to the tender mercies of an Italian frame-maker, who cut all her edges off – a perpetual thought-sore it will be to me'.

Ruskin did not work on his copy of St Ursula in isolation. During the period, J. W. Bunney, Fairfax Murray, C. H. Moore and J. R. Anderson all worked on the picture too. Bunney's copy of the whole picture is once again in the family collection. His copies of the window in the painting, and the corner of the room including her bookcase, both commissioned by Ruskin, are now in the Guild of St George's collection. So too is Angelo Alessandri's study of the saint's head which may have been commissioned by Ruskin but which was not bought by the Guild's trustees until 1893.

In addition to making his reduced copy of the whole painting, Ruskin also made several full-sized copies of details. While some of these may have been worked on *before* the reduced copy was finished, others were made afterwards. They do not appear to have been preliminary working studies for the related copy, but studies in their own right.

On 30 October, we know from his diary, he was working on the Erbe della Madonna – the pot of vervain which stands in front of one of the windows. The plant was identified for him by Daniel Oliver, the botanist at Kew, and Ruskin subsequently gave him this study (No. 347 in Cook and Wedderburn's *Catalogue of Drawings*). On 6 December he told Joan Severn 'I'm getting on well with St Ursula's full head, – I think she'll come velly pitty – She has black eyebrows di ma – did oo ever know a saint with black eyebrows'. He seems to have begun this by 24 November and was still working on it on 19 February of the next year.

Writing to Joan on New Year's Day 1877 he listed his detailed studies – 'the whole, small', the head, full-size with pillow and shield above, the vervain, full size, the water-pitcher and candlestick 'begun more than a month ago'. To Norton a fortnight later he wrote, 'I've nearly now, some three drawings from Carpaccio – one of the entire picture, one of the window with the vervain leaves; the third of the hand – hand and clothes over the breast, full size [this must be the full-sized head on which he was working] – I've been four months at work on these three drawings'. Ruskin was to exhibit this last drawing on 15 November 1884 in his 'Pleasures of Truth' lecture at Oxford, and then he gave it to Somerville Hall (Cook and Wedderburn in their *Catalogue of Drawings*, No. 344; also list, in error No. 346 'Hand' as being at Somerville. This no doubt is the same picture).

Additionally, he made another study of the head, which he gave to C. H. Moore (CW 345), and the bell and tassel at the corner of the saint's pillow (CW 349 – Miss Moore). On 14 March, Ruskin noted that he had 'a prosperous day' on *St Ursula's lamp*, a drawing which I haven't identified. William White, in his *Principles of Art*, says that Ruskin also copied the blue slippers (CW 348). Ruskin refers to the slippers in his description of the painting in *Fors Clavigera* in August 1872 – 'Her little blue slippers lie at the side of the bed – her little white dog beside them… At the door of the room an angel enters (the little dog, though lying awake, vigilant, takes no notice)'.

The dog, in fact, is rather neglected, but Ruskin does refer to it again briefly in *Fors Clavigera* Letter 74, written in Venice on 3 February 1877. '[St Ursula's] own dog, at the foot of the bed is indeed unconscious of the angel with the palm, but is taking care of his mistress's earthly crown' which rests nearby on the dais.

Ruskin's study of the dog seems to have been his last of the group. There is just one reference to it in his diary, noting that on 18 March 1877 he did his 'final work on the Princess's dog'. The drawing never seems to have been used or referred to further by Ruskin, and it remained at Brantwood probably until the 1930-31 sales. Lot 91 in the picture sale at Sotheby's on 20 May 1931 comprised five studies by Ruskin from paintings; four are specified by name and one is merely listed as 'Detail from a Picture by an Italian Old Master'. The lot was bought by J. Howard Whitehouse and it seems probable that the anonymous detail was Carpaccio's Dog. When Whitehouse published *Ruskin the Painter* in 1938, the Dog was catalogued as No. 73 in the Bembridge Collection.

We know from Ruskin's comments in *St Mark's Rest* that he knew

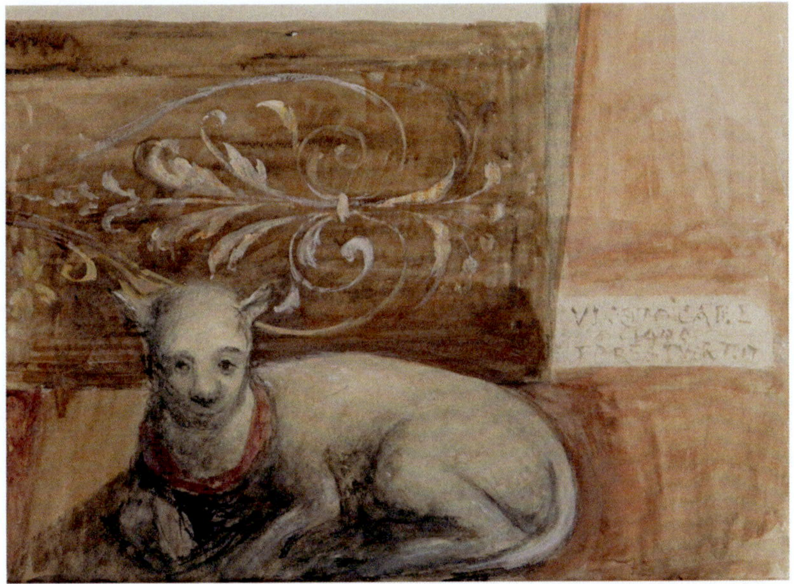

John Ruskin: Study of the Dog from Carpaccio's Dream of St Ursula, *1877. Watercolour, 11.75" x 15.15" (Ruskin Foundation, RF 890)*

the original painting had been heavily restored. In fact, the cycle has undergone ten restorations; *The Dream* particularly has been heavily retouched. The first restoration was undertaken in July 1520, when the paintings were only twenty or thirty years old. In 1546 they were again worked on. We know that *The Dream* was restored in the eighteenth century because of the inscription beside Carpaccio's own name and date, 'Cortinus R[estauravit] 1752'. The most recent restoration of the cycle was carried out by Ottorino Nonfarmale between 1983 and 1985 under the supervision of the soporentendente Francesco Valcanover and Giovanna Nepi Scire, director of the Gallerie dell' Accademia. During this work much of the repainting was removed.

Ruskin was of the opinion that St Ursula's face in *The Dream* had been entirely repainted at some date. If indeed, this is the case, then the most recent restoration has dealt quite gently with her. It did not deal quite so gently with the saint's little dog. We know that the lower

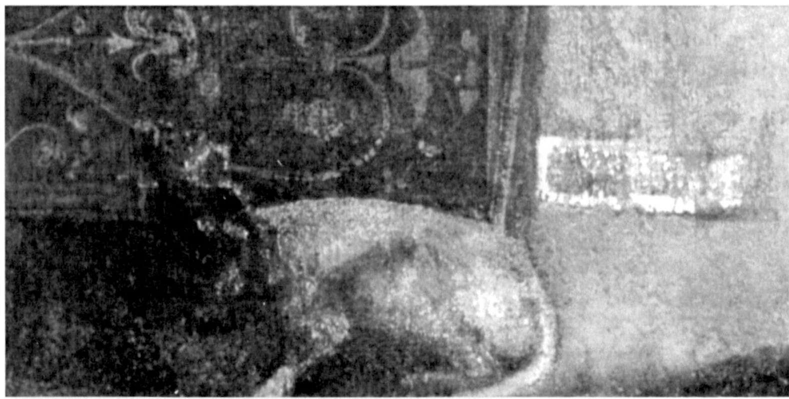

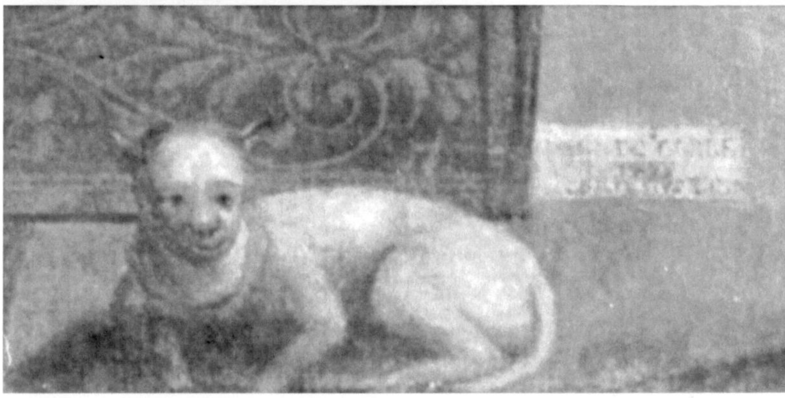

Top, V. Carpaccio: Dog in Dream of St Ursula *(Venice, Gallerie dell' Accademia), photographed before the 1983-5 restoration. (Su concessione del Ministero per I Bene e le Attivita Culturali); Bottom, V. Carpaccio: Dog in* Dream of St Ursula, *photographed after the 1983-5 restoration. (Si concessione del Ministero per I Bene e le Attivita Culturali).*

part of the picture had been damaged, and thus had been overpainted. The dog which Ruskin copied with such care, is now a mere shadow of its former self. The body is still more or less intact. Presumably this is the original Carpaccio. But its face, and indeed its head, on which Ruskin had lavished care, has now almost totally disappeared.

XXIII

SOME GREEN PHOTOGRAPHS

RUSKIN REVIEW AND BULLETIN, VOL. 5, NO. 2, 2009

A RUSKINIAN REVISION AND EXTENSION

There is a well-known photograph of the bearded John Ruskin, leaning against a wall at Brantwood. Cook & Wedderburn reproduce the central part of it as the frontispiece to volume XXXVII of the *Library Edition*. In their 'Catalogue of Portraits' in volume XXXVIII they list the photograph as No. 52, and there and in the caption to the reproduction they date it 1885. The photograph was taken by T. A. & J. Green of Grasmere.

The central element of the photograph, the figure of Ruskin, was frequently reproduced as a postcard. Cook & Wedderburn list it as having been reproduced in 1889 as the frontispiece to volume I of *The Ruskin Reading Guild Journal*, although I have to admit that it is not present in my set of the original parts of that journal. It has also been reproduced elsewhere. When I reproduced the entire photograph as No. 221 in *John Ruskin. A Life in Pictures*, I fear I followed Cook & Wedderburn's lead and dated it as having been taken in 1885.[1]

Dr Jan Marsh has recently been corresponding with me in connection with the Ruskin entries in the catalogue of portraits of late Victorians which she is preparing for the National Portrait Gallery. Thanks to the skill of her Research Assistant, Elizabeth Heath, two further photographs taken by the Green brothers during the same session at Brantwood have now been found, uncatalogued, in the National Archive Image Library.

Perhaps even more important is the information that they were registered, on deposit, at the Public Record Office, on 21 September 1881, and they were probably taken just before their deposit. Thus they were taken four years before the date ascribed to them by Cook & Wedderburn.

This earlier dating is important because it means that these three photographs pre-date my No. 171 photograph by Elliot & Fry taken in 1882, and now must be considered the earliest photographs in which Ruskin appears wearing his beard. As I explained in the note to portrait No. 161 in my portraits book, the silhouette drawn by Ruskin of himself and a gardening party is the first *drawing* showing him with a beard. The first *bust* to show a beard is my No. 164, by G. Atkinson.

In *John Ruskin. A Life in Pictures* the Green photograph is reproduced following a series of ten exposures by Barraud taken in May or June 1885. In my description of the Green photograph I observe that 'on this occasion his beard has been trimmed so that it was nicer to look at' than in the Barraud photographs. It now turns out, of course, that it hadn't been trimmed – it was four years younger!

I would suggest that the slightly more informally posed photograph (opposite, top) was the first of the series taken by Green. Then probably followed the well-known version (opposite, bottom) in which Ruskin looks a little tidier. Probably the next exposure was the group posed on the lawn outside the drawing room windows (see p. 224). It remains to identify all of the figures in this interesting photograph.

We know with reasonable certainty who was at Brantwood in the summer of 1881. Ruskin himself was there for most of the summer, although he did spend a few days at Seascale, returning to Brantwood on 20 July. Sara Anderson (Diddie) seems to have been there for much of the time. Alexander Wedderburn was certainly there on 15 September when Ruskin began keeping his diary again, and seems to have still been there by 26 September.

Other visitors that summer were Peggy and Rosalind Webling, two of the talented daughters of R. T. Webling. In 1881 Peggy was ten years old, and Rosalind was thirteen. Our principal source of information about the Webling girls' visit to Brantwood is Peggy's privately published *A Sketch of John Ruskin*. This undated pamphlet was published in 1914, thirty and more years after the visit, and in it Peggy admits 'mine is the memory of a child's impressions, singularly vivid in some instances, blank and confused in others'. Certainly

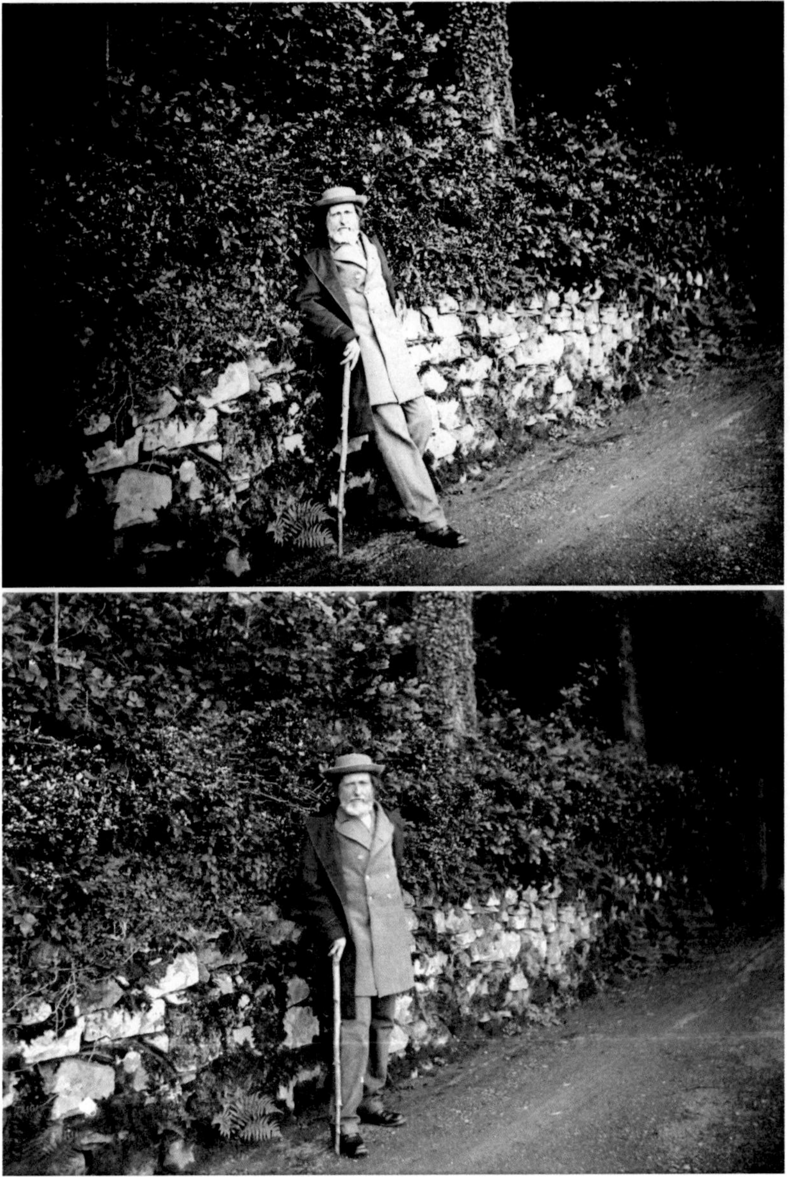

Top, photograph A: Ruskin, in what was probably Green's first exposure.
Bottom, photograph B: Probably the second exposure; the well-known photograph.

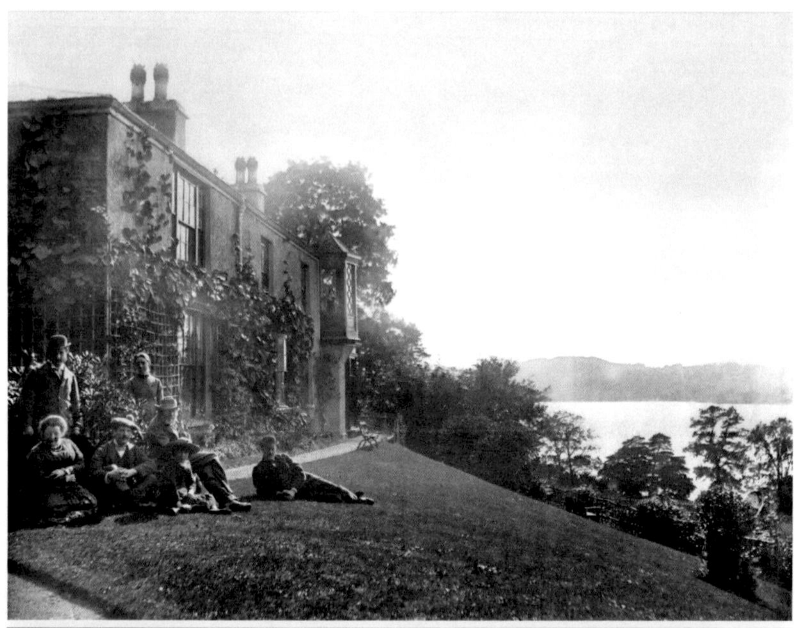

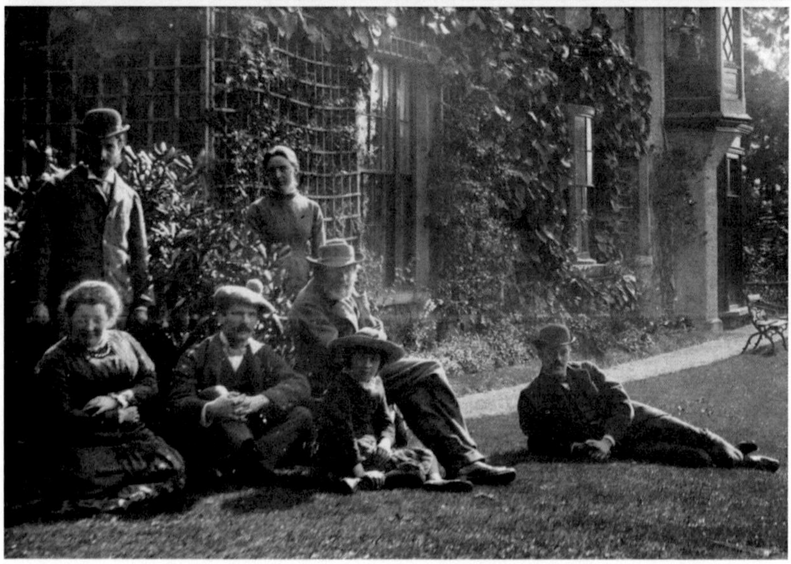

Top, Photograph C: The group on the lawn in front of Brantwood; bottom, Photograph C (Detail)

she wrote a fascinating account of what they did at Brantwood, but we can tell, from other sources, that she does slightly confuse and conflate the events of their various visits.

However, in 1881 they do seem to have been at Brantwood from early August until mid-September. Ruskin's diary for 17 September records 'Peggy and Ros[alin]d go away'. Ruskin's silhouette of the gardening party, to which I refer above, was probably sent by Ruskin to another sister, Josephine, who was at home in London. The diary entry of 15 September ('…happy day with Diddie, and Alic, Rosalind and Peggy. Happy walk on moor before one o'clock') may well refer to this silhouette excursion. I think that the Green photographs were also taken within a day or two of this event.

The two girls in the photograph certainly could be Peggy and Rosalind who were ten and thirteen respectively. (They couldn't be the Severn daughters because Lily was eight and Violet was only one in 1881.) Peggy, sitting on the lawn at Ruskin's feet, is wearing a large hat. We know from other photographs that Rosalind was a tall girl and in her account of the visit Peggy tells us that she was short and fat, with cropped hair; both girls had 'every-day dresses of blue serge, loose and plain, with broad-brimmed hats'.

'Peggy photographed [by Green] at Brantwood', reproduced from her autobiography

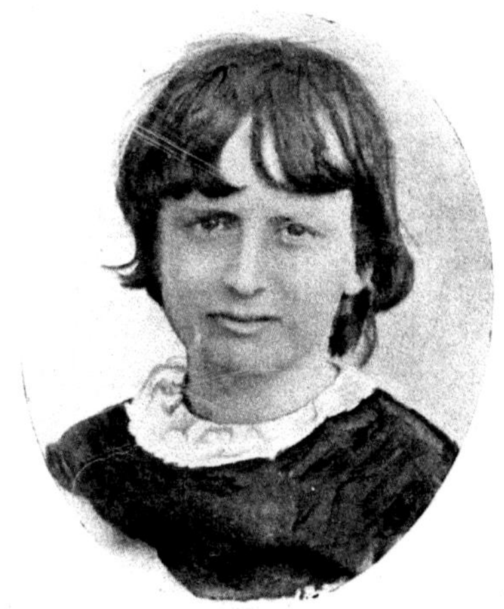

My assumption that the two girls in the photograph are the Webling sisters is confirmed by a few words which I have just discovered in Peggy's autobiography. 'While we were staying with him [Ruskin]', she wrote, 'a man came one day to take photographs. I reproduce one of his attempts, as my family thought it showed in a remarkable way the effect that the Professor had upon me.' (right)[2]

Who are the other people in

the group? Well, Joan Severn, sitting on the lawn at the left of the group is obvious. I think it is Arthur Severn standing behind her. It would be a logical place for him to stand – and the moustache seems to be of the same generous size as in the 1872 Venetian photograph. Sitting next to Joan is, I think, the twenty-seven year-old Alexander Wedderburn. He *was* a Scot – and the figure appears to be wearing a tam-o'-shanter. Ruskin, with Rosalind standing behind him, is wearing the same clothes that appear in the other two photographs, and 'the soft grey hat' remembered by Peggy. The final figure remains a mystery. I think it is either Laurence Hilliard or W. G. Collingwood, both of whom were at Brantwood that summer. It is pure speculation, but I think it is Hilliard.

REFERENCES

1 James S. Dearden, *John Ruskin. A Life in Pictures* (Sheffield: Sheffield Academic Press, 1999).

2 Peggy Webling, *Peggy: The Story of One Score Years and Ten* (London: Hutchinson & Co, [1924]), p. 64.

XXIV
JOHN RUSKIN IN CANADA

THE FRIENDS OF RUSKIN'S BRANTWOOD NEWSLETTER, AUTUMN 2004

❦

Among the pieces prepared for *The Ruskin Newsletter* No.36, which in the event was never published, was the following note on Ruskin, Canada. As many Ruskinians will know, there are several towns in America called Ruskin – for various reasons. But until I received a letter from Rein Gerretsen, a Dutch member of the Ruskin Association and a keen Ruskin collector (many of the books from his collection are now in the *Friends* Library at Brantwood), I was quite unaware of another Ruskin, this time in Canada. It seems, therefore, worthwhile putting on the record what we know.

Of his visit to see his brother in Maple Ridge, east of Vancouver, in June 1992, Rein Gerretsen wrote:

> [My brother] took me around the area as far as Alberta – Banff Park, Lake Louise and Lake Maraine; a marvellous landscape and vast scenery – the most beautiful mountains, snow caps, scenery one can imagine. They live in Maple Ridge and the first evening of my arrival they drove me to the Dam (hydro works) on the Fraser River. It was there I saw the name of a hamlet: Ruskin, and told my brother and sister-in-law about JR and my involvement.

I could tell them JR was never in Canada, but I could not understand how this hamlet Ruskin got its name – so my sister-in-law went to the local library the next day and asked about it. Somebody kindly looked it up in some local history book and found this:

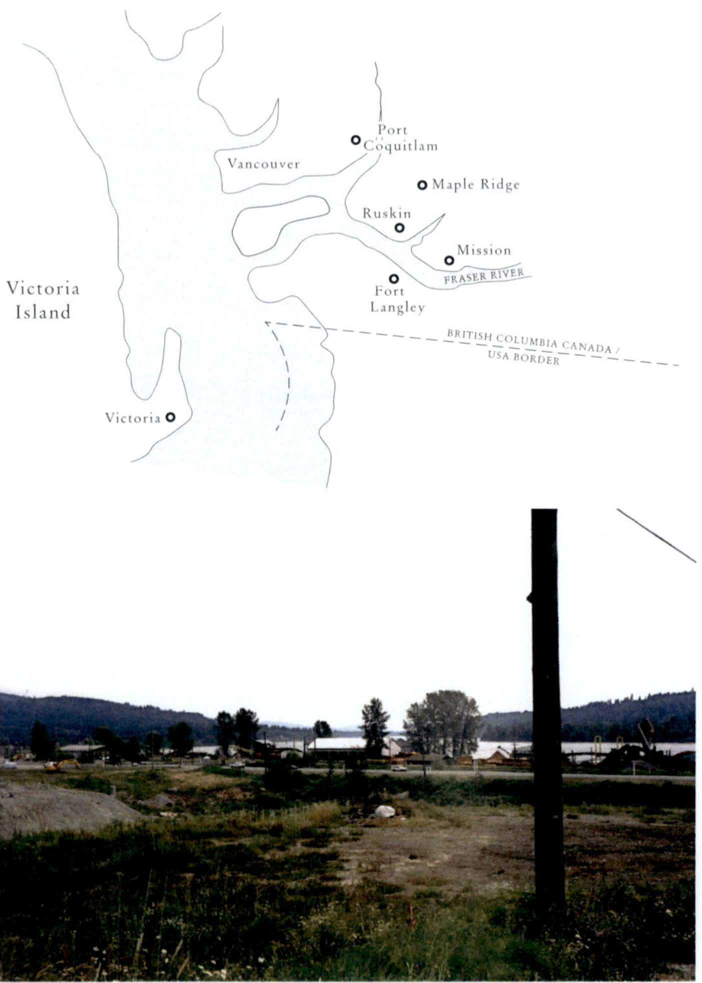

Top, map showing the location of Ruskin; bottom, a Ruskin landscape!

In the 1800s a settler from England came to this area – his name was C. Whetham. He was so impressed with John Ruskin's ideas that he named the settlement Ruskin. He held discussions with people from the area and the town was officially registered as Ruskin in 1895.

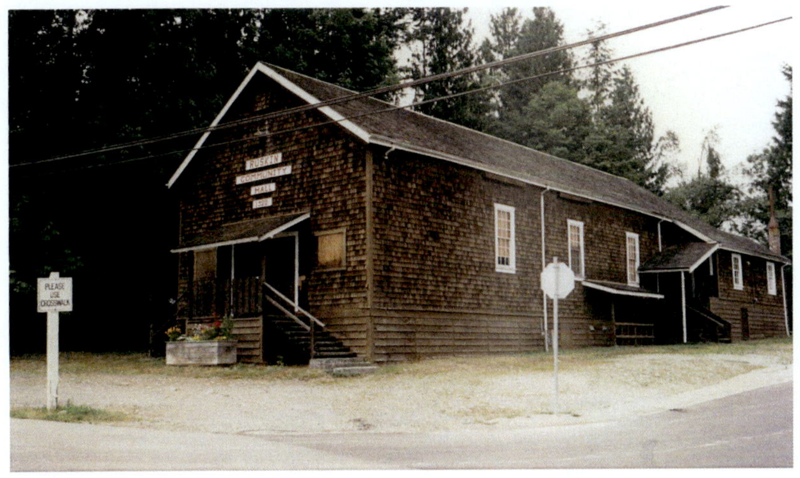

The Community Hall, Ruskin

So we went again to the dam and on to the village – this is what we saw; the wood mill aside the river Fraser gives the impression of the former settlement – lumber is the main industry in Canada and north of the Fraser River are the endless Rocky Mountains! Up the road were two buildings and an electricity station – all power goes on poles. I took some photos; a school and opposite, a brown wooden community hall (1922). That's all – there is not a village to be seen – no shops or anything – this is it! Further back to the Dam are a number of wooden houses – a settlement.

Is it not remarkable? I travel to the other side of the world – 12km high in a Boeing 747 – 800kph speed – outside – 50° – with 450 people – my first flight ever, most sensational! And what I see, right there, is a hamlet called Ruskin – it is a small world after all!

[Since this piece was written, my attention has been drawn to a publication which throws more light on the origins of Ruskin in Canada. I would refer those who are interested in the subject to Sheila Nickols (ed.): *Maple Ridge. A History of Settlement.* This was originally published in 1972 by the Maple Ridge Branch of the Canadian Federation of University Women.]

XXV

JOHN RUSKIN'S VENETIAN GHOST*

THE BOOK COLLECTOR, VOL. 60, NO. 1, 2011

ഗ

It must have been early in 2004 that a friend, who also happened to be a well-known antiquarian bookseller, told me that he had an interesting set of John Ruskin's *Stones of Venice* that he would like to show me in case I could throw light on it.

The next time that we were together was at a meeting in Sheffield in November of the same year and the copy of *Stones* was produced for me. It was nicely bound in nineteenth-century full calf gilt, but the contents were sadly mutilated. The title-pages of volumes 1 and 2 were missing, but the title-page of volume 3 showed that it was the second edition, published in 1867 by Smith, Elder & Co. There was an ownership inscription, 'Oct 3/11 Harold Pilling, 22 Cleaver St, Burnley' on the fly-leaf of each volume. What was immediately obvious in opening the volumes was that they were very extensively annotated, and in almost every case the diagrams in the text were *very* carefully cut out, and then replaced and secured by either stamp hinges or small strips of music tape. The annotations were made by several hands. Two I immediately recognised. The annotations in blue wax crayon were by George Allen and those in red ink were by his daughter Grace; they both habitually used these media.

In a way, this also tied in with the ownership signatures. George Allen died on 5 September 1907. During the next few years his family disposed of Allen's collection of books, engravings, Martinware and other things through a series of catalogues. I have not been able to search the whole of this series, but these three volumes do not feature

* A. W. Pollard once said that when a notice of a printed edition having no real existence had once appeared in print its ghost was never laid.

in the issues that *have* been searched. However, it may be significant that Pilling's ownership date, 1911, falls during the years while these catalogues were being issued.* My reaction to the annotations and excisions was that the set must have been used as the 'copy' for one of George Allen's editions of the book. The page numbers on the contents pages in volumes 1 and 3 have all been revised in black ink by a third hand; the contents page of volume 2 is lacking. Thus it would be a simple matter to compare the revised page numbers with other Allen editions.

Since we were in Sheffield it was an easy matter to visit the Guild of St George's Library at the Millennium Galleries. There we compared the revised page numbers with the 1886 edition, the 1898 'Uniform Edition' and the Ruskin 'Library Edition' volumes of 1903 and 1904. This was clearly not the 'copy' used for any of these editions. Soon afterwards I was able to add a set of the third, 1873-4 'Autograph' edition to my collection. This too was not set from my annotated copy; this however did not surprise me because the third edition was published by Smith, Elder & Co.

This exhausted the options. Allen hadn't published any other editions of *The Stones of Venice*. Then I remembered that in the 1890s, in order to compete with all of the American piracies of Ruskin's books, George Allen had collaborated with the New York publisher Charles E. Merrill in the comprehensive 'Brantwood' edition of Ruskin's works, for which Charles Eliot Norton had written the introductions. Perhaps this was the 'copy' for the American edition. I thought I remembered copies of the 'Brantwood' edition in the Ruskin Library at Lancaster University, but enquiries proved

* Harold Pilling was born in Burnley in 1888; at the time of the 1911 Census, on 2 April, he was a 'book-keeper' living at 22 Cleaver Street with his parents, Willie, a cotton power-loom overlooker, and Edith, a cotton weaver. He is not known to me as a Ruskin collector but such is the nature of these volumes that he could not have been without special interest in him. However, he was a keen member of the Esperanto movement and when he died in 1957 he had been the president of the Burnley Esperanto Society for a number of years. Because of his interest in Ruskin he would probably have owned a copy of the 1910 edition of *La Rego de la Ora Rivero*, the Esperanto translation of Ruskin's *The King of the Golden River*. Pilling was a director of a Burnley cotton mill.

me wrong. They only have a set of the Norton introductions to each volume. I did, however, find a copy of the Merrill & Baker edition on the internet. I ordered it, only to find, when it arrived, that it was not the 'Brantwood' edition but the 'Illustrated Cabinet Edition', *c.* 1899, and nothing to do with George Allen. Eventually I *did* find a set of the 'Brantwood' edition, again in America, and advertised as only two volumes. Even a broken set would be adequate to check against the contents pages of my annotated copy. When it arrived, it *was* the correct edition, but it turned out not to be a broken set. It was, in fact, the two-volume 'Traveller's Edition' – again, nothing to do with my annotated set.

I had to report to my bookseller friend that I had explored all the possibilities I could think of and didn't know what else to suggest. There the matter rested. Finally, in August 2008 he telephoned me. When the enquiry began, I had asked him to offer me the first refusal when he decided to sell the books. Here was the offer. We decided we were not going to get any further and I had the opportunity to add the three volumes to my collection. When they arrived a few days later, I duly wrote their catalogue card. In writing my notes on the card, and listing all of the editions for which it was *not* the 'copy', I realised where logic had so far failed me. If it wasn't the 'copy' for any published edition, then it must be the 'copy' for an *un*published edition.

A search of the small-type bibliographical notes preceding *The Stones of Venice* in the Ruskin 'Library Edition'[1] revealed that it had been planned, around 1876, to include an edition of *Stones* in Ruskin's 'Collected Works' series. In order to understand the status of this series of books it is necessary to understand something of Ruskin's publishers, and his attitude to publishing methods. The firm of Smith, Elder & Co became Ruskin's publishers in 1843 with the first volume of *Modern Painters*. But they did not sell his books in large quantities, and the many plates for the illustrations to *Modern Painters*, *Seven Lamps of Architecture* and *Stones of Venice* were paid for by John James Ruskin, the author's father, so their net income was not great. By 1860, with the publication of the final volume of *Modern Painters*, Ruskin's interests and concerns were turning more and more to social economy. In the field of publishing, Ruskin was becoming unhappy with the current system whereby the publisher set the price of the book to the trade, but the trade then set its own selling price to the public. He determined to make a change, at least with the method of selling his own books. He established George Allen, who had been his assistant since 1857, as his agent, and he undertook his own publishing. Many of his publications from now on were issued in parts, and the selling price was printed on each part. Whereas Smith, Elder had sold only to the trade, George Allen sold to trade and private customers alike, *at the same cover price*, so that the public could see what profit the booksellers were adding. Not unnaturally, Ruskin's sales suffered, and eventually Allen persuaded him to modify the method. As publisher he set the retail price, giving the trade a discount. From this arrangement grew the Net Book Agreement, which governed the method by which books were sold for the next century.

It must have been evident to Smith, Elder that changes were being made with the beginning of the publication of the first 'Letter' of *Fors Clavigera* in January 1871, when Ruskin began to take a more active role in the distribution of his books. Ruskin announced on page 2, in the 'Advertisement': 'For reasons which will be explained in the course of these letters the Author wishes to retain complete command over his method of publication. For the present they will be sold only by Mr G. Allen, Heathfield Cottage, Keston, Kent.' Smith, Elder appear to have continued to print *Fors* until Letter 27. And they continued publishing for Ruskin. In May 1871 a new edition of *Sesame and Lilies* was published, as volume 1 of Ruskin's new 'Collected Works' series. In the Preface to that volume he announced that the series would include 'scarcely anything out of the first and second volumes of *Modern Painters*; and shall omit much of *Seven Lamps* and *Stones of Venice*: but all of my books written within the last 15 years will be republished without change'. Smith, Elder printed the book and their name appears as publisher on the title-page.

The second volume of the 'Collected Works' series, *Munera Pulveris*, was issued in January 1872 with an important change on the title-page, which noted that it was 'Printed for the Author by Smith, Elder & Co. and sold by Mr G. Allen'. Volumes 3, 4 and 5, *Aratra Pentelici*, *The Eagle's Nest* and *Time and Tide*, all appeared in 1872 with the same names on their title-pages, as did volume 6, *The Crown of Wild Olive*, in December 1873. Meanwhile, in January and February 1873 Ruskin had corresponded with George Smith about the publishing of his books and their small returns.[2] Ruskin offered to sell to Smith, Elder all of his pre-1870 copyrights but Smith offered only £2500 and Ruskin replied that this 'was somewhat less than I expected'. He told Smith that he proposed to offer the copyrights to other buyers. In the end, they were not sold, which, as it turned out, was fortunate for the author.

Writing to Ruskin on 11 February 1873, George Smith reminded him that at the end of December 1871 his credit with Smith, Elder stood at £1035 2*s* 0*d*, but it had been 'spent in printing *Fors Clavigera* and the books of your new series'.[3] By February 1873 Ruskin was prepared to make the final break from Smith, Elder and it is clear that from *Fors Clavigera* Letter 28, dated from Brantwood on 20 February – the April issue of the publication – the printing was now being undertaken by a new firm. A short while afterwards, the first chapter of his *Love's Meinie* was also printed by the new printer. The London printers Walter Hazell and George Watson had bought an old silk mill on the edge of Aylesbury and there they opened their country branch in 1867. Ruskin heard about, and approved of, their experiment (although he hated power-driven machinery and would have preferred the printing to have been done by hand). It was to Watson & Hazell that Ruskin transferred his work in 1873. Their imprint was changed to Hazell, Watson & Viney soon afterwards when J. Elliott Viney became a director. The new imprint is first seen in *Fors Clavigera*, Letter LX (December 1875).

Despite the fact that Ruskin had said two years earlier in the first volume of the 'Collected Works' series that the series would include part of *The Stones of Venice*, in October 1873 Smith, Elder published the third edition of *Stones*, known as the 'Autograph' edition because Ruskin signed the Preface in each copy.* Some old sheets of the

* In a letter of 29 November 1885 George Allen told John Hobbs, his brother-in-law, that the 1873 edition was 'set up without his [Ruskin's] leave'. Ruskin subsequently wrote a new Preface for that edition in which he hinted at a future 'abstract' of the book before signing each of the 1500 copies of the edition.

second edition were used in volume 1 which is dated 1873; volumes 2 and 3 are dated 1874. Ruskin's plans for the future of *Stones* were unclear in the mid-1870s. Although Smith, Elder had just published the third edition in a run of 1500 copies (Ruskin considered the state of the plates too worn to print more) he seems to have had the intention to issue another edition. Writing in the November 1875 Letter of *Fors Clavigera* (probably in October) he declared his intention to publish 'in the same form as the geology and botany[4] what I desire to ratify ... of my former writings on art'.[5] In a footnote to this statement he indicated that he referred to *Modern Painters, Stones of Venice, Seven Lamps of Architecture* and *Elements of Drawing*: 'I cut these books to pieces, because in the first three, all the religious notions are narrow, and many false'.

While Queen Victoria's youngest son, Prince Leopold, was an undergraduate at Oxford, Ruskin was the Slade Professor of Fine Art and a friendship had grown between the two men. When the prince was in Venice by April 1876 he suggested in conversation with a mutual friend, Rawdon Brown, that Ruskin should prepare a new edition of *Stones*. Ruskin himself arrived in Venice on 7 September 1876 and on the following day he wrote to Joan Severn: 'I've been correcting my Stones for printer and find it mostly all right, but – it is like editing a volume of baby talk, without any fun in it'.[6] We can tell from two letters[7] written three days later that Ruskin was not merely planning to 'revise' *Stones*, he was planning almost entirely to rewrite it. Writing to Susan Beever, he told her, 'I hope to get my new *Stones of Venice* into almost as nice a form as *Frondes*.' *Frondes Agrestes* (1875) was Susan Beever's volume of selections from *Modern Painters*. And to George Allen he wrote on the same day, '[I] have set to work fairly on the new *Stones of Venice* which will have all the "eloquent" bits in the second and third volumes served up like pickled walnuts, in sauce of a very different flavour.' But Ruskin soon became distracted from his work on this new 'Traveller's Edition'. He devoted much time to copying one of Carpaccio's *St Ursula* paintings, and preparing his *Guide to the Principal Pictures in the Academy of Fine Arts at Venice*. But on 1 January 1877 he wrote to Joan Severn, 'I am very happy this morning and going to begin my new Stones of Venice'.[8] However

Rawdon Brown was *not* happy with what Ruskin was doing. He wrote on 22 March 1877, 'I fetched you to Venice to reprint the "Stones" & to correct their errors, not to add to them'.[9]

The outcome of the affair seems to be that the new edition of *Stones*, advertised for the 'Collected Works' series in December 1876, was abandoned, and instead, interrupted by illness and other work, the two-volume 'Traveller's Edition' was finally published in 1879.

Meanwhile, what of the 'Collected Works' series? By a quirk of circumstances the next volumes of the series to be published were volumes VIII and IX – *Val d'Arno* and *Queen of the Air*, both in 1874 (volume VII did not appear until 1876). By then the change in Ruskin's publishing policy was complete. George Allen's name appeared on the title-page as publisher and they were printed by Watson & Hazell. In December 1876, despite knowing that Ruskin was preparing the 'Traveller's Edition', Allen announced that the three volumes of *Stones of Venice* would appear as volumes X, XI and XII of the 'Collected Works' series.* They would be printed without the plates, but the woodcut 'figures' would be included.† Ruskin had already said in the Preface to the 'Autograph' edition that he was limiting the edition to 1500 copies because of the worn condition of the engraved plates.

In Venice, his plans for the new edition had eventually emerged and on 21 January 1877 he told Allen of his intention to print, same size as *Mornings in Florence*, the introductory chapters and the Local Index of *Stones*, revising and completing them 'For the use of travellers while staying in Venice and Verona'. At the same time he told Allen there would be an accompanying 'St Mark's Rest. The History of Venice written for the Guidance of English Travellers while they visit her ruins'. Writing to Allen from Venice on 17 March 1877

* According to T. J. Wise in his *Complete Bibliography of . . . John Ruskin* (London: printed for subscribers only, 1893), vol. II, p. 64. Wise may have seen the actual announcement, or he may have been told of it by Allen, from whom he did get much help.

† To have included the plates would have incurred a great deal more expense because at this time they were still owned by Smith, Elder, see below.

WORKS BY MR. RUSKIN,

Lately published or nearly ready.

NOW ISSUING.

REVISED SERIES OF ENTIRE WORKS, IN BOUND VOLUMES.

Purple calf (full), gilt leaves, carriage free.

I. **SESAME AND LILIES.**

Three Lectures, with New Preface. Price 18s.

1. Of Kings' Treasuries. 2. Of Queens' Gardens.
3. Of the Mystery of Life.

II. **MUNERA PULVERIS.**

Six Essays on the Elements of Political Economy. Price 18s.

III. **ARATRA PENTELICI.**

Six Lectures on the Elements of Sculpture.
Given before the University of Oxford, in Michaelmas Term, 1870, with 21 Plates.
Price £1 7s. 6d.

IV. **THE EAGLE'S NEST.**

Ten Lectures on the Relation of Natural Science to Art.
Given before the University of Oxford, in Lent Term, 1872. Price 18s.

V. **TIME AND TIDE.**

Twenty-five Letters to a Working Man of Sunderland on Laws of Work.
Price 18s.

VI. **THE CROWN OF WILD OLIVE.**

Four Essays on Work, Traffic, War, and The Future of England.
With added Article on the Economy of the Kings of Prussia. Price 18s.

VII. **ARIADNE FLORENTINA.**

Six Lectures on Wood and Metal Engraving, and Appendix.
Given before the University of Oxford, Michaelmas Term, 1872. With Twelve Plates.
Price £1 7s. 6d.

I.—Definition of the Art of Engraving.
II.—The Relation of Engraving to other Arts in Florence.
III.—The Technics of Wood Engraving.
IV.—The Technics of Metal Engraving.
V.—Design in the German Schools of Engraving. (Holbein and Durer.)
VI.—Design in the Florentine Schools of Engraving. (Sandro Botticelli.)
VII.—Appendix.

VIII. **VAL D'ARNO.**

Ten Lectures on Art of the Thirteenth Century in Pisa and Florence.
Given before the University of Oxford, Michaelmas Term, 1873.
With Twelve Plates. Price £1 7s. 6d.

IX. **QUEEN OF THE AIR.**

Being a Study of the Greek Myths of Cloud and Storm. Price 18s.

X., XI., XII. **THE STONES OF VENICE.**

Revised, and with some additions to the text; but without plates, which the Author does not think necessary to the purpose of the work, and cannot incur the expense of re-engraving.
[*In preparation.*

George Allen's List *for December 1876 advertising the 'Venetian Ghost' at the foot of the page (author's collection)*

Ruskin told him: 'You had better continue the numbers of the great series [I assume he referred to the 'Collected Works' series] – leaving Stones of Venice till its ready …' Allen withdrew the advertisement; *The Two Paths* was published in 1878 as the tenth volume and *A Joy for Ever* in 1880 as the eleventh and final volume of the series. Did Ruskin realise how much work had already been done in preparing *Stones* for the 'Collected Works' series?

To complete the publishing history of *Stones of Venice*, in 1886 George Allen published an imperial octavo edition, 220 copies on hand-made paper and 2000 ordinary copies. The type for this edition was set using Smith, Elder's second edition.[10] In 1898 Allen included *Stones* in the small-format 'Uniform Edition' series of Ruskin's works, in a run of 3000 copies; there were also 1000-run reprints in 1900 and 1902. Finally Allen included *Stones* as volumes IX, X and XI of the Ruskin *Library Edition* in 1903-4.

What evidence, then, does my mutilated copy of the second edition contain and what can we deduce from it? First, it is rubber-stamped in various places by the publisher with the awful warning to the printer: 'Follow copy exactly / Variations will not be paid / for as Corrections'. George Allen's blue wax crayon notes I had seen before in the Whitehouse Collection on the reverse of photographs taken for the 'Library Edition'. He has made a number of annotations, particularly relating to type sizes to be used for appendices and the need for proofs of the index. But particularly George Allen's notes relate to the illustrations. He has noted on most of the plates 'Include foot-line in blue'. As far as the diagrams in the text are concerned, in almost every case he has scored through them and marked them with a deletion sign. But the evidence as to *when* these signs were made is conflicting. Sometimes the crossings-out extend to beneath the re-fixing hinges and sometimes the crossings-out appear to extend *on to* the fixings.

So what do we learn from all of this? The indication from the notes on the plates is that the plates were to be used in the new edition. We know from the December 1876 announcement that the projected 'Collected Works' edition would *not* contain the plates. We also know from George Allen's letter of 4 March 1889 to his brother-in-law

DECORATION. XXII. THE ANGLE. 257

So I shall call the above mouldings beaded chamfers, when there is any chance of confusion with the plain chamfer, *a* or *b*, of Fig. LII.: and when there is no such chance, I shall use the word chamfer only.

§ XI. Of those above given, *b* is the constant chamfer of Venice, and *a* of Verona; *a* being the grandest and best, and having a peculiar precision and quaintness of effect about it. I found it twice in Venice, used on the sharp angle, as at *a* and *b*, Fig. LIV., *a* being from the angle of a house on the Rio San Zulian, and *b* from the windows of the church of San Stefano.

Fig. LIV.

a *b* *c* *d* *e* *f*

§ XII. There is, however, evidently another variety of the chamfers, *f* and *g*, Fig. LIII., formed by an unbroken curve instead of two curves, as *c*, Fig. LIV.; and when this, or the chamfer *d*, Fig. LIII., is large, it is impossible to say whether they have been derived from the incised angle, or from small shafts set in a nook, as at *e* Fig. LIV., or in the hollow of the curved chamfer, as *d*, Fig. LIV. In general, however, the shallow chamfers, *a*, *b*, *e*, and *f*, Fig. LIII., are peculiar to southern work; and may be assumed to have been derived from the incised angle, while the deep chamfers, *c*, *d*, *g*, *h*, are characteristic of northern work, and may be partly derived or imitated from the angle shaft; while, with the usual extravagance of the northern architects, they are cut deeper and deeper until we arrive at the condition *f*, Fig. LIV., which is the favourite chamfer at Bourges and Bayeux, and in other good French work.

I have placed in the Appendix* a figure belonging to this subject, but which cannot interest the general reader, showing

* Varieties of Chamfer.

S

Stones of Venice I, *showing the excises and replaced diagrams, with George Allen's blue crayon deletions. Grace Allen's ink revisions to the Figure reference in the text may be seen. The Aylesbury deletions of full points can also be seen in the headlines*

VII. GOTHIC PALACES 251

there is in every one of them, except the upright arch of the treasury, a small fissure across the marble of the flanks.

Whatley

§ XXVI. Though, however, the Venetian builders adopted these Arabian forms of arch where grace of ornamentation was their only purpose, they saw that such arrangements were unfit for ordinary work; and there is no instance, I believe, in Venice, of their having used any of them for a dwelling-house in the truly Byzantine period. But so soon as the Gothic influence began to be felt, and the pointed arch forced itself upon them, their first concession to its attack was the adoption, in preference to the round arch, of the form 3 *a* (Plate XIV ~~above~~); the point of the Gothic arch forcing itself up, as it were, through the top of the semicircle which it was soon to supersede.

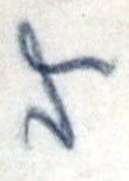

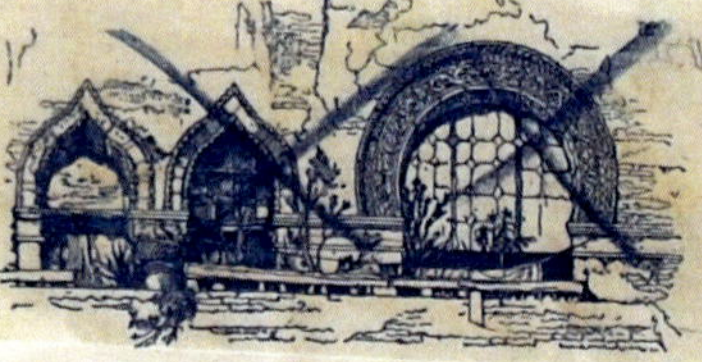

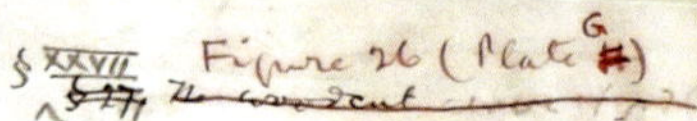

§ XXVII Figure 26 (Plate G) represents the door and two of the lateral windows of a house in the Corte del Remer, facing the Grand Canal, in the parish of the Apostoli. It is remarkable as having its great entrance on the first floor attained by a bold flight of steps, sustained on pure *pointed* arches wrought in brick. I cannot tell if these arches are contemporary with the building, though it must always have had an access of the kind. The rest of its aspect is Byzantine, except only that the rich sculptures of its archivolt show in combats of animals, beneath the soffit, a beginning of the Gothic fire and energy. The moulding of its plinth is of a Gothic

Stones of Venice II, *marked up for Whatley, with deletions and manuscript addition*

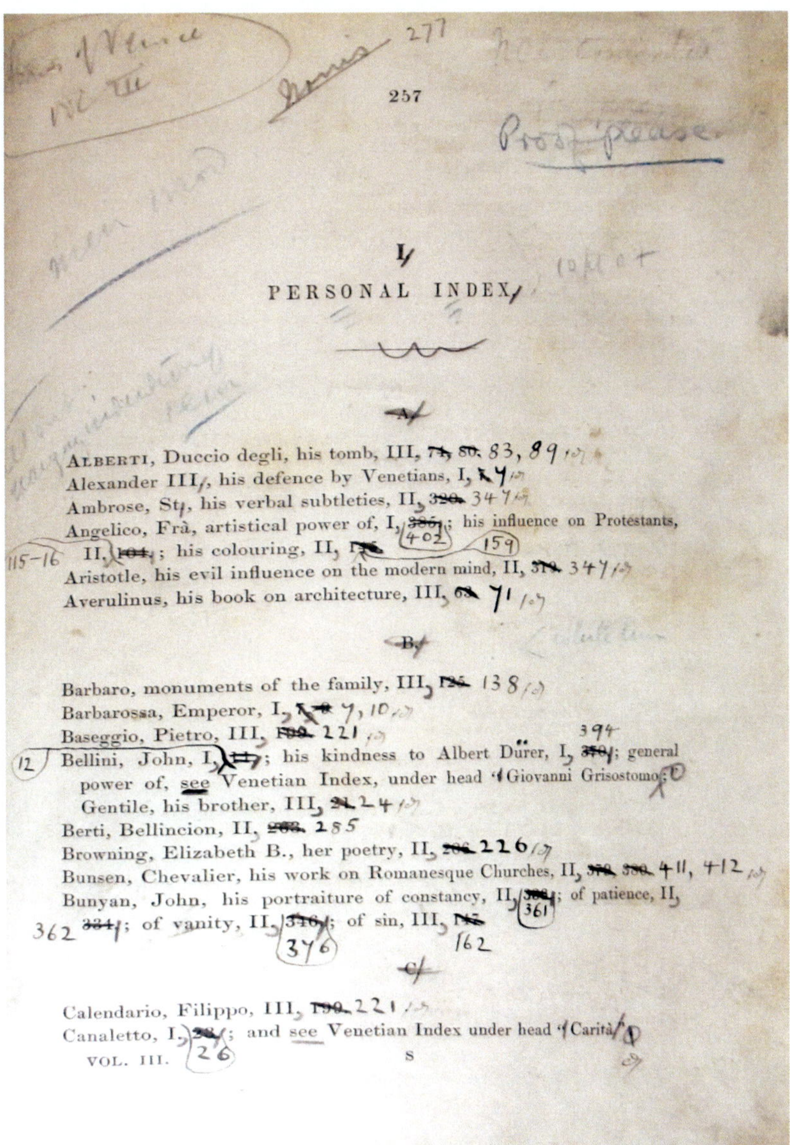

257

I.

PERSONAL INDEX.

A.

B.

C.

VOL. III. S

Stones of Venice III, *showing revisions to the index page numbers, George Allen's request for 'Proof please' and the Aylesbury marking for compositor Norris. Deletions for full points in the headings are also to be seen*

John Hobbs that on 5 September 1878 Allen took 'a special van' and a cheque for 500 guineas to Smith, Elder and brought away the plates and blocks for *Modern Painters*, *Seven Lamps of Architecture*, and *Stones of Venice*, most of which Ruskin's father paid for in the first place. Thus the markings for the plates in my copy could not relate to the projected 1876 edition and *must* relate to the 1886 edition.

While on the subject of illustrations, let us consider Grace Allen's corrections. In almost every case where one reads in the text, for example 'Fig. XXIV', she has deleted this, with a new insertion, 'Fig. 24 (plate G.)', or 'Fig. XXXI' is changed to 'Fig. 31 (plate J.)'. Thus one must infer that the diagrams were to be removed from the text and grouped together on to a series of plates. For example, Figs 1, 2, 3 and 4 are marked up for Plate A; Figs 5, 6, 7 and 8 for Plate B; Figs 9, 10, 11 and 12 for Plate C, and so on. These diagrams were probably cut from the pages in order to send them to have process blocks made, the original woodblocks not being available to Allen until 1878. Because of the text printed on the reverse of the diagrams, I guess that the cut-out diagrams were restored to the volumes *before* the text was set for the 1876 edition. Many of Grace Allen's other corrections relate to the deletion of footnotes or the moving of them into square brackets within the text.

One or possibly two hands seem to have been at work at Aylesbury. One, usually in pencil, marked up what appear to be changes in style – the deletion of full points following ft, ins, St, running heads, and so on, the transposition of full points and asterisks where these occur at the ends of sentences, and the putting of book titles into italics instead of within inverted commas. This same hand has also marked up groups of pages for various compositors, to which I will refer below.

In volumes 1 and 3 (it is lacking in volume 2) the page numbers on the contents pages have been revised in black ink. Those on the Lists of Plates are revised in red ink. I think the red ink is Grace Allen's; I think the black contents pages were revised at Aylesbury. All of the page numbers in the various indices have been revised in black with the occasional use of red ink. These revisions are, I think, by Grace Allen, but they *could* have been written by someone at Aylesbury. The very fact that the page numbers on the Lists of Plates have been revised shows that this was not done for the 1876 edition. No plates were to be included in that edition because they were still in the hands of Smith, Elder. But also the revised page numbers do not conform to the page numbers actually *printed* in the 1886 edition. One can only assume that the position of the plates was revised in proof.

The page numbers on the existing contents pages have been revised upwards. The page number for Appendix 25, the final section of volume 1, has been revised from 398 to 423, In volume 3 the final readable revision is from page 221 to 242. The increase in the number of pages indicates that the new page size must have been smaller. The size of the second edition page is 10 ins x 6 ¼ ins whereas the page size of the 'Collected Works' series is 8 ½ ins x 5 ¼ ins. The most extensive annotations occur in the various indices. At the end of volume 3, pages [253]-362 are four indices: I Personal Index; II Local Index; III Topical Index; IV Venetian Index. Every page number has been revised. This could only have been done working from a set of page proofs of the work. Of the indices in the earlier editions, the 1886 edition only contains an expanded version of the Venetian Index. This really is more a detailed set of notes on various buildings, rather than being an 'index' in the usual sense of the word. The other three indices have disappeared in the 1886 edition, to be replaced by a new index written by Alexander Wedderburn. In order not to confuse the copyright and royalties situation, Allen published Wedderburn's Index as a separate 135-page volume in paper boards, although it is now sometimes found *within* rebound sets of the edition.

From the foregoing it is evident that the revisions to the indices could not have been made for the 1886 edition. Thus, they must have been made for the projected 1876 edition, and as shown above, because of the detail involved, the 1876 edition *must* have reached the page-proof stage. I do not know if any page proofs survived. No copies of the actual edition appear to have been printed.

Let us now consider the various annotations which appear to have been made at Aylesbury. The revisions to the style do not conform to the style of the 'Collected Works' series, where superfluous full points abound after running heads, paragraph numbers, and so on.

Book titles, where they occur in the text, remain in inverted commas rather than being changed to italics. No more has the style of the 1886 edition been changed to conform to the marked revisions, which seem to have been totally ignored. Many of the revisions may have been made when the volumes were in their original Smith, Elder bindings. In their rebound state, several of the annotations disappear into the gutters. But the volumes must have been dismembered in order to distribute sections to the various compositors. In some cases the changes from one compositor to another occur part way down a page. So a *simple* dismemberment and distribution could not have taken place; in some cases the copy must have been passed from one compositor to another.

The principal value of the Aylesbury annotations lies in the names of the compositors marked against different sections of the text. The three volumes have been marked up, perhaps by Henry Jowett.* Generally, the pages were allocated in groups of ten, but occasionally the grouping ran to a little more or less than this figure. Sometimes the final page in a group was the last page of a chapter consisting of only a few lines; frequently the change from one compositor to another occurs part way through a page; thus my counting of the numbers of pages set by each compositor is inevitably approximate. The compositors involved, with the (approximate) numbers of pages they set for each volume, are shown opposite.

From this table it can be seen that the largest number of pages was set by Whatley. Norris and Starr must have been senior compositors because they undertook the more complicated setting of appendices and indices, involving various different sizes and fonts, and of course many figures. Norris, for example, seems to have set all fifty pages of the appendix to volume 1, together with much of the indices of volume 3 which he shared with Starr. Starr also set the nineteen pages of the appendix to volume 2.

The Hazell, Watson & Viney archives, apparently rescued as an afterthought when the business closed down, are preserved in the

* The manager of Hazell, Watson & Viney's works at Aylesbury. I have been unable to compare his known writing with the markings-up of *Stones*.

Compositor	*Vol. 1*	*Vol. 2*	*Vol. 3*	*Total*
Harbottle	48	–	13	61
Hall	50	78	–	128
Whatley	58	116	88	262
Rodgers D.	68	40	88	166
Ayers E.	48	30	28	106
Kite	44	30	46	120
Norris	50	–	70	120
Jelby	–	70	26	96
Starr	–	19	10	29
Ayers H.	–	–	12	12

Centre for Buckinghamshire Studies in Aylesbury. Unhappily, they are very incomplete. The Register of Employees engaged between 1874 and 1930[11] was searched for the names on my compositors list and only Valentine Hall* appears, as having joined the firm on 17 July 1882. We do not know when the other compositors joined. The series of Production Day Books from 1871 to 1910 unhappily has a gap between 1874 and the 1890s. The name of A. E. Starr occurs in a list at the back of the employment register of people who had applied for positions but who had not been engaged – but without a date.

Interestingly, this Albert E. Starr was employed as a bookbinder by Butler & Tanner at Frome† in 1881. His father, William Starr, of 6 Cross Street, was a 'printer's Pressman'. Other names common to my list of *Stones* compositors and the 1881 Frome Census are William Whatley, Printer, who lodged with Sarah Palmer in Bell Lane; her son William was a 'Printers compositor'. William Harbottle, a 'printer

* Hall remained with the company until 1903 when he died.

† This identification was thanks to the skill of my record searcher, Eileen Bartlett, who also searched the 1881 Frome Census.

machinist', was the son of James Harbottle of 31 Naishes Street. Another Starr family of 10 Naishes Street was also much involved with the printing trade; Samuel was a labourer 'at Printing Works', Sarah Ann was a 'folder', Francis James was a 'Painter at Printing Works' and Henry Watson Starr was a 'Printer'. The fact that all of these people were living in Frome and working at Butler & Tanner's works in 1881 does not necessarily mean that they were not with Hazell, Watson & Viney in either 1876 or 1886. But the coincidence of so many similar names in my volumes and in the Frome Census surely shows some movement of workers between the two works. I must add, of course, that Butler & Tanner do not appear to have ever printed anything for Ruskin!

So what does all of the evidence indicate? We know that the three volumes must have been used as 'copy' for the 'Collected Works' series 1876 projected edition because of the extraction of the diagrams and the revision of the indices. We also know that the type for the 1886 edition was set from a copy of the second edition – which this is. The evidence of the compositors is inconclusive, but the fact that Valentine Hall joined Hazell, Watson & Viney in 1882, after the 1876 edition was set but before the work on the 1886 edition, probably indicates that the named compositors were working on the 1886 edition.

All of the evidence would appear to indicate that my three volumes of the second edition of *Stones of Venice* served as the printer's 'copy' for both the ghostly 1876 edition and George Allen's big 1886 edition.

REFERENCES

1. *Works*, IX, lvi.
2. Jenifer Glynn, *Prince of Publishers. A biography of the Great Victorian Publisher George Smith* (London: Allison & Busby, 1986), pp. 104-12.
3. Ibid., pp. 108-9.
4. *Deucalion* and *Proserpina*, which were being published in periodical parts.
5. *Works*, XXVIII, pp. 443-4.
6. *Works*, XXIV, p. xxxv.
7. *Works*, XXXVII, p. 208.
8. Van Akin Burd, *Christmas Story. John Ruskin's Venetian Letters of 1876-1877* (New York: University of Delaware Press, 1990), p. 217.

9. British Library Add MS 36.304 fol. 129.
10. Wise, *op. cit.*, vol. II, p. 64.
11. D/HWV/11/5.

OTHER BOOKS BY JAMES S. DEARDEN

The Parish Church of St Michael, Rampside, privately published, 1949

Printing at Coniston. Bembridge: Yellowsands Press, 1958

The Professor. Arthur Severn's Memoir of John Ruskin (edited). London: George Allen & Unwin Ltd., 1967

A Short History of Brantwood. Twickenham: College of Technology, 1967 (reprinted 1979)

Iteriad, or Three Weeks among the Lakes, by John Ruskin (edited). Newcastle: Frank Graham, 1969

Facets of Ruskin. London: Charles Skilton, 1970

Ruskin and Coniston (with K. G. Thorne). London: Covent Garden Press, 1971

John Ruskin. Aylesbury: Shire Publications, Lifelines Series, 1979 (reprinted frequently)

John Ruskin's Camberwell. St Albans: Brentham Press for The Guild of St George, 1990

A Tour of the Lakes in Cumberland. John Ruskin's Diary for 1830 (with Van Akin Burd). Aldershot: Scolar Press, 1990

Ruskin, Bembridge and Brantwood. The Growth of the Whitehouse Collection. Keele: Ryburn Publishing, 1994

Hare Hunting on the Island. Kingston: Isle of Wight Foot Beagles, 1996

John Ruskin. A Life in Pictures. Sheffield: Sheffield Academic Press, 1999

The King of the Golden River, by John Ruskin, with an essay on its writing and publishing. Freshwater: Coach House Publications, 1999

Brantwood: The Story of John Ruskin's Coniston Home. Coniston: The Ruskin Foundation, 2009

Further Facets of Ruskin. Bembridge: Published by the author, 2009

John Ruskin's Guild of St George. Bembridge: The Guild of St George, 2010

Turner's Isle of Wight Landscapes and the Discovery of Shanklin Chine (with Robin McInnes). Shanklin: Shanklin Chine, 2012

The Library of John Ruskin. Oxford: Oxford Bibliographical Society, 2012

Rambling Reminiscences. A Ruskinian's Recollections. London: Pallas Athene, 2014

LIST OF ILLUSTRATIONS

❦

INDEX

First published 2017 by
Pallas Athene (Publishers) Ltd
2 Birch Close, Hargrave Park,
London N19 5JT
Reprinted 2026

ISBN 978-1-84368-152-6

www.pallasathene.co.uk

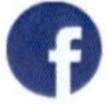 @Pallasathenebooks

 @pallasathene.co.uk

 @Pallasathenebooks

Printed in England by Blissetts